D1736948

The Decline of the Anglo-American Middle East 1961–1969

A Willing Retreat

To My Parents

The Decline of the Anglo-American Middle East 1961–1969

A Willing Retreat

Tore T. Petersen

sussex
ACADEMIC
PRESS

BRIGHTON • PORTLAND

2 4 6 8 10 9 7 5 3 1

First published 2006 in Great Britain by
SUSSEX ACADEMIC PRESS
PO Box 2950
Brighton BN2 5SP

and in the United States of America by
SUSSEX ACADEMIC PRESS
920 NE 58th Ave   Suite 300
Portland, Oregon 97213–3786

British Library Cataloguing in ation Data
A CIP catalogue record for this book is available from the British Library.

Library of Congress Cataloging-in-Publication Data
Petersen, Tore T., 1954–
   The decline of the Anglo-American Middle East, 1961–1969 :
   a willing retreat / Tore T. Petersen.
      p. cm.
   Includes bibliographical references and index.
   ISBN 1-84519-118-8 (h/c : alk. paper)
   1. Middle East—Foreign relations—United States.
   2. United States—Foreign relations—Middle East. 3. Middle
   East—Foreign relations—Great Britain. 4. Great Britain—
   Foreign relations—Middle East. 5. United States—Foreign
   relations—Great Britain. 6. Great Britain—Foreign relations
   —United States. 7. Middle East—Foreign relations—20th
   century.
   I. Title.

   DS63.2.U5P483   2005
   327.73056′09′046—dc22
                                                       2005013610

Typeset and designed by G&G Editorial, Brighton & Eastbourne
Printed by TJ International, Padstow, Cornwall
This book is printed on acid-free paper.

Contents

Cast of Characters

Badeau, John S., American ambassador Egypt, 1961–1964.

al-Badr, Mohammed, Iman of Yemen from September 19, 1962, overthrown September 26, 1962, thereafter leader of Royalist forces.

Ball, George, undersecretary of state, 1961–1966.

Barzani, Mulla Mustafa, leader of Iraqi Kurds to 1975.

Bator, Francis, senior member National Security Council staff, 1964–1967, deputy special assistant to the president for national security affairs, 1965–1967.

Battle, Lucius D., American ambassador Egypt, 1964–1967, assistant secretary of state Near East, 1967–1968.

Brown, George, deputy prime minister, 1964–1968, British secretary of state for foreign affairs, 1966–1968.

Bruce, David K. E., American ambassador United Kingdom, 1961–1969.

Bundy, William P., deputy assistant secretary of defense for national security affairs, 1961–1963, thereafter special assistant to the president for national security affairs to 1966 .

Butler, R. A. (Rab), British secretary of state for foreign affairs, 1963–1964.

Caccia, Sir Harold, British ambassador to the United States, 1956–1961.

Callaghan, James, British chancellor of the exchequer, 1964–1967.

Clifford, Clark, US secretary of defense, 1968–1969.

Davies, Rodger P., deputy director office of Near Eastern affairs, 1962–1963, thereafter director to 1965, thereafter deputy assistant secretary of state for Near Eastern and South Asian Affairs.

Dean, Sir Patrick, British permanent representative to the United Nations to 1965, thereafter British ambassador to the United States.

Eilts, Herman F., officer in charge of Arabian Peninsula affairs, office of Near Eastern affairs, department of state to 1961, thereafter political officer for the Near East and South Asia American embassy, United Kingdom, from 1966 American ambassador Saudi Arabia .

Eisenhower, Dwight D., president of the United States, 1953–1961.

Faisal ibn Abd al-Aziz Al Saud, crown prince of Saudi Arabia, king from 1964 to 1975 .

Fawzi, Mahmoud, foreign minister Egypt to 1964, thereafter deputy prime minister for foreign affairs to 1968.

Fowler, Henry H., US secretary of the treasury, 1965–1968.

Gordon Walker, Patrick, British secretary of state for foreign affairs, 1964–1965.

Greenhill, Sir Denis, counselor British embassy, Washington to 1962, thereafter minister to 1964.

Harlech, Lord (Sir David Ormsby Gore), British ambassador to the United States to 1965.

Hart, Parker T., American ambassador to Saudi Arabia to 1965.

Healey, Denis W., British minister of defense, 1964–1970.

Heath, Edward, British prime minister, 1970–1974.

Home, Lord (Alexander Frederick Douglas-Home), British secretary of state for foreign affairs, 1960–1963, thereafter prime minister to 1964, foreign secretary 1970–1974.

Hussein I, ibn Talal, king of Jordan, 1952–1999.

Jenkins, Roy, British chancellor of the exchequer, 1967–1970.

Jernegan, John D., deputy assistant secretary of state for the Near East and South Asia, 1963–1965.

Johnson, Lyndon B., vice president of the United States, 1961–1963, president, 1963–1969.

Johnston, Sir Charles H., last British governor of Aden, 1960–1963.

Jones, Curtis F., principal US officer Aden, 1965–1967.

Kamel, Mustafa, Egyptian ambassador to the United States, 1961–1967.

Katzenbach, Nicholas deB., undersecretary of state, 1966–1969.

Kennedy, John F., president of the United States, 1961–1963.

Khrushchev, Nikita Sergeyevich, leader of the Soviet Union, 1957–1964.

Kissinger, Henry A., National Security Council advisor to president Nixon, 1969–1973.

Kitchen, Jeffrey C., deputy assistant secretary of state for politico-military affairs, 1961–1967.

Komer, Robert W., senior staff, National Security Council to 1965, thereafter deputy special assistant to the president for national security affairs to 1966, thereafter special assistant to the president to 1967.

McNamara, Robert, US secretary of defense, 1961–1968.

Moore, George C., officer in charge of Arabian Peninsula affairs, bureau of Near Eastern and South Asian Affairs, department of state, 1964–1966, thereafter acting country director for Arabian Peninsula affairs, 1966–1969 .

Nasser, Gamal Abdul, president of Egypt, 1954–1970.

Nixon, Richard, president United States, 1969–1974.

Pahlavi, Mohammed Reza, shah of Iran, 1941–1979.

Qassim, general Abdul Karim, prime minister Iraq, 1958–1963.

Rostow, Walt W., special assistant to the president, 1966–1969.

Rusk, Dean, US secretary of state, 1961–1969.

Sandys, Duncan, British secretary of state the commonwealth, 1960–1964.

Saqqaf, Sayyid Omar, deputy foreign minister Saudi Arabia, 1962–1964, minister of state for foreign affairs, 1964–1974.

Saud ibn Abd al-Aziz, king of Saudi Arabia, 1953–1964.

Saunders, Harold H., senior staff, National Security Council, 1961–1969.

Stevens, Sir Roger B., deputy undersecretary British Foreign Office to 1963.

Stevenson, Adlai E., Jr., US permanent representative to the United Nations to 1961–1965.

Stewart, Michael, British secretary of state for foreign affairs, 1965–1966, 1968–1970, deputy prime minister, 1966–1968.

Talbot, Phillips, assistant secretary of state for Near Eastern and South Asian Affairs, 1961–1965.

Trend, Sir Burke, British secretary of the cabinet, 1963–1973.

Trevaskis, Kennedy, British high commissioner Aden, 1963–1964.

Wilson, Harold, British prime minister, 1964–1970.

Acknowledgments

I wish to thank Hans Otto Frøland, Per Hernæs and Roar Madsen at the Norwegian University of Science and Technology for reading parts of the manuscript. Professor Edward Ingram has as usual, provided much encouragement and support. Anthony Grahame, Editorial Director at Sussex Academic Press, has expertly and expeditiously guided the manuscript to publication. I am grateful to the Norwegian University of Science and Technology for partially supporting the research for this book. Last but not least, many thanks to Leif Inge for cheerfully and effectively assisting me in the archives.

Abbreviations

AEI	Associated Electrical Industries
ARAMCO	Arabian American Oil Company
BAC	British Aircraft Corporation
BOAR	British Army on the Rhine
CAB	Cabinet papers, Public Record Office, Kew
CF	Country File
CFNSF	Country File, National Security File
DEF	Defense
CIA	Central Intelligence Agency
DDE	Dwight David Eisenhower
DDEL	Dwight David Eisenhower Library, Abilene, Kansas
FCO	Foreign and Commonwealth Office
FLOSY	Front for the Liberation of South Yemen
FO	Foreign Office records, Public Record Office, Kew
FRA	Federal Regular Army, Aden
FRUS	Papers Relating to the Foreign Relations of the United States
IRG	Inter-Regional Group
JFK	John Fitzgerald Kennedy
JFKL	John Fitzgerald Kennedy Library, Boston, Massachusetts
LBJ	Lyndon Baines Johnson
LBJL	Lyndon Baines Johnson Library, Austin, Texas
MGB	McGeorge Bundy
Mc	memorandum of conversation
MP	memorandum to the President
MPMGB	memorandum to the President by McGeorge Bundy
MPWWR	memorandum to the President by Walt W. Rostow
NARG	National Archives; Record Group
NLF	National Liberation Front for Occupied South Yemen
NSC	National Security Council
NSF	National Security File

POL	Political Affairs and Relations
PREM	Prime Minister's Office, Public Record Office, Kew
PRO	Public Record Office, Kew
PRSY	People's Republic of South Yemen
SHSC	special head of state correspondence
UAE	United Arab Emirates
UAR	United Arab Republic
YAR	Yemen Arab Republic
WWR	Walt W. Rostow

Introduction

The Anglo-American Middle East, 1961–1969

When the Labour Government of Harold Wilson announced the with-drawal of British forces from the Persian Gulf by the end of 1971, president Johnson protested the decision on January 11, 1968: "Our own capability and political will could be gravely weakened if we have to man all the ramparts alone."[1] As the Vietnam war deepened, Lyndon Johnson and his secretary of state, Dean Rusk, were unwilling for the United States to serve as a world policeman and saw great value in a responsible ally projecting military force into areas where the US government had limited military capability. Britain possessed a string of bases extending from the Middle East to the Indian Ocean and the Far East, supplementing and comple-menting American bases and an ability for force projection. This complex of bases, labeled Britain's role east of Suez in the 1960s, made the United Kingdom a global military power.[2]

The Johnson administration placed great store in a continued worldwide role for the United Kingdom. American concerns about British policy were three-fold: prevent devaluation of the pound sterling; avoid reductions in the British army on the Rhine (BOAR); and for the British to remain east of Suez. American policy makers considered the pound the first line of defense for the dollar. If the British devalued, international speculators might turn their attention to the dollar, forcing a devaluation of the American currency. Maintaining the value of sterling created numerous difficulties for Britain: it required high interest rates, which had a defla-tionary effect on the domestic economy, and the giving of economic and military aid to keep new states like Malaysia within the sterling area. All these factors contributed to straining scarce British reserves of gold and dollars.[3] Equally unacceptable to the Americans was a reduction in the BOAR or withdrawal east of Suez to restore the British balance of payments and prevent devaluation. When Wilson announced the termina-tion of the British position in the Persian Gulf, the Johnson administration's attempt to manipulate British policies by economic subsi-dies foundered as Labour's ideological juggernaut dismantled the empire. In the end, American policy toward Britain ended in dismal failure, the pound was devalued, the British army on the Rhine reduced, and the commitment east of Suez terminated. In this book I argue that Wilson and the Labourites were intent, all along, on ending Britain's overseas commitments for reasons of ideology; the poor shape of the British economy was just an added inducement to speed up the withdrawal process. While the Wilson government was determined to end the British role east of Suez, it was flexible in the ways and means the decision was implemented. In the meantime, east of Suez and the ever wobbling pound were useful tools by which to pressure the Americans for money and other concessions. In fairness to the United States in failing to detect the Labour government's determination to end British overseas commitments, leading Labour politicians had hidden their intentions in rhetoric committed to empire. It is perhaps in this context that Wilson's rather extravagant claim, "Our frontiers are in the Himalayas", must be seen.[4] While paying lip service to close Anglo-American relations and a continued British role east of Suez, Labour, in the end, did not care much for either.

Given the American interest in a continued British presence east of Suez, why did the Johnson administration acquiesce in the precipitate British withdrawal from the Middle East? British minister of defense, Denis Healey, thought the Americans wanted the British to stay, but not for reasons of grand strategy:

> The United States, after trying for thirty years to get Britain out of Asia, the Middle East, and Africa, was now trying desperately to keep us in; during the Vietnam war it did not want to be the only country killing coloured people on their own soil.[5]

Apart from Healey's racist allegations, a continued British presence east of Suez grew in importance with the intensification of the Vietnam war. As Saki Dockrill observes: "Paradoxically, however, the deeper the American commitment in Vietnam enhanced the importance to the USA of Britain's military presence both East of Suez and in Europe." For British politicians the Vietnam war had almost the opposite effect, lessening American power and authority in their eyes.[6] Labour's policies may also be seen as a not so subtle attempt to liberate the United Kingdom from the special relationship. Foreign minister George Brown exclaimed to his fellow ministers, in July 1966, that Britain should break with the United States, devalue the pound, withdraw its forces from east of Suez and join the Common Market.[7]

The process was helped along by the Johnson administration's questioning of American commitment to the Middle East. The president's advisors wondered why Johnson should take an interest in the area at all, particularly since years of conciliating Egyptian leader Gamal Abdel Nasser and other Arab radicals had done nothing to prevent their strident anti-Americanism and tilt toward the Soviet Union, while moderate Arab regimes grew more critical of American policy. While the Johnson administration seemed to have had little leverage over the UK Labour party, the Eisenhower administration pressured a much stronger British government into concession after concession prior to the Suez crisis. Eisenhower tolerated little or no opposition to American policies in the Middle East: he ousted the Iranian prime minister Mohammed Mossadeqh in August 1953, pressured Britain into a humiliating withdrawal from Suez in November 1956, and invaded Lebanon in July 1958, to prevent the Iraqi revolution from spreading. During the Kennedy/Johnson era, the United States desisted from forceful intervention in the Middle East, a point not lost on the Arab nationalists. In the 1960s, there were few, if any, Eisenhower-type penalties for crossing the Americans, thus reducing the cost and dangers of challenging the United States.

Still, before the British withdrawal, Britain and the United States, despite occasional disagreement and sometimes differing emphasis, cooperated effectively in the main to maintain their influence in the Middle East. I have termed the British and American areas of common interest in the region the Anglo-American Middle East, which reached its heyday and decline during the Kennedy and Johnson eras. The term is flexible, changing continuously with differing patterns of Anglo-American interactions in the area. Since Britain always wanted American support or understanding for its positions, the Americans, whether they wanted it or not, were drawn into Britain's sphere of influence. While separate policies in the Middle East existed, most importantly the special American interest in Israel, it should be noted that the British were extremely skillful in coopting and channeling American initiatives for their own purposes. Independent American policies in the region were, therefore, few and far between. When Kennedy became president, the Anglo-American Middle East was largely confined to relations with Egypt, Jordan and the Arabian Peninsula.

So far as I am aware, the Anglo-American Middle East is a new term. While the term certainly may be applied to the entire post-war period, the 1950s were a particularly tempestuous time for Anglo-American relations in the Middle East. A far more harmonious relationship grew out of this strife under Kennedy and Johnson, each power supplementing and complementing each other's role in the Middle East. When both powers were in basic agreement, they had little trouble in maintaining their influence. This study, then, is an attempt to describe, analyze and explain the Anglo-American Middle East, how and why it reached its high point early in the Johnson administration, and from thereon rapidly declined. Empire takes various forms and shapes. The term Anglo-American Middle East may possibly be successfully applied to the period after the British withdrawal from the Persian Gulf in 1971, but that was an empire without fixed points or possessions. While we may see a communality of Anglo-American interest after 1971, as in the 1991 Gulf war and 2003 invasion of Iraq, the extent of Anglo-American cooperation is much more difficult to delineate than in the earlier period. The Anglo-American Middle East is therefore highly appropriate as a conceptual framework to analyze Anglo-American area interaction in the period 1961–1969.

Before Labour's electoral victory in October 1964, the Conservatives under Harold Macmillan (prime minister 1957–63) and Alec Douglas-Home (1963–64) believed Britain's continued role as a great power depended on the British position in the Middle East. They followed the well-trod path of their Conservative predecessors, Winston Churchill (prime minister 1951–55) and Anthony Eden (1955–57), in trying to keep the Middle East within the British sphere of influence. The Suez crisis was not the end of the British presence in the Middle East. On the contrary, the period after Suez saw an increase of British military activity, particularly on the Arabian Peninsula. The Tory leadership was well aware of the need for reform in their dependencies and areas of interest, but came increasingly to rely on military measures against the forces opposing a continued British presence in the Middle East. Unfortunately for Britain, although it won battles, Arab nationalism in its various shapes and forms was not a force that could be defeated on the battlefield.

John F. Kennedy's approach differed from the Tory hardline toward the Middle East. The president sought rapprochement with Nasser through warm personal letters and generous supplies of food aid. American farmers, at one point, fed 40 percent of the Egyptian population.[8] While accommodating the United States on minor points, Nasser refused to trade his position as the chief spokesman of Arab nationalism for American wheat, sometimes pursuing policies at cross purposes with the Kennedy administration. To avoid being tainted by past American association with reactionary Arab regimes, the United States kept the conservative monarchies at arm's length, believing them to be brittle constructions, out of touch with their own masses and with only the dimmest prospects of survival.[9] At the same time, well aware of Britain's significant military contribution to Middle East stability, the Kennedy administration assisted in maintaining British areas of interest. Courting Arab nationalists and supporting the British position in the Middle East were inherently contradictory policies: by refusing to give priority to either, Kennedy harvested the benefits of neither.

Standard accounts of the American–Israeli relationship hold that Eisenhower avoided close association with Israel, threatened sanctions to force Israel to withdraw from Sinai, refused it security guarantees, and provided little economic support; all of which changed with Kennedy.[10] But as Abraham Ben-Zvi shows, the shift in American policy began earlier, after the American invasion of Lebanon in July 1958, when the United States perceived Israel as a potential counterbalance to Egypt. The decisive shift, however, came with the sale of Hawk missiles to Israel in August 1962. It was originally conceived as compensation to Israel for the American tilt toward Egypt, as well as an attempt to broaden and solidify Jewish support in the November 1962 elections to Congress. In return for the Hawks, the United States expected Israel to accept the return of up to 100,000 Palestinian refugees. Despite sending ambiguous signals prior to the sale, the Israeli prime minister, David Ben-Gurion, took the Hawks but refused to budge on the refugees. Kennedy engineered a major shift in American policy toward Israel through the sale of Hawks, but did not obtain a modification of Israeli policy in return.[11]

While American–Israeli relations grew distinctly warmer under Kennedy, the relationship never blossomed into a full-blown alliance. In fact, the United States enhanced Israeli security while continuing its rapprochement with Egypt. The Jewish state never took precedence in Middle East politics before the Six Day War and was not a major Anglo-American concern before that time either. For Britain, relations with Israel were almost a non-policy; concerned with Israel's security, its main goal was to stay aloof of the Arab–Israeli conflict. After the Suez crisis, Britain made but little effort to broker any peace between Israelis and Arabs.[12] As Robert McNamara notes: "Britain was content to remain on the periphery, balancing supplies of Centurion tanks to Iraq and Jordan with similar quantities to Israel."[13]

Lyndon Johnson claimed that he was one of the best friends Israel ever had. According to Douglas Little: "Lyndon B. Johnson would consummate the Israeli–American reconciliation initiated by Eisenhower and accelerated by Kennedy." While there is ample testimony to the president's sexual prowess, it is hard to visualize Johnson cementing American–Israeli relations in this manner. Besides, as Little later admits, the relationship was not that close after all: "Despite the pro-Israeli complexion of his new administration, the president was not eager to expand US military assistance."[14] In fact, the Johnson administration struggled to stay on an even keel with respect to the Arab–Israeli conflict. Hal Saunders, Johnson's point man on the Middle East in the White House, reported to the president on June 24, 1966: "We have succeeded in maintaining satisfactory working relationships on all sides of a series of local disputes that have threatened to drive us and the USSR into opposing camps." To offset increased Soviet arms sales to radical Arab regimes and prevent Israel falling behind in the arms race, Saunders explained the president, the United States sold weapons both to the Arabs and the Israelis, which succeeded in temporarily restoring the deterrent balance. "Our purpose is to buy time for an Arab–Israeli accom- modation."[15] While Johnson failed miserably in warding off the Six Day War in June 1967 (more on the war in chapter 4), Israel's stunning victory led the president falsely to believe that the Jewish state could serve as a strategic asset helping the United States contain increased USSR influence in the region as well as the resurgence of a militant Nasser.[16] Sadly, for Johnson and his successors, Israel has shown little willingness to align its policies with the United States. On the contrary, its militancy and aggression are the chief obstacles to an Arab–Israeli peace today.

Scholars have virtually neglected the government of British prime minister Sir Alec Douglas-Home, which served from October 1963 to October 1964, not to mention UK foreign policy in general and its Middle Eastern policy in particular. American scholars claim that, in the same period, the Middle East was not very high on Lyndon Johnson's list of concerns. There were no crises in the area demanding the president's attention. The president was "preoccupied with domestic reform", Warren I. Cohen explains, "the election campaign of 1964, and Vietnam".[17] Rusk observes: "During the Kennedy years and up until 1967 the Middle East presented few major problems for me as secretary of state."[18] The memoirs of the other protagonists are of limited value; as foreign minister Rab Butler's concerns regarding the Middle East were restricted to a colorful account of his meeting with Lyndon Johnson that follows closely (in an abbreviated form) the British records of the talks.[19] Lord Home avoids saying anything useful or informative about his premiership, while Anglo-American relations in the Middle East are largely neglected in Lyndon Johnson's memoirs, as well as in the two recent biographies of the president.[20] Yet despite the neglect by scholars and the relative complacency of the Johnson administration, the United States was challenged by assertive and aggressive British policy in the Middle East. Throughout the first half of 1964, the Butler and Home governments conducted several military operations in their Aden Federation in an effort to subdue anti-British guerillas. The Home government was so concerned about unrest in Aden and its position in the Middle East, that their role east of Suez took precedence over seeking closer ties with the European Common Market.[21]

Despite the rapid British dismantling of empire after Labour's electoral victory in October 1964, scholarly opinion holds that Wilson and the Labour government had every intention of maintaining the British position east of Suez. Unfortunately, balance of payments problems and weakness of the pound eventually forced a withdrawal in a desperate attempt to restore the health of the British economy. Scholars argue that upon taking office in 1964, the new Labour government was unpleasantly surprised by a £800 million deficit. The refusal to devalue tied the government to a life and death struggle for economic survival and forced British withdrawal east of Suez in order to cut expenses.[22] "Not since 1945, when a bankrupt nation faced the imminent end to Lend-Lease," Ben Pimlott observes, "had an incoming administration faced so severe a crisis."[23] But as Austen Morgan points out, when the Conservatives returned to power in 1951 they faced a deficit of £700 million, much larger in real terms than the 1964 deficit. Still, the 1951 deficit would be paid up within a year. According to Morgan, Wilson's handling of the deficit was largely a self-inflicted wound:

> But he proceeded to play politics with the deficit, partly to blame the outgoing Conservative government. He would later use the argument about an inherited crisis to justify his own government's tawdry performance. Nothing was sprung on Harold Wilson when he entered Downing Street, but he chose to behave in a dramatic fashion. This only made the crisis worse.[24]

The deficit gave Labour, intentionally or not, extreme flexibility of policy. Failures could be blamed on their predecessor, economic problems used to squeeze money out of the United States, and finally, any predisposition to liquidate the empire hidden by the fig leaf of financial exigency. Minister of housing Richard Crossman's diaries confirm that pressures on Wilson from the left and right wing of the Labour party, left the prime minister "free either to withdraw from East of Suez or to extract a higher price from the Americans for standing staunchly by them".[25] The pound and the British role east of Suez were intimately tied to Anglo-American relations: in order to gain American assistance to maintain the stability of the former, the British pledged to remain in the latter.[26]

Arab nationalism emerged as a political force in the Middle East after the breakup of the Ottoman empire following the First World War. The boundaries drawn by the European powers were mainly to ensure their control of the area, and disregarded, according to the Arab nationalists, the Arab nation and common Arab culture existing across these frontiers.[27] The Arab nationalist movement was anti-imperialist, seeking to abolish the artificial frontiers imposed by the great powers.[28] While Nasser did not invent Arab nationalism, he successfully appropriated Arab resentment of the colonial powers, emerging as its chief spokesman after the Suez crisis of 1956. But Nasser was never able to monopolize Arab nationalism, as the belief that all Arabs were members of one Arab nation was more a myth than reality.[29] The Arab nationalists disregarded regional and ethnical diversities, as well as differences in economic and social development and political experience. Arab unity should transcend and overcome these difficulties, but reality proved otherwise. While anti-colonialism remained a potent force in Arab nationalism, after 1958, with Egypt's union with Syria and the Iraqi revolution, Arab unity was more and more linked to the idea of revolutionary socialism. The enemies of Arabism were the reactionaries, the kings, shahs and the pashas with their supporting cohorts of oligarchic politicians and wealthy landowners and businessmen who kept the Arab world divided and cooperated with the colonial powers.[30]

Unfortunately, many American scholars, preoccupied with Nasser, overlook many of the nuances, and the extent of Anglo-American cooperation in the area. If the Middle East was quiet for most of 1964, the potential for trouble remained great, and it was in Egypt where the potential was greatest. "It was Nasser, always, Nasser", Cohen insists, "who made it impossible for Johnson to ignore the Middle East", investing the Egyptian leader with almost supernatural powers:

> The central role in the Middle East drama, from November 1963 to January 1969, was played by Gamal Abdel Nasser . . . Virtually every event of consequence bore his imprint as he rallied Arab masses, manipulated American presidents and Soviet premiers, terrified local potentates, and ranted against Israel. [31]

Burton Kaufman believes that during his first two years in office the president "paid relatively little attention to problems in the Middle East, which for the most part did not seem to require much".[32] But Nasser's lack of gratitude for the sizeable American food aid, and increasing challenge to American interests in the Middle East, alienated Johnson from the Egyptian dictator. Kaufman as well as Ethan Nadelmann and William Burns emphasize the personality factor: Johnson and Nasser simply did not like one another. "While one can easily overstate the importance of the Kennedy–Nasser relationship in Washington's relations with Cairo", Kaufman explains, "one can just as easily understate the significance of the personal animus between Johnson and Nasser."[33] Douglas Little argues that Nasser, by supporting the Palestine Liberation Organization and Marxist rebels in Aden, "helped bring Egypt's relations with America to the breaking point" in 1964.[34]

Burton Kaufman is also preoccupied with Nasser, and shares the belief in the unimportance of the British in the Middle East,[35] while William Burns points out that as Nasser's truculence increased, the United States lost interest in placating him through American food shipments. Besides, even with food aid generously supplied, the United States had only limited influence on the Egyptian dictator's behavior: "despite a clear need for American economic assistance, the Nasser regime was psychologically and politically unprepared to make the sorts of concessions that the American government expected in return for its aid." All this suggests that, for all the irritation and anger at what was mostly rhetoric from Nasser's side, he was basically a minor irritant to the Johnson administration.[36] Robert W. Stookey confirms this point:

> Nasser's extravagant denunciations of the United States, amply publicized by the press, turned the American public, the business community, and the Congress

against Egypt. Administration spokesmen, on the other hand, reacted in low key or not at all; the implication that the United States government now regarded him as at most a minor nuisance wounded Nasser's pride.[37]

Assessing Nasser's career, Malcolm H. Kerr observes that whatever successes the Egyptian leader had enjoyed they were largely illusory.[38] Kerr's impression is confirmed by the archival record: when the Egyptians let Congolese students in Cairo burn down the American Library in protest against US policy in Congo, and a plane owned by a friend of Johnson was shot down by the Egyptian airforce, the administration's response was muted. McGeorge Bundy, National Security Advisor to LBJ, noted:

The President, as guardian of the national interest, may share the anger of Americans when our libraries are burned, but he is careful and restrained in his actions and his words, because experience has proven that anger is not a good guide to action with these nationalists.[39]

In Cairo, reality looked different. The Egyptian leadership was convinced that Johnson was too pro-Israel and had little or no interest in continuing the Kennedy rapprochement with Nasser. Not only that, the Egyptians were convinced that the United States sought the overthrow of their government. From this perspective, Nasser had little incentive and much to lose by continuing the Egyptian conciliation of the United States.

This book is a study of Anglo-American relations in the Middle East between 1961 and 1969. The policies and concerns of Arab governments are of relevance only insofar, strictly speaking, as they pertain to the main topic of this work. With this focus, I have made no attempt to do research in area archives in the Middle East. Events in the region are analyzed from the vantage point of British and American archives and perspectives, supplemented by the printed primary sources available and published scholarly accounts.

During my research, I have had the benefit of consulting recently declassified material in the Public Record Office, Kew, England, the National Archives in College Park, Maryland, and the Kennedy and Johnson Libraries in Boston, Massachusetts and Austin, Texas, respectively.[40] I have found, to my amazement, that British and American archives are riddled with derogatory comments about the Arabs – and this under the Johnson administration, which emphasized racial equality and civil rights, and the Wilson government with its ingrained dislike of empire and colonialism. "Arabs have a 'band wagon' instinct" and will follow what is popular "in an exaggerated degree" high commissioner in Aden, Kennedy Travaskis, opinionated to colonial secretary Duncan Sandys on February

20, 1964,[41] and Parker T. Hart, American ambassador to Saudi Arabia, claimed in a dispatch to the State Department on January 17, 1967, that Arabs were incapable of constructive action.[42] Further examples of this paradoxical Anglo-American attitude will be provided and quoted as the story unfolds.

Despite the impression left behind by British and American civil servants, closer inspection of the archival record gives a more favorable assessment of many Arab leaders. King Faisal of Saudi Arabia, the Persian Gulf rulers and Adeni sheiks emerge as honorable men struggling to do their best in an often hostile and always difficult environment. The evolvement of Faisal is particularly instructive. He started out as the typically fire-eating Arab radical, being, among other things, the chief instigator of the occupation of the Buraimi oasis, souring Anglo-Saudi relations in the period 1952–1963. Increasingly alienated by Nasser and his confrontational policies, Faisal deeply regretted supporting him against the conservative monarchs in the 1950s. King Hussein of Jordan was the chief victim of this early Egyptian–Saudi alliance. As the Egyptian–Saudi rift widened, Faisal became a staunch supporter of Britain and the United States and his fellow conservative monarchs in the Middle East. On February 16, 1967, the Foreign Office reported that, in the current difficulties, Faisal would back Hussein in Jordan to the hilt. "When you had a true friend this was the least you could do and Saudi Arabia now bitterly regretted the support she had once given, to her shame, to Nasser's attacks on Jordan."[43] In the era of Wilson and Johnson, Faisal patiently and courteously solicited British and American support, only to be rewarded by the precipitous British withdrawal from Aden and the Gulf, despite repeated assurances to the contrary, leaving him to face his enemies alone. Although the United States was concerned about the future of the Gulf, it refused to take over the British security commitments, the American aloofness being interpreted as disinterest by Faisal. While there is a certain justification to Faisal feeling abandoned by his benefactors, it could be argued he was somewhat remiss in protecting his own interests, doing little or nothing to support moderate forces in Aden before Britain withdrew, passively watching Aden fall to Marxist–Leninist guerillas. Faisal feared the consequences of having a revolutionary government at his southern border, but he refused to involve himself in the civil war, doing nothing but providing sanctuary for deposed Adeni sheiks.

Prologue

The Great Powers and the Middle East, 1952–1961

Edward Ingram, professor of imperial history, takes a dim view of the Anglo-American 'special relationship', comparing it to "an alliance of restraint in which the weaker partner commits suicide by inviting its stronger partner to strangle it. In Britain's case, the United States was all too willing to oblige."[1] Certainly, whatever benefits accrued from the partnership, preservation of the British empire was not one of them. Despite the endless scholarly debate on the British decline, there was nothing inevitable about the end of empire in the Middle East and no question of the British willingly handing over its area of influence to the United States.[2] On the contrary, by 1952 Britain still had major influence in the area and was determined to hold on to its areas of interest, its control of vast oil reserves propping up its status as a great power. British assets were considerable: 80,000 troops manned the Suez Canal base complex; there were naval facilities in Aden; air squadrons in Iraq; the Arab Legion in Jordan; rear bases in Cyprus and Malta; they controlled Iranian oil production and owned the world's largest oil refinery in Abadan; and finally, Britain was in charge of the defense and foreign policies of a string of protectorates along the Persian Gulf.[3]

The British position was precarious: revolutionary officers under Gamal Nasser took power in Egypt in 1952 and demanded British withdrawal from the Suez Canal. Prime minister Mohammad Mossadeq of Iran nationalized the Anglo-Iranian Oil Company (AIOC) in 1951, breaking diplomatic relations with Great Britain in 1952 in retaliation for Britain effectively barring Iranian oil from world markets. Finally, Saudi Arabia, with the aid and assistance of the Arabian American Oil Company (ARAMCO), occupied the Buraimi oasis in October 1952, on the southeastern tip of the Arabian Peninsula. The oasis, believed to contain oil, was jointly controlled by the British protectorates Muscat and Oman and Abu Dhabi. Strategically located at important crossroads, whoever held Buraimi could easily overwhelm the small sheikhdoms controlling the oasis. The Saudi occupation of Buraimi, then, could potentially undermine the British position in the Persian Gulf region, from Kuwait in the north around the Arabian Peninsula to Aden. Between 1945 and 1950, the United States replaced Britain as the leading western power in Saudi Arabia. Owing to its enormous oil reserves and its air base at Dahran, the United States had a greater interest in Saudi Arabia than in any other Middle Eastern state. Thus, the dispute over Buraimi became a festering sore in Anglo-American relations in the period 1952–1957.[4]

The British predicament elicited little sympathy or aid from the Americans, who believed British misfortunes were of their own making. The United States, the Eisenhower administration claimed, had only limited interest in the Middle East. Great Britain's failure to maintain area security and to come to terms with Arab nationalism, the president argued, forced a larger role on the United States, lest the Middle East be lost to the Soviet Union by default. Meanwhile, political involvement led to mercantile ambition, and the US government decided to supplant British with American oil companies. The British all along believed that commercial considerations moved American policy, given the absence of a credible Soviet threat or indigenous Communism in the Middle East.[5]

In almost every strategy document produced by Anglo-American policy makers in the 1950s and 1960s, a central goal was to prevent Soviet influence, penetration and control of the Middle East, without much elaboration of what the Soviet threat entailed. Steeped in the politics of the cold war, Anglo-American leaders and administrators probably had little need to explain to each other the consequences of increased Communist influence in the Middle East. The irony is, despite much expenditure of treasure and efforts, the Soviets were largely unsuccessful in the Middle East. Even after the Six Day War, when the Soviet Union lavished military assistance on its clients Egypt, Syria and Iraq in an effort to compensate for its failure to prevent the Arab defeat at the hands of Israel, Soviet influence and control in the Middle East was tenuous at best. By 1970, the Soviet Union had acquired air and naval bases in Egypt, and port rights in Syria, Sudan, Iraq and North and South Yemen. But at what cost? As one authority notes: "In return for enabling the Soviets to claim influence, the Arabs expect Moscow to supply loans, weapons, technical advice, diplomatic support, and favorable terms of trade. The obvious question is, Who is exploiting whom in this relationship?"[6] Why, then, the Anglo-American concern about the Soviet Union in the Middle East? The Soviet Union effectively exploited anti-colonial sentiment in East and Southeast Asia; there was a genuine fear that they could successfully duplicate that policy in the Middle East. For the most part, then, the Soviet threat was more potential than real in the Middle East.[7]

Soviet policy towards the Middle East rested on a defensive and an offensive foundation. Defensively, because of the proximity of the Middle East to the Soviet southern border there was a vital interest in preventing the region from being used as a base for an attack on the Communist motherland. Offensively, the goal was to dominate the Middle East to deny area resources, most importantly oil, and strategic location to the United States and its allies. In addition, the Soviets justified their efforts in the Middle East by their claim to leadership in the 'world revolutionary' and the 'national liberation' movements. While Stalin was too cautious to risk confrontation with the West in the Middle East, his successors made a determined effort to increase Soviet influence in the area. Key to the Soviet efforts were large amounts of economic and military assistance, as well as diplomatic support to its most important clients and allies in the Middle East, like Egypt, Iraq and Syria. Despite large arms sales, the Soviet Union failed to gain control of the recipient countries' policies. Most notably, the Soviet leadership under Nikita Khrushchev failed to protect local communists in Egypt, Iraq and Syria. While receiving aid from the Soviet Union, Nasser declared the Egyptian Communist Party illegal and kept its members in prison. When Khrushchev tried to intervene on their behalf, Nasser denounced the attempt as an intolerable interference in Egypt's internal affairs. Despite all their efforts, the Russians had little success in undermining Anglo-American influence in the Middle East.[8]

In both Egypt and Iran, the United States perceived itself as caught between British colonialism and Middle Eastern nationalism. For the Americans, Britain's reliance on kings and pashas to keep order in the Middle East was outdated. Unavoidable social change in the region was to be encouraged and steered in a pro-Western direction, to avoid giving the Soviet Union opportunities for increasing its influence. United States secretary of state John Foster Dulles warned, on March 17, 1954, that unless Great Britain showed greater flexibility on Egypt and Iran, the United States would take unilateral action there and elsewhere in the Middle East. America forced Britain out of its prized possessions in Egypt and Iran by threatening to provide unilateral aid to Egypt, thus excluding British influence and establishing an oil consortium in Iran to replace AIOC without British participation. The Anglo-Egyptian agreement of October 1954 forced Britain to evacuate the Suez Canal base complex by June 1956. The only residue of British influence left in Egypt, where it previously held the dominant position, was (as the future would show) a meaningless pledge by the Nasserite regime that Britain could reactivate the base in case of external aggression to the Middle East and Turkey.[9] In Iran, Britain caved in to American demands, reluctantly accepting a 40 percent share of the new oil consortium, where only a few years previously AIOC had been in a monopoly position.[10]

Despite the loss of British pre-eminence in Egypt and Iran, British politicians had no intention of withdrawing from the Middle East: they planned to increase Britain's influence, contemplating intelligence operations, in 1955–6, aimed at overthrowing the governments of at least Saudi Arabia, Egypt, and Syria.[11] By that time, Anthony Eden, who had consistently advocated a line in the Middle East independent of the United States, had succeeded Winston Churchill as prime minister. On October 4, 1955, he told the cabinet:

> Our interests in the Middle East were greater than those of the United States because of our dependence on Middle East oil, and our experience was greater than theirs. We should not therefore allow ourselves to be restricted overmuch by reluctance to act without full American concurrence and support. We should frame our own policy in light of our interests in the area and get the Americans to support it to the extent we could induce them to do so.[12]

The chosen vehicle to preserve British influence was the Baghdad Pact, which Britain joined April 5, 1955, with Turkey, Iraq and Pakistan forming an anti-Communist alliance. Having encouraged the formation of the Pact, the United States held back, feeling that Britain had transformed the organization to preserve its influence in the Middle East. When Britain, against American advice, tried to entice Jordan to join the Pact, it became the beginning of open Anglo-American dissension in the Middle East. Dulles opposed including Jordan because Nasser would consider it an affront to his plans of forging an Arab nation, whose support, Dulles argued, was indispensable in any negotiations for a comprehensive Arab–Israeli peace. The British scheme backfired when the plan became public. Encouraged by Radio Cairo, Jordan erupted in riots, making its pro-British king Hussein barely able to cling to the throne. All thoughts of Jordan's joining the Baghdad Pact were given up.[13]

Barely a month after the last British soldiers left their Suez bases, in accordance with the Anglo-Egyptian treaty of 1954, Nasser nationalized the Suez Canal Company in July 1956. The Egyptian dictator claimed that the nationalization was in retaliation for the humiliation inflicted upon him when the United States, with British concurrence, publicly refused to finance the building of the Aswan Dam. American military aid offered to Egypt, after the conclusion of the Anglo-Egyptian agreement, came with too many strings attached, in too small quantities to suit Nasser, and was foolishly used by Dulles as a lever with which to induce Egypt to make peace with Israel. The attempt backfired when Nasser turned to the Soviets, who eagerly supplied him with arms in large quantities. To contain the Soviet Union and secure Egypt's friendly disposition towards the West, Britain and the United States offered to finance the building of the Aswan Dam. But when Nasser continued his anti-Western propaganda and recognized Communist China, Dulles withdrew the offer to finance the Dam. Recognizing Nasser's nationalization of the Suez canal as a challenge to British preeminence in the Middle East, president Eisenhower firmly and consistently opposed military action to rectify the nationalization of the canal, claiming resort to the methods of yesteryear would set the entire Middle East aflame. The United States embarked on numerous meetings and conferences to dampen British and French belligerency and ultimately deflect any military action against Nasser. France joined the British, believing Nasser was the main source of support to Algerian rebels in its core colony in French North Africa. France exaggerated the importance of the Egyptian threat to North Africa, as Nasser was rather long on propaganda, but short on economic and military assistance to the Algerian rebels. Tired of American procrastination, England and France teamed up with Israel and attacked Suez on October 29, 1956, taking unilateral action without informing the United States. Britain and France suffered a humiliating defeat in Suez. The Americans orchestrated a censuring of British actions in the UN, speculated against the pound, and embargoed Western hemispheric oil to Europe at the onset of winter. Furthermore, an enraged president Dwight Eisenhower effectively forced Eden out of office.[14]

Buraimi played an important part in the Anglo-American rift over Suez. It was on Buraimi that Britain chose to draw the line against American pressure, threatening twice during the spring of 1954 to kill any Americans found in the oasis, believing ARAMCO's wish to start drilling for oil was only a subterfuge to bribe local tribes to switch allegiance to Saudi Arabia. Later, in October 1955, Britain reoccupied the oasis and evicted the Saudis without informing or consulting the United States, much to the annoyance of the Eisenhower administration. During the Suez crisis, senior officials in the Eisenhower administration attributed the strain in Anglo-American relations to Buraimi: Dulles complained that "the recent chain of events in the Middle East had very largely stemmed from the British action in the Buraimi oasis". Under-secretary of state Herbert Hoover Jr. believed that Anglo-American differences "had gone a great deal deeper than people imagined: It had started a long time ago even before Suez as far back as the Buraimi incident". In a conversation with the British ambassador, Sir Harold Caccia, Hoover expressed his resentment of Britain's habit of acting without warning the United States: "There had been Buraimi; then Jordan, and now Suez."[15]

The Suez crisis threatened a serious cleavage in the Atlantic Alliance. Confronted with increasing anti-Americanism in the United Kingdom, Eisenhower, perhaps belatedly, realized that Britain was a far more important and reliable ally than Egypt or Saudi Arabia would ever be. The president therefore took immediate steps to restore the alliance, while in Great Britain Eden's successor, Harold Macmillan, was equally willing to reestablish ties with the United States. Eisenhower and Macmillan met in

Bermuda in March 1957, where they reviewed the whole range of Anglo-American relations. Great Britain conceded hegemony of the Middle East to the United States in return for continued dominance of the Persian Gulf. United States concern for Saudi Arabia was no longer allowed to disturb Anglo-American harmony, as can be seen in the passivity of the United States when Britain suppressed a Saudi-sponsored rebellion in Oman between 1957 and 1959. The new post-Suez Anglo-American relationship was succinctly summed up by a US National Security Council Paper of January 10, 1958: "The major phenomena affecting the United States since the British–French–Israeli invasion of Egypt in November 1956 have been the emergence of the United States as the leader of the Free World interest in the area, and tacit recognition of that by our British and French allies in all areas except the Persian Gulf and the Aden area." This, of course, carried implications for Anglo-American relations, the paper concluded: "Our objectives with the British in the area will no longer revolve around the usefulness *per se* of the British position in the area. Rather will they be conditioned by our very real interest in maintaining Britain as a strong and prosperous member of the Western alliance."[16]

While the potential for the Soviet Union to exploit Western disagreements was great, American fears of increased Communist influence after Suez were probably exaggerated. Towards the end of Eisenhower's administration, the Middle East was relatively quiet. Khrushchev's open support and espousal of, particularly, Egyptian communists gave Nasser cause for concern. Soviet–Egyptian relations thus became distinctly colder at the end of the 1950s. In 1958, Nasser celebrated his greatest triumph, achieving union with Syria, calling his new creation the United Arab Republic (UAR), retaining the name even after Syria dissolved the union in 1961 because of Egyptian high-handedness. Much to Khrushchev's chagrin, Nasser clamped down on the Syrian Communist Party, the largest and most influential Communist Party in the Middle East.[17] Violently deposing the Iraqi monarchy in 1958, Iraqi dictator Abdel Karim Qassem at first sought an alliance with his fellow radical in Egypt. The Iraqi–Egypt rapprochement soon soured, deteriorating into a competition for leadership of Arab nationalism. Nasser would brook no challengers, and Qassem, taking no particular liking to playing second fiddle, severed the Iraqi–Egyptian axis. Nasser tried to overthrow Qassem by subversion, when that failed he waged an all out propaganda war against the Iraqi leader. Iraqi Communists supported Qassem, earning Iraq Moscow's aid in pointed rejoinder to Egypt. Nasser's struggle with Iraq, then, was indirectly a fight for influence in the Middle East with the Soviet Union. The Egyptian campaign against Arab Communism eased the pressure on the United States and the United Kingdom and their allies in the Middle East. The newfound Anglo-American agreement and Nasser's preoccupation with Iraq made it possible for other Arab regimes to focus on their internal affairs. For the West, the Middle East gave little cause for concern when Kennedy became president.[18]

Challenging the conservative Arab regimes, and Western dominance of the Middle East, was the handsome, charismatic, eloquent figure of Gamal Abdul Nasser, taking power at the age of only 34, emerging as an effective speaker and rallying point for Arab nationalism, and a major leader in the nonalignment movement. His successes were astonishing, being the first native-born Egyptian leader in 150 years, having forced the British out of the Suez Canal bases, and surviving the Anglo-French onslaught during the Suez crisis. He was revered by millions of Arabs in the Middle East.[19] The United States courted Nasser after he took power in a military coup in 1952, believing his anti-Communist and anti-colonial rhetoric made him a valuable ally in the cold war, only to be weaned from this policy after the Egyptian leader acquired arms from the Soviet Union in 1955. Nasser thus opened the Middle East to Soviet penetration, a policy the Eisenhower administration had sought to prevent at all costs through its assiduous courtship of Egypt. In the early stages of the Suez crisis, the State Department evaluated the roles Nasser played in the Middle East. He posed as a progressive military dictator seeking to modernize Egypt and promote Egyptian leadership in the Arab world; he clearly wanted to be a symbol of Arab nationalism. The dark side was that he was "an aspirant for power on a large scale, utilizing without scruple and without regard to the interests of his own or other peoples the tensions, resentments and capacities for trouble that exist in the Middle East and Africa". The nationalization of the Suez Canal Company in July 1956 suggested that Nasser's third role dominated:

> Developments of the past few weeks, however, point clearly to the conclusion that Nasser is an international political adventurer of considerable skill with clearly defined objectives that seriously threaten the Western world, though probably with no definitely planned tactics or timetable. . . . Nasser intends to make full use of the resources of the Arab world, notably the Suez Canal and the oil, the resources and turmoil of the entire African continent, and the support of Muslims in Indonesia, China, Malaya, Siam, Burma and elsewhere, "to wield power without limit". . . . It must be concluded that Nasser is not a leader with whom it will be possible to enter into friendly arrangements of cooperation or with whom it would even be possible to make any feasible accommodations.[20]

Still, president Eisenhower sided with Nasser in the ensuing Suez crisis. Humiliating Britain and France, Eisenhower correspondingly boosted the power and prestige of Nasser among the neutral countries and in the Middle East. The US president was evidently of the opinion that a successful Anglo-French military operation was a greater detriment to American interests than enhancing Nasser's stature.

In his book *The Philosophy of the Revolution*, Nasser argued that Egypt was the center of three concentric circles embracing the Arab, Islamic, and the African worlds. Nasser believed it his duty to rid these areas of Western influence and colonialism, which in his parlance also included American interests. If successful, much power would have redounded to the Egyptian leader. Only belatedly did Eisenhower try to rein in Nasser. The American intervention in Lebanon in 1958, on the heels of the Iraqi revolution in July the same year, was an effort to stabilize the situation in the Middle East and contain Nasser's influence. In addition, President Eisenhower sought to impress on Nasser the extent of American military power and Soviet impotence to come to his assistance.[21] But soon thereafter, Eisenhower reverted to his original policy of placating the Egyptian dictator, believing friendly relations and aid would prevent the renewal of close Egyptian cooperation with the Soviets and take the edge off Nasser's most strident anti-Western propaganda and activities. Douglas Little and William Burns argue that President Eisenhower pursued a quiet détente with Nasser after the Lebanese invasion.[22] This rapprochement, Jeffrey Lefebvre notes, began as early as November 1958 in northeast Africa.[23] But as William Henry Brands points out, even during the best of times Egypt and the United States did not see eye to eye: "Normalization of relations between the United States and Egypt meant that the leaders of the two countries were talking, but it certainly did not mean that they were agreeing about much."[24] Little did it matter; for all Eisenhower's attempts to improve relations with Egypt, Nasser remained deeply suspicious of the United States. American aid totaling $400 million from 1952 to 1960 failed to alleviate these suspicions. Eisenhower pursued a more nuanced and sophisticated policy towards Nasser and Arab nationalism, not just treating the Middle East as a pawn in the global cold war as claimed by Kennedy.[25]

On the eve of the Kennedy administration, Nasser's parting words to the president in a speech celebrating the Egyptian revolution was a rejection of everything Eisenhower represented. The American embassy in Cairo reported on December 24, 1960: "US has not come in for such sharp and specific criticism for long time."[26] Whatever the Americans did, Nasser refused to give up his independence and his priorities to subordinate Egypt to American and British interests. From his point of view, he often detected hostile intent from the West, fearing that the ultimate American goal was his violent overthrow. From the American point of view, Nasser's unwillingness to heed its major Western benefactor in any matter of importance soured Nasser's relations with United States as the American government grew tired of giving aid in return for abuse when Lyndon Johnson was president. Nasser feared, probably rightfully so, that aligning himself too closely with the United States or making peace with Israel could jeopardize his claim to be the leader of Arab nationalism. When the union with Syria broke up in 1961 with much loss of face, Nasser reacted by declaring political and diplomatic warfare against the conservative Arab regimes, turning to socialist reconstruction at home. Despite the stridency of his rhetoric and his confrontational policies, Nasser failed to topple any of the conservative monarchies, succeeding only in polarizing the Arab world.[27] When civil war broke out in Yemen in September 1962, Nasser intervened in support of the revolutionary forces. Gaining a bridgehead on the Arabian Peninsula threatened oil-rich Saudi Arabia and the British colony in Aden. Despite American warnings to keep his hands off both, Nasser persisted. Unfortunately for the Egyptian leader, his forces were caught in the seemingly endless quagmire of the Yemeni civil war, draining Egypt's treasury and manpower. Fighting his fellow Arabs in Yemen cost Nasser much standing and prestige in the Middle East and internationally, while his socialist experiments at home brought the Egyptian economy close to bankruptcy.[28] As the 1960s proceeded Nasser's status as the chief spokesman for Arab nationalism lacked much of its former luster.

I

John F. Kennedy Confronts the Middle East

A New Beginning?

When John F. Kennedy became president, the Middle East was relatively quiet and the new American leader intended it to remain so. While the Soviet Union, despite prodigious efforts, had made relatively little inroads in the area, their potential for undermining Western interests was always great. Nasser patched up his relations with Moscow when his union with Syria fell apart in September 1961. The Soviet leaders became disillusioned with Quassem after he turned against his erstwhile allies the Iraqi Communists.[1] The new president had reason to fear that the renewed friendship between the Soviet Union and Egypt might cause further destabilization of the volatile Middle East. Kennedy had to contend with the impulsive, mercurial and unpredictable Nikita Khrushchev, who sought recognition from and superpower parity with the United States, strangely by adopting an often aggressive and threatening posture against the Americans. After successfully launching Sputnik on October 4, 1957, Khrushchev boasted that Soviet factories churned out missiles "like sausage". In reality, his Rocket Strategic Forces consisted, as late as 1959, of only four unwieldy missiles. Believing his threat of using nuclear weapons had forced the Anglo-French withdrawal from Suez, Khrushchev routinely rattled his nuclear arsenal when talking to Western leaders.[2] After the implosion of the Soviet empire in 1991, we know today how frail this Communist utopia was, but Khrushchev (as was the case with his predecessors) radiated Soviet power even from a position of inferiority. While much less powerful than the United States, the Soviet Union still could inflict horrifying damage on the West in a nuclear war. The possibility of a nuclear holocaust led the Western powers to tread warily around the Soviet leader. Enamored with his own successes, Khrushchev loudly proclaimed the construction of Communism in the USSR by 1980, pledging to overtake the United States economically by that time. While announcing victory in the economic competition against the West, Khrushchev also declared his support of wars of national liberation, intending to wrest the third world from Western dominance.[3] In the Middle East, this potentially heralded a concerted Soviet effort to side with Arab radicalism to drive out the vestiges of British and American influence in the area. The cold war and related issues consumed much presidential time and attention. John F. Kennedy approved the abortive attempt to overthrow Cuban dictator Fidel Castro at the Bay of Pigs, successfully maintained Western access to Berlin in the face of repeated challenges from Khrushchev, and faced down the Russian leader during the Cuban missiles crisis of October 1962, while dramatically escalating the American military commitment to Vietnam.[4] In this context, it was important for Kennedy to prevent the Middle East from becoming another flash point in the global cold war. The president's bold and innovative stroke was seeking rapprochement with Nasser, hoping to prevent the renewed Egyptian–Soviet entente from blossoming into an alliance that could destabilize the Middle East and turn the Egyptian leader towards domestic developments and away from his confrontational policies.

In his address accepting the nomination as candidate for the presidency by the Democratic Party, Kennedy introduced the concept of the new frontier. After paying tribute to the pioneers and their struggles, and describing the disappearance of the old frontier, Kennedy told the party faithful that the new frontier of the 1960s was a frontier of opportunities and hopes, as well as threats: "The new frontier of which I speak is not a set of promises – it is a set of challenges." In the Middle East the new frontier was on the Nile with Nasser leading the great trek into the future. The new frontiersmen were a versatile lot and would try anything; Arthur Schlesinger notes that the majority were professional men, "but ordinarily they used it as a springboard for general meddling".[5] When making Nasser the pivot of their Middle East efforts, the new frontiersmen casually dismissed his anti-American policies. The young Turks of the new frontier should therefore have been well aware of what Little labels "Nasser's shrill calls for Arab unity"; making Egypt key to American efforts in the Middle East was more than a little reckless.[6]

In all fairness to the new frontiersmen they were well aware that a rapprochement with Nasser was fraught with difficulties. Robert Komer, Kennedy's point man on the Middle East in the White House, noted in a memorandum for the president on December 8, 1961:

> The best we could achieve from a more forthcoming policy toward Nasser would be a strictly limited marriage of convenience; our interests run sharply athwart each other at too many points. At least in the early phases, moreover, we would be giving a lot more than we would get in return. Nor can we woo Nasser away from being a neutralist and nationalist (any more than Moscow could). But what

we might hope to achieve through a more professedly forthcoming policy is to create a vested interest in his part in better US/UAR relations, which would in itself inhibit him from taking actions which would upset it.[7]

The Kennedy approach to Nasser was a gamble, and the administration knew it, but believed the odds more favorable than they turned out to be. The Yemeni civil war undermined the fragile foundation of the Egyptian–American rapprochement. Nasser's dispatch of troops to support fellow Arab radicals in need was a potential bridgehead against Saudi Arabia and the British colony in Aden. Egypt's involvement in Yemen starkly highlighted the fundamental misconceptions behind American policy toward Nasser. While willing to modify his policies on minor points in deference to American wishes, Nasser refused to be derailed from issues he considered important, like the spread of Arab radicalism. The chance to extend his influence on the Arabian Peninsula was of greater priority than placating the Americans. Putting the conflict with Israel in the 'ice-box' was a gesture that gained him much in the eyes of the new frontiersmen, but cost him little. Being preoccupied with fighting his Arab rivals, Nasser had in the early 1960s neither the time, interest or resources to provoke a war against the Israelis. The Syrian secession from the UAR in 1961 was a tremendous loss of face for Nasser, and he reacted by trying to undermine the conservative regimes in the Middle East. The result was that by "the end of 1963 more Arab states were at each other's throats at once than ever before".[8] Not only that, during most of the Kennedy administration Nasser was isolated in the Arab world. After the breakup of the union with Syria, he refused to recognize the successor regime there, while his difficult relations with Iraq continued. To give credence to his fight against the conservative monarchies, Nasser broke off relations with Jordan and denounced the regime in Saudi Arabia. Intervening in Yemen, and killing fellow Arabs, did nothing to endear him to the populations in the Middle East. Egyptian–Soviet relations improved after 1961, and Nasser freely and happily accepted military and economic aid from Moscow; he did not in any sense become a Soviet stooge. Furthermore, Khrushchev had not necessarily picked a winner for increased USSR influence in the region by wagering on the Egyptian horse in the fractious Arab world. Nasser's isolation in the Middle East and independence of the Kremlin begs the question why the Kennedy administration thought a personal relationship with the president and large amounts of food aid were the panacea to the ills of the Middle East. By competing with the Soviet Union in wooing Nasser, the United States helped him overcome many of the disadvantages of his self-imposed isolation. By playing off his superpower benefactors against each other, Nasser increased his prestige in the Middle East. With the fundamental weakness of the Soviet agricultural sector, the Kremlin would probably have been reluctant to embark on more or less perpetual subsidies of Egypt, since Nasser did not portray any willingness to subordinate himself to Moscow in return for the gifts bestowed upon him. Given these circumstances, the Egyptian leader extracted a heavy price for a service that was available for free from the Kennedy administration.

Concomitant with Kennedy's tilt towards Egypt, the progressive power in the Middle East, the United States kept the conservative Arab regimes at arm's length. To prevent the evolvement of Nasserite-inspired elites and to secure oil supplies, the United States encouraged reform and modernization. Ironically, reform and modernization would often lead to the development of the newly educated classes most susceptible to Nasser's appeals. Pushing reform may have prevented radical Arabism from making inroads in Jordan, Saudi Arabia and Iran, but their effects were neither lasting nor particularly impressive. While feeling abandoned by the United States, the conservative monarchies could not afford to alienate the Americans. Great Britain was the chief beneficiary of this American policy: casting about for an alternative to American protection, Saudi Arabia restored relations with the United Kingdom in January 1963. Saudi Arabia had broken diplomatic relations with the United Kingdom in protest against the British reoccupation of Buraimi in October 1955 and the British invasion of Suez in November 1956. Fearing the Egyptian bridgehead in Yemen, the Saudis believed they might be the next victims of Nasser's suborning activities and therefore sought to ally themselves with Britain whose Aden colony was exposed to Egyptian expansionism. Britain, however, was far more concerned with challenging the American arms monopoly in Saudi Arabia than providing the regime with military protection.

While Anglo-American relations were much improved after their nadir during the Suez crisis, the powers approached the cold war issues somewhat differently. Great Britain was generally more conciliatory towards the Soviet Union, fearing nuclear war would mean the total obliteration of Britain as well as being apprehensive about the potential consequences of a resurgent Germany. To prevent either and to encourage East–West détente, Britain was more inclined than the United States to offer concessions to the Soviet Union. In addition, Britain was willing to placate Moscow to facilitate top-level summits and disarmament talks and defuse tensions over Berlin and Germany. The British government was firm in excluding China from the United Nations, but was pressured by British public opinion in favoring admission of the People's Republic of China. The State Department feared the erosion of British support for its China policy. But it was the Middle East, always the Middle East, where the potential for divergence of Anglo-American policies was greatest. Britain was far more sensitive to the security of its oil supplies than the United States, expressing a willingness to employ military force on the Arabian Peninsula, whereas the Americans thought political measures sufficed.[9]

To secure the uninterrupted flow of oil to the West, and maintain pro-Western regimes in oil-rich countries like Kuwait, Britain wanted to prevent Nasser and the Soviet Union from making inroads in the Persian Gulf. From a bridgehead in the Gulf, they could, the British feared, undermine the entire Middle East. Britain therefore placed a high value on area political stability. The Foreign Office explained the rationale behind British Middle East policy in this way:

> H.M.G. necessarily regard their position in the area as a closely knit whole. This is so for both military and political reasons. Militarily to carry out their obligation to defend Kuwait they need the use of a number of bases in the Arabian Peninsula. To ensure the use of these bases they need both the military power to protect them and the confidence of the Rulers, in whose territory they lie, that they will defend their independence. The Rulers are for the most part very conscious that Arab nationalism would sap their positions if given a chance; they attach importance to the preservation of the present system of government throughout the Gulf and look to us to help them. This explains why we sometimes have to react very firmly against apparently unimportant nibbling attempts to change the present position in one or another part of the area.[10]

After the Suez crisis in 1956, Britain had moved its military headquarters in the Middle East to its Aden base, an effort that would eventually account for the bulk of the more than 30,000 air, army and navy personnel stationed in the Middle East. A smaller British contingent from all the three services was stationed in Bahrain. The British position in Aden and its hinterland was complex; the Aden colony consisted essentially of Aden town and base, while the hinterland (the Aden Federation) had the status of protected states, similar to Britain's relations with the Persian Gulf sheikhdoms, whereby Britain was in charge of their defense and foreign policy. The Aden colony and Federation were merged on the initiative of London. Hadramut, or the Eastern Aden protectorate, chose to remain aloof of this merger.[11]

Despite the British military build-up on the Arabian Peninsula, and being granted hegemony in the Persian Gulf by the United States, the British position in 1961 faced several challenges. The Imam of Yemen, harboring irredentist ambitions in the Aden colony hinterland, deeply resented British attempts to build the Aden Federation. From the mid-1950s to the early 1960s, Yemeni tribesmen repeatedly pestered Aden with armed incursions, while at the same time dissident tribesmen in Aden received money, arms and encouragement from Yemen. Before the revolution in Yemen, Britain easily withstood these pinprick attacks; indeed, they proved beneficial to Britain as they encouraged the hinterland sheiks into the Federation for protection against Yemeni aggression. In revenge for the British reoccupation of Buraimi, crown prince Faisal of Saudi Arabia encouraged an uprising in Oman with money, men and military supplies. Britain, with the support of the sultan of Oman's armed forces, crushed the rebellion between 1957 and 1959. While no longer a threat, some rebels remained at large, and after 1961 the rebellion had degenerated into a bothersome terrorist campaign. Finally, Anglo-Saudi relations remained frozen from 1956 to 1963. The British made little or no effort to open lines of communication with Saudi Arabia after the Suez crisis, arguing they had no further concessions to offer and that the Saudis had to take the first step. While Buraimi ceased to be an Anglo-American point of contention after the Suez crisis, it did not for Faisal. Being the chief architect of the Saudi occupation of Buraimi, the prince suffered a terrible loss of face when Britain reoccupied the oasis – a humiliation Faisal found difficult to forgive and forget. Even after the restoration of diplomatic relations between Britain and Saudi Arabia in January 1963, disagreement over the oasis caused continued friction in Anglo-Saudi relations. Before resuming relations with Britain, the Saudi government actively sought to undermine the British position in the Persian Gulf, after the rebellion in Oman proper petered out, by encouraging an uprising in Dhofar in western Oman on the border of the Aden Federation. The reoccupation of Buraimi in October 1955 forced a reevaluation of British defense policies in the Gulf; thereafter the position from Aden to Kuwait was considered a close-knit whole. The British, then, had ample reason and the will to project their military power in the area. They would get their chance when Iraq laid claim to Kuwait in June 1961.[12]

The Kennedy administration shared the British concern about access to Middle East oil, and believed the best approach to secure oil resources was to conciliate Nasser to avoid nationalist turmoil in the Middle East.[13] From an oil policy perspective, the 1960s remained strangely tranquil compared to the turbulent 1950s, when Great Britain and the United States were often at loggerheads over the control of oil, and to the oil crisis 1969–1979, when oil prices shot from $1.20 per barrel to $41 per barrel, causing massive dislocation to the industrial economies of the West. The United States and Britain were lulled into a sense of complacency, falsely believing that they held the upper hand because of the producer countries' dependence on a global market for their oil. The Anglo-American oil companies and their governments easily brushed off attempts by the oil-producing nations in the Middle East to use oil as a political weapon as late as after the Six Day War in 1967. When the Middle Eastern oil producers tried to embargo oil as a punishment for Britain and United States supporting Israel, the embargo collapsed within months. The United States cranked up its own domestic production, which, with increased Venezuelan production, made up the shortfall of Middle East oil production. This, combined with the loss of revenue for the oil producers, forced the termination of the embargo. But the very success in containing the oil producers also led Anglo-American policy makers to view questions of oil with less urgency than their predecessors. While Kennedy had no intention of leaving the Middle East (in fact he sought to enhance US interests and secure a continued Anglo-American presence in the area), he set in train motions that decreased American influence and contributed to the oil crisis of 1969–1979.[14]

In addition to turning Nasser away from the Soviet Union, securing the oil supply and supporting the British, Kennedy encouraged the conservative states – Jordan, Iran and Saudi Arabia – to reform and modernize their societies to better withstand the onslaught of Arab nationalism. While American encouragement went along with Faisal's mildly reformist impulse, the shah of Iran chafed under American pressure.[15] Kennedy's ideas of reform and modernization were neither new nor novel. British foreign minister Anthony Eden (1951–55) warned the cabinet on February 16, 1953, of the need for modernization in the Middle East:

> In the second half of the 20th century we cannot hope to maintain our position in the Middle East by the methods of the last century. However little we like it, we must face that fact. Commercial concessions whose local benefit appears to redound mainly to the Shahs and Pashas no longer serve in the same way to strengthen our influence in those countries, and they come increasingly under attack by local nationalist opinion.[16]

Needless to say, Eden's modernist inclinations foundered on the reoccupation of Buraimi and the Suez crisis. While being well aware of the dangers of backwardness, Britain still relied on "the Sheiks and Pashas", having done little to encourage reform in the Persian Gulf and Aden. Indeed, the British presence was often extremely limited in the hinterland, apart from the occasional bombing foray to keep restless tribesmen in check. The main American client, king Saud of Saudi Arabia, was the most reactionary of all.

Much of the stability of the renewed Anglo-American relationship after Suez and the more limited, but restored, British position in the Middle East hinged on the personal friendship between the British prime minister, Harold Macmillan, and president Dwight D. Eisenhower. But in 1961 Eisenhower retired, leaving Macmillan to ponder how to establish a working relationship with the new American president. For Macmillan, while he believed in the special relationship, close relations with the United States were a way to maintain Britain's position as a great power. Macmillan's official biographer has written a rather amusing account of how Macmillan charmed himself into Kennedy's good graces, so that according to Jacqueline Kennedy, the president "could speak almost to an equal". Macmillan's success at ingratiating himself with Kennedy was the result of a long-term and planned effort. In a memorandum, the prime minister wrote: "I must somehow convince him [Kennedy] that I am worth consulting not as an old friend (as Eisenhower felt) but as a man who, although of advancing years, has young and fresh thoughts." Macmillan and the Foreign Office worked assiduously in soliciting an invitation to Washington early in president Kennedy's tenure, in order for Macmillan "to establish good personal relations with the President". This was desirable because, foreign minister Lord Home noted, apart from gaining influence, in case of disagreement between Britain and the United States "it is easier to limit its effects if personal relations between Heads of Government are good". But the new president had to be approached carefully, because whereas Macmillan appealed to Eisenhower's sense of "sentiment and comradeship", which "was more effective than intellectual argument", this was not the case with Kennedy. Here "cosy chats" were of no value; Macmillan needed practical and useful plans to gain the president's ear. Always the dissembler, Macmillan wrote in his memoirs: "Apart from a formal telegram of good wishes I decided to wait, unlike some of my European colleagues who were already pressing their claims to visit Washington."[17]

According to Arthur Schlesinger and Theodore Sorenson, Kennedy had a closer personal relationship with Macmillan than with any other foreign leader.[18] The price of Macmillan's friendship was a constant pleading for American support for British policies in their colonies and dependencies, with the underlying threat that unless American support was forthcoming, it would damage Anglo-American relations. The special pleading paid off handsomely, secretary of state Dean Rusk assuring Home at one point that he "hoped the United Kingdom Government realised how much the United States Government valued their special relations with the United Kingdom". The Americans seemed to have developed a considerable respect for Macmillan's personal qualities.[19] Sometimes, Macmillan was driven to near hysteria by perceived or imagined American threats to empire. The prime minister complained to Kennedy on April 28, 1962 that if American officials put any value on British military presence in the Near and Far East, "they should refrain from encouraging the anti-Colonial pressures which were making it increasingly difficult for us to maintain our bases overseas". In fact, the United Kingdom was entitled to American support in its overseas role. The president disclaimed any effort on part of his administration to undermine British colonies. "He would be very interested to hear of any recent expression of responsible American opinion which had embarrassed the United Kingdom Government in the discharge of their Colonial responsibilities."[20] Despite being sometimes annoyed by Macmillan's constant pleading, the president supported British policies. Indeed, the United States was very solicitous of its British ally, in large part because of lingering memories of the Suez crisis, memories Macmillan eagerly recalled at times of Anglo-American disagreement. John Darwin observes that after Suez "successive American administrations showed a surprising tenderness towards British pretensions to remain a great power".[21]

It was a crisis in Kuwait that became the first test of the newly established Macmillan–Kennedy partnership. The British had wasted no time in approaching the new American administration seeking support for its position on the Persian Gulf. But while having no hesitation in approaching the Americans and wanting to remain in the Persian Gulf, there emerges from the diplomatic record a curious ambiguity among British policy makers. There is a certain defensiveness in the British position, almost an embarrassment over still having areas of influence. But whatever doubts they harbored privately, Macmillan and his successor Douglas-Home pursued with great intensity Britain's traditional policy of maintaining, and if possible even enlarging, its area of interest in the Middle East. Great Britain acknowledged Kuwait's independence and terminated its agreements with that country in June 1961. Shortly thereafter, Qassem announced his intention to incorporate Kuwait into the republic of Iraq, claiming that Kuwait had been part of the Basra province under the Ottoman empire. The United Kingdom promptly informed the ruler of Kuwait of its willingness to assist him, with force if necessary. Kuwait was Britain's chief concern on the Persian Gulf because of its large oil production, which favorably assisted the British balance of payments, and because of Kuwait's willingness to accept and hold pound sterling. With the dispatch of British troops went the usual requests for American aid and assistance. The United States was in complete accord with British policy, Kennedy approving American political and logistical support at a National Security Council meeting on June 29, 1961.[22]

The British wanted their military presence in Kuwait to be a demonstration of overwhelming power. The American consul in Kuwait reported to Washington:

> Kuwait is being treated to impressive display British military might. Carrier BULWARK and two frigates presently Kuwait bay and one tank landing ship (MEON) unloading trucks and tanks in suburb Shuwaikh. Troops of Marine Commando unit (British battalion strength) with plenty fire power and transport being transported, some by helicopter, to assembly area at new jet air port south of town. Meanwhile squadron Hunter jets from Bahrain thunder overhead.[23]

A total number of 5,000 British troops were landed in Kuwait. The

American embassy in London later described the landings as a "well-developed plan . . . put quickly and effectively into operation".[24] Military success and unconditional American backing did not suffice for the British who immediately tried to micromanage the American effort in the Gulf. This was in line with previous Anglo-American cooperative ventures in the Middle East where the British spent much time and energy in tailoring American actions to their own specifications.[25] Home cabled Rusk on July 2, 1961 requesting an American naval presence outside Kuwait: "Our own naval forces in the area are still rather thin and reconnaissance by the U.S. destroyer could be of great help – particularly if at the same time the second destroyer were to be moved round Bahrain from Aden." Rusk believed that British area forces sufficed and declined closer military association. The crisis eventually blew over when British troops were replaced by a mixed force from the Arab League, principally Saudi Arabia, Jordan and Egypt. Privately, the British admitted to being very pleased with the American assistance during the Kuwaiti crisis. American diplomats later wondered if there had been a genuine threat to Kuwait, but that is almost beside the point, as the crisis was eminently suited to display British military prowess.[26]

Nasser seemed to be of two minds about the British intervention in Kuwait: on the one hand, he welcomed the slapping down of his Iraqi rival; on the other hand, he clearly resented the successful display of British military power. Accordingly, the Egyptian dictator stepped up his campaign against the British-supported feudal rulers on the Persian Gulf. Meeting with Philips Talbot, assistant secretary for the Near East, Denis Greenhill of the British embassy in Washington speculated: "one reason the UAR had singled out the UK for propaganda abuse in recent weeks is that the UK is one of the few countries left to which Nasser can still be rude with 'impunity'". But neither the United States nor Britain expressed much alarm at this last twist of Nasser's propaganda machine.[27]

Egyptian–American relations reached its high point during the summer of 1962. Nasser had kept the Arab–Israeli dispute in the 'ice-box', hosting a very moderate conference of African neutralists and pledging to Kennedy to keep differences with the United States 'within limits'.[28] Although the United States was committed to the survival of Israel from 1948, its relations with Israel first grew close after the Six Day War. The United States declined to align itself with Israel before 1960, believing too close identification with Israel could jeopardize American relations with the Arab states. Eisenhower used economic and political pressure to force Israel to withdraw from the Sinai peninsula, occupied after Israel's invasion of Suez in 1956. Furthermore, Eisenhower refused to give Israel a security guarantee and gave it little economic support. American–Israeli relations grew warmer under Kennedy and Johnson, in part because of the

Democratic president's dependence on the Jewish vote. Kennedy was the first president to define United States–Israeli relations as special, pay close attention to Israel's security problems and sell a major defensive arms system to Israel.[29] Kennedy sought good relations with both Israel and Egypt. "The fact that the security and integrity of Israel are of deep and lasting concern to the US", Kennedy wrote Nasser May 27, 1963, "is not a matter which has up to this point prevented the growth of friendly US–UAR relations, and I hope it will not do so in the future". The United States opposed all aggression in the area: "We mean not only Arab aggression against Israel but any Israeli aggression as well. We showed this in 1956, and mean it just as much today."[30] The president signaled very clearly that the United States gave priority to its relations with Egypt over Israel. The breakup of the Egyptian–Syrian union and Nasser's conflict with the conservative Arab states reduced the pressure on Israel as the common enemy of the Arabs, and allowed Kennedy to give extraordinary guarantees to Israel. Even Lyndon Johnson, a self-professed friend of Israel, declined to let the relationship blossom into an alliance to compensate for deteriorating American relations with Egypt. Until Nasser broke relations with the United States and Britain, alleging that British and American airplanes assisted Israel in the Six Day War, president Johnson worked hard to avoid a breakdown in American relations with Egypt. When the United States sold arms to Jordan and Saudi Arabia to counter Soviet arms supplies to Egypt, Iraq and Syria, Johnson was forced, by domestic pressure, to supply Israel as well. Only after the Six Day War, and the advent of Richard Nixon, did Israel become an important American strategic asset in the cold war against the Soviet Union.[31]

American policy makers confidently predicted that long-term food aid would make Nasser more amenable to the United States; they disregarded British objections that subsidizing Egyptian food imports freed Egyptian resources for Nasser to pursue policies in opposition to Anglo-American interests in the Middle East. But even John Badeau, American ambassador to Cairo and one of the chief architects of the American tilt towards Egypt, sometimes found Nasser's independence difficult to swallow: "We have had to wink at the wasteful diversion of resources into mutual efforts at subversion."[32] However, fear of forcing a too close Egyptian alignment with the Kremlin limited the pressure the United States could put on Egypt "to contain UAR's overweening ambition". Nasser's brand of Arab radicalism was, in any case, much preferable to increased Communist influence in the Middle East, which would be totally antagonistic to American interests while Nasser seemed more attuned to American policy. Furthermore, as the State Department believed the conservative Arab regimes only had the dimmest prospects of survival, rapprochement with Nasser emerged as a sensible policy.[33]

The most important tool for improving American relations with Egypt was the Food for Peace program or Law (PL) 480, initiated for disposing surplus agricultural commodities. After the Lebanese invasion, the Eisenhower administration offered Egypt PL480 aid in six-month install-ments. Nasser's moderate behavior in American eyes in 1961–62 encouraged the Kennedy administration to implement a large three-year effort with PL480 in October 1962, part of "a sophisticated, sensitive effort", Talbot argued, "to establish a more affirmative relationship" with Egypt. In addition, the United States offered continuation of its aid program with about $200 million annually, and "assiduous promotion of the personal relationship between President Kennedy and President Nasser through correspondence". Talbot vigorously defended the policy against British objections that American aid financed Nasser's anti-Western ventures, and that the Egyptian economy would collapse without American assistance. Privately, high administration officials were well aware that the United States sustained the shaky Egyptian economy. Talbot explained to his British counterpart Roger Stevens in May 1962 that the aid made it possible for the American embassy in Cairo "to talk to the Egyptians about a wide range of issues and to tell them frankly about aspects of their policy which they disliked", in contrast to the previous year. The United States promised to provide Egypt with $431.8 million in food aid for the next three fiscal years. By 1963, Egypt had become the world's largest per capita consumer of American food aid. Even with this substan-tial aid, the State Department could not tie political conditions to the assistance, or make Egypt cease its propaganda against Israel. American officials hoped to persuade Egypt "to undertake further policy changes in its own interest", to turn Egypt towards domestic development, away from the Soviets and towards a less confrontational stance to the West.[34] The hope was to shift Egyptian policies gradually away from confrontation with the West, encouraging Nasser to think that he would reap greater benefits by being friendly than by being hostile. Unfortunately, the American experiment toward Egypt went awry because in the end both parties had incompatible interests, beginning largely with the conflict in Yemen. But during the summer of 1962 the signs were promising, as Nasser went to some length to accommodate the Americans.

2

Kennedy, Nasser, Macmillan and the War in Yemen

1962–1963

When the aging but ruthless Iman Ahmad, leader of Yemen, died on September 19, 1962, his far less capable son, Mohammed al-Badr, succeeded him. Yemen under Ahmad was distinctly medieval, the Iman endeavoring to isolate the country from outside influences. The pressure for reform and modernization was substantial, particularly among army officers inspired by Nasser's version of Arab nationalism. The more radical of the officers, under the leadership of Colonel Abdullah Sallal, believed al-Badr incapable of reforming Yemen and ousted him in a coup only a week after his father's death. Unfortunately for Sallal, al-Badr escaped the assassination attempt and rallied mountain tribes under the Royalist banner in a guerrilla war against the revolutionaries. Fearing the spread of Nasser's revolution to their homeland, the Saudis supported the Royalists.[1] There is ample evidence that Nasser inspired and instigated the coup. The Egyptian leader soon dispatched troops to assist the revolution, an effort that would eventually total 70,000 soldiers.[2] Having little or no interest in Yemen, and through no fault of its own, the United States was caught in the crossfire of placating the Egyptians, reassuring the Saudis and supporting a continued British presence in Aden and the Persian Gulf. Whatever blame was assigned to Nasser for the civil war in Yemen, Kennedy refused to give up the rapprochement with Egypt. The United States signed the three-year PL480 agreement after learning about Egyptian involvement in Yemen. Komer observed, "Nasser probably wants the agreement now so he can show the US backs him despite Yemen. Saudis and others may interpret this the same way." Kennedy approved a long-term PL480 on October 5, 1962 "but desired every effort to insure minimum publicity".[3]

With no fundamental interests at stake in Yemen, the main American concern was to avoid involvement in the Yemen civil war. The United

States wanted to contain the conflict and prevent the war from spilling over into Saudi Arabia. Although the Kennedy administration kept the regime at arm's length, Saudi Arabia's strategic location and large oil reserves could not be overlooked. To prevent a Saudi–Egyptian confrontation over Yemen, the United States pressured the Saudis to cease assisting the Royalists and planned to use Saudi compliance to encourage Egyptian withdrawal from Yemen. The United States and Great Britain feared that the Soviet Union would exploit the war to extend its influence into the Arabian Peninsula. The fragile Aden Federation, with its disenfranchised cosmopolitan town and backward hinterland, was a fertile ground for Nasser's nationalist agitation, and, the British feared, for Moscow's influence. To contain the Nasserite bridgehead in Yemen, Britain and the Adeni sheiks surreptitiously supported the Royalists with arms and matériel. The United States warned Egypt against encroaching on Aden, where the US had a vital interest.[4]

In almost all their communications, American policy makers expressed fear that being too antagonistic to Nasser would only turn him towards the Soviet Union. If not careful, the Yemen war could be the entering wedge to increased USSR influence on the Arabian Peninsula. Ironically, while persuading the Kremlin to supply his Yemen operation, Nasser jealously guarded his clients, thereby preventing the Soviet Union from gaining any credit for their efforts.[5] In other words, Nasser, for his own reasons, in the early stages of the Yemen war, prevented the Soviet Union from gaining much influence. While effectively keeping Moscow at bay, Nasser cleverly played on American fears that unless they reined in the Saudis, Egypt and Yemen would have no other choice than to turn to the Soviet Union. As American ambassador to Saudi Arabia between 1961 and 1965, Parker Hart notes that: "in those days of the Cold War Washington believed that Soviet spheres of interest in a backward land as Yemen would quickly evolve into spheres of control".[6]

Assessing the civil war in Yemen at the end of Lyndon Johnson's administration, the State Department outlined the wider issues of the conflict for the United States; one of the main concerns of American policy was to maintain peace and stability in the volatile Middle East. Arab radicalism, Nasser style and Communist efforts on the Arab Peninsula emerged as the main challenges to American policy. As the Yemen civil war deepened, Soviet and partly Chinese Communist influence increased among the Yemeni radicals. The United States therefore promoted modernization and reform as a counterweight to Communist assistance to friendly Arab regimes:

> The case of Yemen has been a focal point of our concern. United States interest in this remote Arab country – which in 1962 was still an isolated medieval kingdom in a mountainous corner of the Arabian Peninsula – quickly burgeoned

when Yemen subsequently developed into a hotbed of angry and dangerous confrontation between radical and conservative forces in the Arab world.[7]

American ties with Saudi Arabia embarrassed the Kennedy administration. Compared to Egypt, Saudi Arabia was a backward country; indeed, slavery was still a legal institution in the early 1960s.[8] Thus when Faisal paid a state visit to Washington in the fall of 1962 to seek American support, the president was forced into a delicate balancing act. Kennedy's special assistant for the Middle East, Robert Komer, outlined the alternatives in a briefing memorandum for the president; the Saudis feared that if Nasser succeeded in establishing a bridgehead on the Arabian Peninsula, they would be the next victims of his suborning activities. Despite Saudi and British support of the Royalists, American policy was to maintain its non-involvement in the conflict. The United States had but little leverage, Komer argued; besides, the archaic Imanate of Yemen did not merit American intervention on its behalf. The United States firmly backed the territorial integrity of Saudi Arabia, with the exception of the Saudis needlessly provoking Nasser into attacking them. Yemen was not an issue of sufficient magnitude to jeopardize American relations with Egypt. In an attempt to calm Saudi apprehensions, Komer asked the president to explain the rationale behind US policy toward Egypt:

> [O]ur policy toward Nasser is designed (a) to turn him inward; and (b) to increase US leverage on him so that we can encourage policies less antagonistic to our interests and those of our friends. We do not think US aid (mostly food) is keeping Nasser in power. If we didn't help, he'd merely turn to the Soviets, which would be emphatically against US and Arab interests.

Besides, modernization and development were "the best antidote to Nasserism". The signs from Saudi Arabia were encouraging, but Komer urged for an acceleration of the reform process. Most importantly, from Faisal's point of view, the president assured him of continued American support.[9] Kennedy, in return for American security guarantees, urged Faisal to abolish slavery, limit the extravagance of the Saudi Royal family and the power of the mullahs, and institute fiscal and judicial reforms and make a determined effort to include educated Saudi youths in the Royal administration.[10] But Faisal was cautioned as the war in Yemen intensified: "We wish Faysal fully understand our commitment to Royal Family as such contingent upon progress and reform in Saudi Arabia and does not connote preservation of Saudi Royal Family at all costs."[11]

With the revolutionaries in apparent control, the State Department persuaded president Kennedy to recognize Yemen on December 19, 1962, provided the new regime kept its international obligations and refrained from meddling in Aden. Recognition was also extended to continue the

American rapprochement of Egypt, and to facilitate the withdrawal of Egyptian forces from Yemen. For Kennedy recognition was an instrument to contain the conflict. While the United States considered recognition, Egypt bombed Saudi border areas on November 2, 1962, despite repeated assurances from Nasser that he did not have any designs on Saudi Arabia. In part the bombing was a defensive measure from Nasser, as Saudi intervention in the conflict soon showed up in the capture of American-made weapons by the Yemeni republicans and confirmed observations of Saudi officers with the Royalist forces.[12] Nevertheless, Saudi Arabia was a major American concern. The United States expressed grave concern to Egypt, and pledged support of Saudi Arabia. In this, the State Department set the pattern for further American reactions to Egypt under Kennedy and Lyndon Johnson. Despite a clamor from Congress, the American public, Britain and Israel for punishment, both presidents wanted good relations with Nasser and refused to apply sanctions against Egypt. Unfortunately, Nasser seemed constitutionally unable to stop his propaganda against Western imperialism regardless of what policy emanated from Washington and London. But if he had acknowledged publicly the friendly Anglo-American policy toward Egypt, much of his position internationally would have evaporated as Nasser had built his reputation fighting Western imperialism.[13]

Nasser's categorical assurance "that the United Arab Republic will not use Yemen as a springboard for invasion against Saudi Arabia" sufficed for the United States to recognize the Yemen Arab Republic (YAR), as the new regime in Yemen called itself. Besides, Talbot argued, since Egypt was the largest and most powerful state in the Middle East, its behavior could be kept within tolerable limits by involving it with the United States. Alienating Egypt could be dangerous: "If the UAR were to direct its power against US interests, it could damage these seriously." Superpower competition for his favor gave Nasser additional leverage; Talbot feared American pressure or denial of aid would only result in Nasser turning to the Soviet Union, increasing its influence in the Middle East. The United States still had many cards to play. Egypt's aversion to foreign control and desperate economic situation opened up constructive use of American aid, giving the United States potential influence in a key Middle Eastern country.[14] But the gamble in recognizing Yemen did not pay off; the YAR was the most fragile of political creations, being propped up by Egyptian bayonets, and having little or no independent foundation of its own. Recognition as an inducement for Egypt to disengage was a failure, as Nasser had no intention of withdrawing until he had secured the survival of the YAR.[15]

The Saudis did not play their part; Faisal distrusted Nasser and responded to the American recognition of Yemen by increasing his aid to the rebels, as did king Hussein of Jordan, fearing that a Nasserite bridge-head on the Arabian Peninsula could be used to undermine all the pro-Western regimes in the Middle East. Egypt retaliated by a more or less continuous bombing campaign of rebel bases in Saudi territory, but to little military effect. As part of the American package proposal in recognizing Yemen, Egypt pledged to begin withdrawing its forces. The bombing campaign was thus in clear violation of Egyptian undertakings. But Kennedy was intent on maintaining American ties with the UAR, and declined to pressure Egypt. Writing to Nasser on January 19, 1963, the president categorically assured the Egyptian leader that the United States was not playing a double policy in Yemen. "We have done and will do what is necessary to protect our important interests in the Arabian Peninsula, but this has been most carefully calculated not to support Saudi policies in Yemen." As the United States refused to pressure Egypt, it refused to pres-sure Faisal. Egyptian bombings of Saudi Arabia and the concomitant propaganda campaign were not helpful, but Kennedy wanted to continue working with Egypt to bring about disengagement from Yemen. The pres-ident concluded: "Many people in both our countries question whether good relations between us are really possible. I think they are wrong, but it is up to us to prove them wrong."[16]

In fact, both Saudi Arabia and Egypt operated on the mistaken assump-tion that they were hurting each other. Nasser believed the Saudi regime weak and ripe for revolution, but the bombing campaign and Egyptian propaganda offensive did not seriously undermine the monarchy. The Saudis thought that by aiding the Royalists they were bleeding Egypt dry. On the contrary, foreign currency costs were low, as were Egyptian casu-alties, while Nasser's army gained valuable combat experience. To prevent further Egyptian incursions into Saudi Arabia and assure the nervous Saudis, Kennedy committed a token air squadron of eight F-100 planes and 500 troops (operation Hard Surface) in Saudi Arabia from July 15, 1963 to January 1, 1964. The president kept the planes on a tight leash, they were only allowed to return fire in self-defense. All other actions had to be personally authorized by Kennedy.[17] Operation Hard Surface was also in response to an Egyptian air drop of arms and ammunition in Saudi Arabia on February 16, 1963 – a clear indication that Nasser believed it possible to encourage domestic unrest in the kingdom. Saudi authorities foiled this rather amateurish attempt at subversion.[18] The air squadron was condi-tioned on the Saudis refusing aid to the Royalists and denying use of Saudi territory for operations in Yemen. American military assistance to Saudi Arabia was presented to Nasser as an inducement for Faisal to disengage.[19] The shielding of Saudi Arabia, the Americans told Faisal, meant he could safely disengage from Yemen now that Saudi was being protected by the United States. Furthermore, in a communication to Faisal on February 22,

1963, Kennedy again stressed the need for internal reform in Saudi Arabia, claiming continued involvement in Yemen would only serve to undermine the fabric of Saudi society.[20] As an additional incentive to secure Saudi cooperation, the president authorized American assistance to build Saudi air defense capabilities.[21]

Aware of American plans to recognize Yemen, the British refused to follow suit. Macmillan claimed to Kennedy on November 15, 1962 that recognition would undermine the British position in Aden. The prime minister's arguments did not impress the president, who believed that Nasser would do whatever it took to ensure victory, if necessary calling for Russian support, thus opening South West Arabia (Aden town and protectorates) to the influence of the Soviet Union. Besides, Kennedy observed that neither the United States nor Britain was willing to intervene with military forces. The president feared that Saudi Arabia and Jordan would be the losers in a major Arab war, because of the strength of Nasserism in their respective countries. The British had no confidence in any assurance Nasser gave, believing he fobbed the Americans off with empty promises. Kennedy declined to write off the rapprochement with Egypt, "trying to see whether we could not exert more influence on Nasser by being friendly than by being hostile". The president assured the Egyptian leader on December 24, 1962: "I regard the very substantial aid we are providing the UAR as a token of our serious intent to establish a new and more constructive relationship between our two countries." Still, to placate the British, American recognition of Yemen depended on Nasser pledging withdrawal of Egyptian forces; a token Egyptian unit promptly was withdrawn once Jordan and Saudi Arabia ceased aiding the rebels. For Yemen, the price of recognition was to adhere to the international obligations signed by the Imanate. That is, accepting the Aden–Yemen boundary agreement of 1934. With these commitments, Kennedy aimed to secure a continued British presence in Aden and the Persian Gulf. From reading the diplomatic record, it is hard to avoid the impression of a president being very solicitous of Macmillan and the British.[22]

As a result of the Yemen imbroglio, Saudi Arabia and Britain overcame years of estrangement and resumed diplomatic relations on January 17, 1963. Thereafter, the British pursued an aggressive commercial policy towards Saudi Arabia, including pushing and selling large quantities of military hardware. Faisal feared a Saudi army filled with officers with Nasserite sympathies, and sought British assistance to create and train a 'White Army', that is a National Guard loyal to the regime. Faisal intended to use the White Army to prevent and crush any uprising from the regular forces. Britain, with Macmillan's approval, encouraged British officers to serve as instructors in the White Army. Britain's resumption of relations with Saudi Arabia represented a dramatic resurgence of British influence in the Middle East since its nadir after the Suez crisis. Slowly, the British had built themselves up to real power and influence, through military intervention in Oman 1957 to 1959, landing forces in Jordan in 1958 and Kuwait in 1961, and, finally, conducting small-scale operations against Yemeni incursions, mostly in the late 1950s, but also in the early 1960s. The British military presence was substantial, so much so that the Joint Chiefs of Staff noted in a memorandum to secretary of defense Robert McNamara: "The UK forces in the Middle East can conduct effective military operations anywhere in the Arabian Peninsula. The combination of coordinated US and UK military capability represents a responsive and flexible force for establishing a credible deterrent."[23] In Cairo, Britain resuming relations with Saudi Arabia while refusing to recognize the Yemen Arab Republic was seen as a hostile act, another example of Britain continuously working against the interests of the United Arab Republic.[24]

With the resumption of Anglo-Saudi relations, and merging of the Aden colony with the surrounding protectorates into the Aden Federation, Kennedy believed it was time for Britain to recognize Yemen. The president explained to Macmillan on January 26, 1963 that it would help to insure respect for the Anglo-American position elsewhere on the Arabian Peninsula. Recognition would isolate Faisal, because, in the face of a united Anglo-American front, the Saudis were hardly in a position to continue aiding Yemeni rebels. If Saudi assistance ceased, Nasser could no longer justify the presence of an Egyptian army in Yemen. Chances for a Royalist victory were remote, the president argued, and recognition might forestall aggressive moves against Saudi Arabia and elsewhere. Recent Egyptian bombing of Saudi Arabia was stopped only by strong American protests. Kennedy continued:

> Once Nasser is deprived of an excuse to maintain a heavy presence in Yemen, natural Yemeni distaste for what is really an alien occupation should soon reassert itself. We doubt that Nasser will find the Yemenis willing tools, any more than he found the Syrians or Iraqis so. But if we force the UAR to reinforce rather than reduce its presence in Yemen, and give the Soviets a chance to do so too, we may end up with a situation far more threatening to us.[25]

Kennedy's request set off a fierce debate in the Macmillan administration, pitting the colonial office against the Foreign Office. The British governor in Aden, Sir Charles Johnston, argued that, to appease Nasser, the Americans wanted to 'kill' the Royalist forces. Britain, however, had no need to placate a Nasser threatening the Aden colony; a Royalist victory in Yemen was therefore much to be preferred to the country under Egyptian control. American policy was conceptually wrong, Johnston claimed; only by making life difficult for Nasser could an Egyptian withdrawal from Yemen be achieved. Non-recognition therefore remained

British policy.[26] Informing the president of Britain's unwillingness to recognize Yemen, Macmillan regretted the divergence of British and American policies, "But as I see it this is due more to differences in our circumstances than divergences in objectives."[27] Despite repeated American entreaties afterwards, Britain refused to recognize Yemen during the remainder of the Kennedy presidency.[28]

Johnston thought the Americans rather condescending, when the State Department persistently argued that only by Nasser's withdrawal could Saudi Arabia's survival be ensured. While the Saudi regime was unstable "at all times and could blow up tomorrow", Faisal was no fool and fully capable of acting in his own best interest. The Saudi monarch was firmly convinced that contrary to American claims, continued hostilities in Yemen were less of a risk to Saudi Arabia than victory of the Republican forces. After all, the Saudis were far less committed in Yemen than Egypt. It was all rather patronizing of the United States to assume it knew the interests of Saudi Arabia and Jordan better than their leaders.[29]

As the British men on the spot distrusted the Americans, US officials in Yemen and Aden harbored a lingering suspicion of British intentions. Despite firm denials from the Foreign Office, the State Department received reports that Britain surreptitiously supported the Royalists with arms and other assistance. To American observers on the ground, the British establishment in Aden had a completely unrealistic assessment of the situation in Yemen, thinking the Royalists were on the verge of a major military break-through. The American consul to Aden, John T. Wheelock, observed in January 1963:

> The reporting officer cannot refrain from speculating that a deep-seated hatred of Nasser and all his works, long accumulated frustration over British withdrawals from former colonial areas, and not a little irritation with U.S. "interference" in the Near East evoking memories of Suez, play part in the construction of this dream world.

In sharp contrast to the often tempestuous Anglo-American relations over the Middle East in the 1950s, local conflict or disagreement was never allowed to disturb the close relationship established between Macmillan and Kennedy.[30] Despite the Anglo-American disagreement over Yemen, there is no doubt that the powers were in fundamental agreement concerning the Middle East.[31] The American ambassador to London, David Bruce, reported to the State Department on April 4, 1963: "As Dept aware, Yemeni problem has created some impression in both official and public circles here that US and UK policies toward ME . . . diverge more than they in fact do. In part at least, adverse affects such suspicions have been bridged by our close and continuous consultation with HMG both in Washington and here."[32] The closeness of policy was confirmed in the talks on the Persian Gulf between American and British officials on April 23 and 24, 1963; the American embassy concluded in its report to the department of state: "The talks showed a general identity of views between the US and UK on Persian Gulf and related problems."[33]

Part of the reason for continued good Anglo-American relations was perhaps more sophisticated reporting from many sources during the Kennedy administration, most of them without the often anti-British slant of the Eisenhower administration. Reporting from London on March 16, 1963, first secretary of the American embassy Hermann Eilts (later ambassador to Saudi Arabia) observed that British concern in Yemen was largely caused by the potential consequences for the Persian Gulf. While the Labour opposition was sharply critical of the decision not to recognize Yemen, the colonial office believed that the war in Yemen retarded the progress of the Aden Federation. The colonial office was supported by many Conservative backbenchers. If not successfully contained, British authorities feared that Yemeni revolutionaries would use terrorism in Aden, and that Britain might be forced to retaliate inside Yemen. Eilts was therefore well aware that disagreement over Yemen could spill over into Anglo-American friction:

> USG has pressed HMG hard re recognition of YAR, thus far unsuccessfully. Our pressure has created some irritation here. Happily, this largely counterbalanced by our close consultation with HMG re Yemen and our demonstrable efforts to take British views into account maximum extent possible.[34]

Both parties took care to downplay conflicts and maintain good Anglo-American relations.

Time and again, the British stressed the importance of the Persian Gulf. During talks with Talbot in late April 1963, British deputy undersecretary of state Roger Stevens explained why his government was so concerned with the Persian Gulf. The British believed their presence in the area prevented Communist penetration, ensured the availability of cheap oil for the West, and finally, contributed to Middle East peace and stability. Cheap oil was the paramount concern: disruption of supply could do serious damage to the British balance of payments. Eilts reported the essence of the talks to the State Department on May 31, 1963: "The focus of British interests is Kuwait, and the entire elaborate, costly structure of British military deployment in the Arabian Peninsula is geared to implement, on the request of Kuwait, the Anglo-Kuwaiti defense agreement of 1961."[35]

The pressures on the Kennedy administration increased when American oil companies began to question American policy towards Egypt. Kermit Roosevelt, of CIA fame from operations in Iran and Egypt under Eisenhower, now vice president of the Gulf Oil Company, claimed the

United States to be opposed to monarchies and ruling families on principle. The American tilt toward Egypt was unfortunate, as Roosevelt had learned from his own experience, Nasser was entirely untrustworthy. Later, countering Socony Mobil Oil Company's claim that American assistance prevented the overthrow of Nasser, Robert Strong, director office of Near Eastern affairs, explained that Nasser "was far too committed to Yemen to have pulled out even if he received no assistance from the United States". The United States did not care who ruled Yemen; American concerns were for Saudi Arabia and the British position in Aden. Once the UAR was persuaded to leave, things would quiet down in Yemen. US oil policy remained as before, that the exploitation of the oil resources should be left to the companies already operating in the Middle East. "To this end we support the British who have prime defense responsibility in the Gulf," Strong explained, "but we have informed the UK that we are prepared to back it up as required."[36]

Despite assurances to the contrary, Nasser continued the Egyptian engagement in Yemen, reneging on his commitment to withdraw troops. Privately, the president questioned the wisdom of recognizing Yemen, since Nasser did not reciprocate, and the United States came somewhat on a collision course with friendly governments like Great Britain. Kennedy instructed Badeau to deliver the following oral message on March 2, 1963:

> President would like you to point out to Nasser that he has personally made great effort for improved relations with the UAR and has taken this course in face of much opposition in the US. He has recognized the new Yemen republic and accepted UAR action there. He has sought to bring the UK to a similar course, and has made strenuous efforts to persuade Faysal to disengage. He has now sent [ambassador Ellsworth] Bunker as his personal emissary to Saudi Arabia for this later [latter?] purpose. In these circumstances, continued UAR attacks on Saudi Arabia are bound to produce very grave consequences in opinion in the US, and the President personally would be placed in a most difficult position.

Kennedy wanted Nasser to cease his more or less continuous bombing campaign against Saudi Arabia, otherwise he might be forced to reassess American policy towards Egypt, indicating that American aid to Egypt might be in jeopardy. Although rattling the aid weapon, the administration had no immediate intention of using it. Badeau was relieved that the United States rejected the overthrow of Nasser or economic pressure on Egypt. Badeau recommended deployment of American forces in Saudi Arabia, to operate within Saudi territory and engage any forces in said territory: "What is essential is to establish credible deterrent to UAR and to remove all possibilities of miscalculation of our intentions. Present vague threats to reexamine US–UAR relations or plaintive discussions of our domestic congressional and press problems will not do the job." Still, the ambassador was uneasy: "We realize that what we in effect are proposing is that we continue to feed a nation against whom we may be forced to take some military action." In a letter to Kennedy of March 10, Nasser made it clear that he wanted continued good relations with the United States, but reserved the right to take whatever action he deemed necessary to halt outside intervention in republican Yemen.[37] And he did, for on March 12, 1963 Egyptian planes bombed Jizan in Saudi Arabia. American protests had little or no effect on the Egyptians.[38] Despite growing disillusion with Nasser, the president refused to change policy toward Egypt. Throughout the remainder of 1963, the United States persisted without success to promote Egyptian disengagement, either by a special envoy or through the United Nations.

The war continued through the summer and fall of 1963. In return for operation Hard Surface, Faisal ceased assisting the Royalists, but Nasser had no intention of withdrawing Egyptian troops, unless the survival of his clients in Yemen was ensured.[39] Nasser's determination was apparently strong enough for him to use anti-personnel bombs, napalm and nerve gas. The British ambassador in Saudi Arabia reported extensive bombing of Saudi Arabia including anti-personnel bombs and poison gas.[40] Nasser admitted the use of chemical bombs to the American ambassador on July 11, 1963. The Kennedy administration protested against Egypt's use of poison gas on July 15, 1963. Even one of the main architects of the American tilt towards Egypt, Robert Komer, was becoming exasperated by Nasser's continued intransigence. "I hate to sound defensive, but even I confess that staying on an even keel with slippery UAR is hard."[41] Still, when summing up the situation on September 20, 1963, Komer argued that the United States had achieved a great deal:

> We've kept a peanut war confined to Yemen and forestalled a direct UAR/Saudi confrontation. . . . In so doing, we've protected the rickety Saudi monarchy and our oil investment (something the oil men don't seem to grasp). . . . We've done so while still preserving our influence with Nasser and Faysal – no mean feat. . . . We've helped keep the Soviets from achieving paramount influence in the YAR (an objective we share with Nasser).[42]

Even with these apparent victories, Kennedy had grown disillusioned with the Egyptian leader. Faisal had ceased assisting the rebels in order to keep the American jet squadron in Saudi Arabia. In his last communication to Nasser on October 19, 1963, the president explained that Britain and Saudi Arabia had stopped aiding the Royalists: "I therefore have no leverage with Faysal when, having carried out his end of the bargain, he continues to see Egyptian troops in Yemen and hear expressions of hostility from Cairo." Kennedy accused Nasser of bad faith, making the president lose credibility in Congress and in public opinion. The president concluded his message by warning that continued Egyptian operations in Yemen might disrupt American–Egyptian relations. Rusk had, just prior to the president's letter, bluntly told the Egyptians that continued aid depended on disengagement from Yemen. In response, the Egyptian ambassador to the United States, Mustafa Kamel, threatened that Egypt, in addition to turning to the Soviet Union, would use its influence among the oil workers to destabilize ARAMCO and sabotage its oil installations in Saudi Arabia.[43]

By now, Congress was coming into play; on November 7, 1963, the Senate voted to deny PL480 aid to any nation engaging in aggressive military action. While not mentioned specifically, Egypt was the target. The Kennedy administration was not bound by the Senate legislation, which contained an 'escape clause' that allowed the president to judge the aggressive intent of aid recipients. The legislation sent Nasser a strong message, to which he complained bitterly about the United States using aid to pressure him. Nasser said "that the UAR emerged from the Suez crisis convinced that it could not depend on the Western world, but that American policy in this Administration had made him hope that this judgment could be reversed. It now seemed clear that he would have go back to 1957".[44]

Kennedy's Middle East policy reveals an essentially careful and cautious manager; although the Yemen war disrupted the American rapprochement with Egypt, Kennedy's friendship with Nasser remained intact. The president was, perhaps, little wiser about his Egyptian counterpart but American relations with Egypt improved during Kennedy's presidency. Nasser had avoided closer relations with Moscow, a net gain for the United States, and kept relations with Israel in the 'ice-box'. The president moved closer to Israel than any of his predecessors, supplying it with a major weapons system, without jeopardizing relations with Nasser or the conservative Arab states. Unfortunately, Kennedy was unable to obtain any modification of Israeli policy in return. It took only eight planes (operation Hard Surface) to reassure the Saudis, protect American oil in the kingdom and contain the conflict in Yemen. The president was equally successful in preventing the Soviets from making further inroads in the Middle East, and they were unable to exploit the turmoil in Yemen for their own benefit. In this American and Egyptian policy ran along parallel lines: Nasser, despite substantial aid from the Soviet Union, effectively shielded Yemen from Russian penetration. Containing the Yemen conflict contributed to area political stability and ensured the continued flow of oil. The British claimed that if American aid to Egypt were cut off, the Egyptian economy would collapse, preventing Nasser from pursuing the war in Yemen and anti-British policies.[45] But despite disagreement over Egypt and Yemen,

Anglo-American relations were good, and the British base in Aden secure as well as the British position in the Persian Gulf. The United States warned Egypt against encroaching against Aden, the president repeatedly making clear that maintenance of British influence was a vital American interest. The president often successfully conciliated conflicting and contradictory interests while at the same time prevented a major flare-up in this volatile area. Towards the end of the Kennedy administration, the United States was on friendly terms with the major protagonists in the Middle East.

3
The Flickering Embers of Empire

Douglas-Home, Lyndon Johnson
and the Middle East

The Kennedy assassination was a profound shock to the American body politic, but the Middle East remained tranquil. "I know of no problems in the NEA", Talbot minuted to Rusk on November 23, 1963, "that will require the immediate attention of the President".[1] Stressing continuity and trying to console the nation, Johnson kept most of the Kennedy foreign policy team. The president's advisors saw little reason to alter a Middle East policy that was largely successful from their point of view. The new president's willingness to adhere to their council secured continuity of policy. Ironically, a president famous for the 'Johnson treatment' – persuading his interlocutors in one on one encounters, with an impressive range of domestic legislative victories to his credit, dominating Congress, aides and assistants – Johnson emerges from the archival record studied here as the most scripted of presidents.[2] The lack of initiative or interest pertaining to the Anglo-American Middle East did not manifest itself in Johnson avoiding all things related to US foreign policy. On the contrary, the president took a keen interest in how the United States waged war in Vietnam, micromanaging the bombing campaign by deciding on individual target selection.[3] In the documentation used for this book, I have only found one instance where Johnson exceeded his brief, when the president met king Faisal in Washington in June 1966. At this meeting, the president applied his famous skills, leaving the king overawed and dispelling any suspicions Faisal might have had regarding American commitment to Saudi Arabia. In other archival documentation used in this book, despite his reputation for dominating the policy process, Johnson religiously followed his briefs when meeting foreign dignitaries. The Kennedy foreign policy team adhered to their successful script in the Middle East, and Johnson saw no reason to deviate from it.

When Macmillan was forced to resign for medical reasons in October 1963, he was succeeded by Sir Alec Douglas-Home. The first priority for the Home government was for the prime minister to establish close personal relations with the president. Rusk explained to Johnson on February 7, 1964:

> Sir Alec wants to establish a personal relationship with you for two reasons. First the *close U.S–U.K association* [emphasis in original] is the most important single factor in British foreign policy. Second, with a general election rapidly approaching, Sir Alec needs to enhance his image as a world statesman.[4]

Perhaps an example of wishful thinking on the British part, Home's most recent biographer D. R. Thorpe argues that the president and the prime minister "were temperamentally poles apart", and the man in the White House had little faith that Home would survive long as prime minister: "Johnson regarded Macmillan's successor as a stop-gap, and was looking to a new relationship with Harold Wilson before the year was out."[5] While this became the established wisdom among scholars and the Johnson administration, initial American assessment of Douglas-Home was far more positive. The American embassy in London believed that Douglas-Home was "a new Conservative leader of remarkable charm and toughness".[6]

Whatever else, Sir Alec was a British conservative of the old school concerned with preserving British influence in the world.[7] Douglas-Home and his foreign minister, R. A. Butler, preferred, like their predeccesors Eden and Macmillan, military means to maintain the British position. Apart from Butler's vacillation at the height of the Suez crisis, Home and Butler seem to have been in complete agreement with Eden and Macmillan's forceful approach to the Middle East.

Within the framework of close Anglo-American cooperation, the British pushed for greater support of their Middle Eastern policy. The Home government focused attention on four main areas where it wanted American support. First, the British urged the United States to reduce or preferably terminate aid to Egypt to discourage Nasser's anti-Western policies in Yemen and elsewhere in the Middle East. Secondly, if the Americans insisted on preserving their relationship with the Egyptian leader, they should unleash Faisal and give him a free hand in supporting the Royalist forces in order to tie down ever larger Egyptian forces in Yemen. If successful, Nasser's scope for independent action elsewhere in the region would be much reduced. Thirdly, the Home government was firmly convinced that Nasser inspired and supported the embryonic rebel movement in their Aden colony and Aden Federation. Home and Butler repeatedly pleaded for American support of military operations in Aden, or even military reprisals against Yemen. Fourthly, the British government deliberately challenged the American hegemony in Saudi Arabia, particularly to muscle in on the lucrative Saudi arms market at the expense of

American companies. While loath to seek an open confrontation with the Americans over Saudi Arabia, it was the potential of having to take over the Western security guarantees to the Kingdom that was the main reason for the restraint shown by an already overstretched Britain. Underlying all the above was the British concern of having cheap and readily available oil. Time and again, Butler stressed to the Americans that oil was the single most important factor in British Middle East policy.

Unfortunately for the Home government, its Middle East policy was both flawed and contradictory. Even if they had succeeded, through the Saudi proxy, to tie down ever larger forces in Yemen, there was no guarantee this would prevent Nasser from confronting Britain elsewhere in the Middle East. Typically, the Egyptian leader redoubled his efforts when facing set-backs or defeats. After the dissolution of the Union with Syria, he embarked on a vigorous campaign against the conservative Arab regimes, and after five years of Yemeni civil war, with the Egyptian economy close to bankruptcy, he deliberately provoked a crisis with Israel in the spring of 1967. Encouraging Faisal to increase Saudi support for the Royalist forces carried dangers of their own. True, if embarked on, Saudi military intervention in Yemen might lead to profitable orders for British arms manufacturers in Saudi Arabia. But keeping the Arabian Peninsula in turmoil endangered the very oil supplies Britain was so concerned about, particularly if the crisis were to spill over into the Persian Gulf area. Besides, there was a distinct limit to British support of Saudi Arabia; although happily seeking access to the arms market, Britain had no intention of taking over American security guarantees and other political commitments to the regime. Finally, the main problem in the Aden Federation was not Egyptian subversion, but lack of political reform. Most of the population was disenfranchised; while in the backcountry, Britain relied on sheiks, emirs and pashas with uncertain popular backing, providing fertile ground for Arab nationalist propaganda. Throughout the first half of 1964, the Home government sought to quell unrest by military pacification campaigns and even a cross-border raid into Yemen. The campaigns were militarily successful but political failures, because while defeating rebels in the field, Arab nationalism still remained a potent force.

American policies remained much the same under Johnson as under Kennedy. The overarching goal was to prevent the Soviet Union from expanding its influence in the Middle East. But the perceived potential for the USSR to threaten American interests was far greater than its realization. Typical is the fact that large-scale investment in Yemen failed to translate into tangible political gains for the Soviet Union. "So far, the preeminent position occupied by the Egyptians has prevented the Soviets from converting the goodwill into substantial influence with respect to internal affairs."[8] Despite investing heavily in Egypt, Syria, Iraq and Algeria, the Soviet Union had little to show for their efforts. Local Communist parties were proscribed and their members were arrested. As one authority has noted: "Although Arab leaders often joined the Russians in denouncing 'imperialism', all had fairly good relations with the Western powers, and Russia was unable to control any of them."[9] In 1964, then, there was a distinct limit to Soviet influence in the Middle East. The rapprochement with Nasser continued, but American–Egyptian relations cooled towards the end of 1964, because the Egyptian leader stepped up his propaganda campaign against the United States. In Yemen, the United States promoted disengagement of Egyptian forces with little success. To prevent the war from escalating, the Americans refused to unleash Faisal or countenance British military operations across the border from Aden. The Johnson administration acquiesced with great reluctance to British attempts to crush local rebels in the Aden Federation with force, and urged political reforms as the solution to the ills of the Aden colony. While still concerned about the territorial integrity of Saudi Arabia, the Saudi acceptance of British courtship caused not only concern in the United States, but also a waning of American interest in the kingdom.

"There are already ample signs," Komer warned Bundy on April 2, 1964, "that the Home government is going to launch an attack on our Arab policy." The Conservative government wanted aid to Nasser reduced, and support of British policy on Yemen. "I suspect Tories think LBJ team an easier work than New Frontier. But unless we bite back, we're going to be under gradually increasing pressure (at least till Labor [sic] gets in)."[10] Internally, the British doubted the vulnerability of Nasser; Butler told Home that while the dictator's maneuverability might be restricted by the Yemen war, it posed no economic or security threat to his regime. Besides the stalemate in Yemen had only limited repercussions for the security of Aden.[11] As was the case with administration policy towards Nasser, lower echelons of the Johnson administration seriously doubted American policy on Yemen. Herman Eilts observed from London on December 19, 1963:

> Seen in perspective, the surprising thing about the British position is not that they have demurred in going along with us on Yemen all the way; it is rather that despite their immediate and great direct interests in Southwest Arabia, they have gone along with us as far as they have.

Once Egyptian troops were withdrawn from Yemen, Eilts predicted an end to the Anglo-American discord.[12]

Despite rumblings of opposition, Komer insisted that the United States continue its rapprochement of Egypt. To Komer it made no sense to pressure Nasser, past experience had shown that to be counterproductive:

As for tougher line toward Nasser, the overriding argument is that it will cost us more than we gain. The Aswan Dam episode and refusal of US military aid in 1955–56 is a case in point. They led directly to Soviet entry into the Arab world, and Nasser's seizure of the Suez Canal. We've spent some years digging out of that hole, why get into it again.[13]

Faulty history aside, Komer's conclusions were wrong. Nasser had acquired arms from the USSR in October 1955, and it was the Egyptian dictator's repeated challenges to American interests in the Middle East that led to the cancellation of the Anglo-American offer to finance the Aswan Dam. Still, Eisenhower rescued him from the consequences of his policies by forcing Britain and France to withdraw from Suez in 1956. Despite critical voices not only outside the administration, but also from within, Komer remained convinced that the United States should continue to conciliate Nasser. Parker T. Hart observed on November 30, 1963 that when Nasser brought relations with the United States to breaking point in 1956–8, it had few, if any, repercussions: "He failed seriously to impair single important US interest and with his enemies in the Arab world now far more numerous than in earlier years, I do not believe he can do so today."[14] Nevertheless, Komer's thesis carried the day. Briefing the president for his meeting with Butler in late April 1964, Komer and Bundy noted: "The main topic Butler wants to take up is the Mideast (it's a commentary in itself on UK policy that when they say Mideast they mean Aden and Yemen)." Johnson's advisors were distinctly unenthusiastic about Britain wanting to take the offensive against Nasser in Yemen and in the United Nations. This was simply not the time to challenge the Egyptian leader, as Nasser probably would up the ante by sending more troops to Yemen, and by increasing his propaganda campaign against British bases in the Middle East. Komer and Bundy feared that the result would be an all-out Anglo-American confrontation with the Arabs in the Middle East. "They'd all back the UAR as a matter of Arab solidarity if we backed the UK against the UAR." The president should therefore seek to persuade Butler to the American point of view, a view, incidentally, also shared by the diplomats in the Foreign Office, who according to Komer worried "over the bloody-mindedness of their ministers". Hopefully, things would improve when the like-minded Labour Party won the general election in October 1964.[15]

Meeting Rusk and the president in late April 1964, Butler pushed for American censure of Nasser. To Rusk, Butler explained that Britain had every intention of holding on to the Aden base, as it was vital to the British position in the Gulf and the Middle East.[16] "The British economy depended heavily on oil", Butler claimed, "which at present we could obtain at reasonable rates from Kuwait and the other Gulf producers." The British wanted American assistance to demarcate and demilitarize the Yemen/

Aden border, and American support in the UN for international observers in the area.[17] This would be one of the last times in the Kennedy/Johnson era senior British officials expressed concern about Middle East oil. This is in sharp contrast to the Eisenhower presidency when oil was a paramount Anglo-American concern. Reporting to Home, Butler found the president sympathetic to British concerns about Nasser and oil. Johnson pledged not to increase aid to Egypt, but believed a total cut-off of aid would be counterproductive.[18]

The Home government persisted in pressuring the United States to its very end to coordinate policies designed to deflate the Egyptian president. Even with Nasser struggling with a deteriorating Egyptian economy, the war in Yemen and against the conservative Arab states, for Britain he was almost the personification of all their problems in the Middle East. Magnifying the importance of Nasser, British leaders exaggerated his influence. Meeting Rusk on August 21, 1964, British chargé Denis Greenhill argued: "HMG views situation in broader context policy re Nasser who having wave of successes throughout area, Cabinet believes time has come to set him back; appropriate way is to force him come to political compromise with Faisal over Yemen." In addition, the British wanted American clearance for Faisal to increase aid to the Royalists, arguing: "Continuation of split and strife-torn country is preferable to Nasser inspired Yemen", and for the United States to offer tangible support by return of the American air squadron to Saudi Arabia. Operation Hard Surface had left Saudi Arabia on January 1, 1964. While pushing for American assistance to Saudi Arabia, Britain refused any military commitments to the kingdom: "HMG does not intend to deploy aircraft in Saudi Arabia or take any other military measures [to] defend Faisal from UAR attack."[19] Rusk explained the American major concern was Saudi Arabia, but would not write a blank check if Saudi Arabia "provokes confrontation by aiding royalists". American security guarantees did not cover a Saudi Arabian campaign in Yemen. The United States urged the UAR to stop overflights "and not react unnecessarily to Saudi frontier mobilization". Rusk concluded that the British position was rather inconsistent: "British were not prepared become militarily involved but were asking us to add to our already large portfolio of military commitments throughout world."[20]

Writing Butler, Rusk observed that the United States shared British concerns about Saudi Arabia and Yemen, but believed unless Faisal intervened more actively in Yemen, Egypt would refrain from attacking Saudi Arabia. "We are making urgent representations to the United Arab Republic," Rusk claimed, "to stop its overflights and to refrain from rashly reacting to Saudi defensive moves on the frontier." As usual, mere diplomatic exchanges did little to deter the Egyptians from forcefully protecting their interest in Yemen. "In the total framework of Anglo-American coop-eration throughout the world," Rusk believed, "our differences of view toward Yemen are a friction which it would be good if we could elimi-nate."[21] Butler felt that Rusk's letter "did not take into consideration complexities situation in Middle East and difficulties for both US and UK involved in Nasser's continued successes throughout the area". It was necessary for Nasser to 'suffer check'. Best method to achieve this was by unleashing Faisal in stepping up aid to the Royalists. Butler's plea failed to impress Rusk and the State Department; resumption of aid "could lead to US and UK being pitted against whole Arab world". While willing to let Faisal take his chances by giving aid to the Royalists, Butler again discounted any British military involvement.[22] Asking for presidential intervention to calm the British, Komer observed:

> If the Saudis resume aid to the Yemeni royalists, Nasser would no doubt resume bombing Saudi supply bases, in which case Faysal will scream for help. The British, who strongly disagree with our policy of pouring oil on troubled waters, have been at us hard to unleash Faysal, even at the expense of our relations with other Arabs.[23]

But despite pressure from Britain, Saudi Arabia and others, the United States refused to jeopardize its relationship with Nasser in 1964.[24]

British policy did not only manifest itself as pressure on the Americans. The Home government made a determined effort to pacify the Aden Federation hinterland. British forces easily defeated the motley crew of irregulars, tribesmen and guerillas in direct confrontation, but had greater difficulties in maintaining permanent pacification of the rebellious area. The term 1964 opened with operation "Nutcracker" in Radfan in the Dhala protectorate of Aden. The operation was militarily successful, and estab-lished the power and prestige of the Aden Federal Government in the area. But as soon as military forces were withdrawn, the rebels returned with a corresponding increase in dissident morale.[25]

Rusk's warning on March 17, 1964 that increased tensions on the Yemeni border posed a threat to joint US–UK interests did little to deter the British from retaliating against border incursions from Yemen.[26] Repeated Yemeni overflights, strafing and bombing of Aden's border areas, raised a clamor for countermeasures. The raids persisted, despite British warnings, and when provoked beyond endurance by the killing of two camels and the destruction of a similar number of tents, London approved retaliatory bombing of the Yemeni frontier fort Harib, which took place on March 28, 1964.[27] Britain was partly motivated by placating local reaction to the Yemeni raids. The sharif of Beihan, leader of the Beihan protectorate in Aden, reminded Britain pointedly "that he was staking his whole future on British support for the Federation against

Nasser, and that so far this support had not been in evidence".[28] The high commissioner in Aden, Kennedy Trevaskis, was elated by the bombing, claiming it "restored confidence generally amongst our friends and given our enemies cause for despondent reflection".[29] But Trevaskis' jubilation was premature. Having argued in favor of retaliation against Yemen, he failed to anticipate the violent international and domestic opposition the Harib bombing provoked. The bombing was condemned in the United Nations, the Arab League and large segments of the British press:

> It was bad enough our having to put British lives at risk in Radfan to protect these petty feudal despots, so the general theme ran, but to be coerced into committing what amounted to an act of war on behalf of such demanding and questionable allies was too much.[30]

Trevaskis and British commander in chief General Harrington urged retaliation against Harib in order for Britain to maintain its influence with South Arab Federation rulers, as the new construct in Aden was called. The British government did not consult the United States about the action, and informed the Johnson administration, in general terms, only one day prior to the bombing. Still, when faced with massive international opposition and condemnation in the UN Security Council, the Home government wanted American backing.[31] The British request for support split the Johnson administration. Komer, in his indomitable fashion, was against aligning the United States too closely with the United Kingdom on Harib:

> The UK retaliatory attack on Harib, designed to counter repeated UAR/YAR peanut air raids along the border (designed in turn to warn off the longstanding UK clandestine support of Yemeni royalists) will result in quite a stink before we're through. Gyppos [Egyptians] will make maximum propaganda of this 'assault on Arabism', of which the SC complaint is only a foretaste. They'll publicize UK covert activities in Yemen, focus spotlight on Aden, encourage other Arabs to cause trouble, etc. Though UAR assures us [US airbase Libya] Wheelus won't be attacked, we'll inevitably suffer. Whole Yemen disengagement question, and US/UK differences over Yemen, will also be raked up. I'm afraid that once again [Colonial Secretary Duncan] Sandys–Trevaskis gunboat diplomacy is going to turn out a net loss . . . a loss we'll share. Do we really make time with London by not bridling at this sort of thing?[32]

American ambassador to the United Nations, Adlai Stevenson supported the resolution condemning the Harib bombing. The United States consistently opposed reprisals and strikes like Harib; the attack was out of proportion to the provocation; American abstention would provoke a host of third world countries; and, finally, Stevenson was already on the record with State Department approval against the British. Rusk was firm in his opposition to Stevenson; Butler had fought the hard-liners in the cabinet and secured British abstention, not a veto in the UN. Besides, Yemeni provocation was of greater magnitude than Stevenson believed, and that:

> The U.S. itself may have to respond to provocations of a more serious but technically similar sort either in Cuba or in Vietnam . . . We have other business with Sandys which makes this no time for a Suez-type reaction from hard-line British Tories.

Summing up the discussion, McGeorge Bundy reluctantly supported Rusk, but alerted that Home should be warned that this was a one-time act of solidarity, since the United States was not consulted before the bombing, in order to "support the wise Butler against the foolish Sandys".[33] Overruling Stevenson, Rusk explained to the American UN ambassador that the British position in South Arabia was very important to the United States and the British needed American help in the present situation. "If the United States voted for this resolution," Rusk warned, "it would undermine reasonable and moderate elements in London and make it difficult to get British help in other matters."[34] Still, on the American side there was a lingering suspicion of being set up by the British. Summing up the episode, Sam Belk of the White House noted to Bundy on May 29, 1964: "Is it possible that the British planned to hit us hard at the last moment on the theory that there would be no time for planning and they could more easily enlist our support?"[35] Thanking the president for his support, Home argued:

> I should now like to build on this decision and see whether we cannot achieve a sense of common purpose and align our policies more closely over the whole problem of the Yemen and Aden. Experience has shown that the general Western interest, as well as the particular British and American interest, are best served when British and American policies are in harmony.[36]

"I, of course, have no illusions about Nasser," Johnson replied, "or the mischievous game he is playing. But I quite frankly doubt that at this point in time abrupt challenges to the Arabs are useful for our joint interests." The president, too, wanted to align policies with Britain over Aden and Yemen: "We both have such great interests to guard in that tortured part of the world that we cannot afford to pursue divergent policies."[37] Butler followed up the exchanges when meeting president Johnson on April 28, 1964. Johnson agreed to Britain soliciting UN assistance in demarcating and demilitarizing the Yemen/South Arabian frontier.[38] Harking back to earlier days, Butler claimed to Rusk that the British economy depended heavily on cheap oil from the Persian Gulf, making a continued British presence in Aden of vital importance.[39]

While Butler and Home had succeeded in gaining the Johnson administration's support for British military operations on the Arabian Peninsula, local American opinion was skeptical. The American consul in Aden, John T. Wheelock, claimed that British policies in Aden left much to be desired, particularly the reliance on sheiks and carefully selected conservative leaders. The British had failed seriously to address the problem of making the Aden Federation a viable entity and let the situation drift dangerously. Wheelock's remedy was, as usual, to press Britain to recognize Yemen as the panacea to remove all ills on the Arabian Peninsula; barring that, to take a hard, close look at the value of the Aden base to the security of the West. The consul believed "that the political cost of keeping the base will within the next few years begin to outweigh its usefulness".[40]

The American acquiescence of Harib was immediately parlayed into acceptance of a British military operation in the Radfan area of Aden. Nutcracker and the Harib bombing had failed to eliminate rebel activity in the Radfan area.[41] Combined with the military campaign was a concerted effort to convince the Americans of the seriousness of Nasser's threat to Aden. The British believed Nasser wanted to eliminate the British presence on the Arabian Peninsula and establish friendly regimes there. Short of direct military action, the Foreign Office argued that Nasser had engaged in "international political action; massive propaganda, encouragement of the Yemenis in trouble-making within the Federation; and direct assistance in that trouble-making".[42] The international political action was financing the Aden Trade Union Congress and the People's Socialist Party in Aden "in opposition to British and Federal policy". Compared to the Viet Cong in Vietnam, the Egyptian effort was small scale:

> In local conditions, however, its impact is very considerable. The backwardness of the hinterland of Aden, the venality of the tribesmen who constitutes most of the population (and whose loyalty is to the tribe, not to the Federation), and the limited compatibility between Aden state and the rest of the Federation make administration difficult and law and order difficult to preserve.[43]

Operation Radforce began on April 27, to open the Aden/Dhala road and suppress dissident tribes. The Radfan protectorate of the Aden Federation was an almost inaccessible area which Britain had left to its medieval slumber as long as the local tribesmen were more inclined to fight one another than to challenge British colonial authority. But now, infiltrated by Nasserite agents and less tractable to traditional colonial methods of pacification (i.e. bombing from the air), ground operations were necessary. The Aden rebellion proved a new and unusual challenge to British hegemony. Air Chief Marshall Sir David Lee observed that policing the empire was easier in the good old days, when dissidents could be bombed into submission at a suitable interval after warning leaflets had been dropped on the rebel village.[44] Unfortunately, those tried and tested methods no longer worked in the Southwest Arab Federation. "Consequently dissident outlawry has become a thing of the past," the ministry of defense warned Home on May 2, 1964, "and we are confronted by an infinitely more sophisticated and menacing enemy." The operation required substantial British forces, in addition to the Aden Federal army, and troop transfers from Great Britain as well.[45]

When military operations petered out during the summer of 1964, the most hard-core rebels remained undefeated, forcing British troops to guard Radfan for the remainder of the British presence in the Aden Federation. Army chief General J. Cubbon explained to Wheelock that the British strategy was "the holding of strategic agricultural areas and dominating mountain peaks in most of the Radfan plateau, in hope of forcing dissidents to give themselves up to avoid starvation".[46] Butler had grown skeptical of the British strategy, explaining to Home:

> To the extent that future United States/United Kingdom interdependence in round-the-world strategy may require land-based facilities, we should look for points where the local political scene has no anti-colonialist or anti-Western complexes, or, preferably, where there are no inhabitants at all.[47]

Butler's observation drives home the curious ambivalence in the Conservative administration's attitude to British areas of influence in the Middle East. Having every intention of remaining in the Middle East and little reluctance in applying military force to do so, the policy just was not working. Nutcracker and Radforce were the last of a long string of technically successful British military operations in the Middle East, but while the United Kingdom won on the battlefield, Arab nationalism still remained a potent force. In short, military force did not seem to be the solution to Britain's problems in the Middle East. The American approach of seeking an understanding with the forces of Arab nationalism and of providing Egypt with food aid, was equally unsuccessful. This proved to be the unresolved legacy of Conservative Middle East policy in the period 1951–64. The failure to create area stability wore the Conservative commitment down, making it easier for the successor Labour government, perhaps, to dismantle the empire in the Middle East.

The long-term consequences of Nutcracker and Radforce notwithstanding, Trevaskis, however, was concerned about the short-term consequences of the lack of stability in Southwest Arabia. In an important dispatch of February 20, he warned about the rapidly deteriorating situation in Aden. The high commissioner's report set off a flurry of activities in London aimed to address the Aden problem, and galvanized the prime minister into action. Still, when the dust settled, Britain was no closer to a political settlement. Trevaskis warned that once Nasser had established himself in Yemen, only extraordinary measures could save Aden. Neglect of necessary reforms in Aden before the revolution in Yemen in 1962 had now created a serious situation for Britain. Even more so because the "Arabs have the 'band wagon' instinct in an exaggerated degree" and would therefore join the rebels, "being intimidated by threats of reprisals if they do not do so". Unfortunately, the Federal government was no serious alternative to the rebels, seen locally as a wholly British subsidiary, and not even remotely as a genuine Arab government. One of the federal ministers in Aden succinctly explained to Trevaskis the contradictory nature of British policy: "One can only rule Arabs through fear or favour. You will not permit us to rule through fear, nor will you provide us with the means to do so through favour."[48] In this precarious situation, Britain was left with stark choices. To remain required undertaking stern repressive measures: crushing unrest by suppressing civil liberties, placing opposition leaders in detention, censuring the press and expelling all of the local workforce hailing from Yemen, in addition to intensifying military operations in the hinterland of the Federation. Short of disengagement and withdrawal, Trevaskis saw only two possible alternatives to give the Federation immediate independence to prove itself as a genuine Arab government, while the British turned a blind eye to the necessary but distasteful repressive measures after independence. Alternatively, they thought they could seek accommodation with Nasser and Yemen but in that case, they would have to be prepared to evacuate the Aden base, as the base would have limited utility to Britain in such a situation.[49]

Trevaskis' dispatch shook the complacency in London, the government firmly intended to stay in Aden, and to use the local feudal rulers to do so. The cabinet secretary, Burke Trend, believed repression unacceptable to the ministers, and the colonial secretary opposed full independence in the immediate future, leaving only to accede to the enemies of the Crown, according to Trevaskis. There was no reason to believe that a reversal of policy would make the Aden base more secure than relying on the 'semi-feudal' governments in South Arabia.[50] "I think that the moment has now come for us to make a real effort," Home wrote Butler, "to get to grips with the situation in Arabian Peninsula." The Persian Gulf was a vital British interest, and the prime minister believed that the United Nations could help defuse the crisis, because "trouble always redounds to Nasser's advantage and not to ours, since it always rallies to him popular support, not least in Aden itself". Home wanted UN involvement, and the border with Yemen fixed and/or demilitarized. "In Aden, we really have to make a serious effort to make our presence there worthwhile to the local inhabitants." The British had achieved no success so far, which put the future of the Aden base in jeopardy. Home therefore wanted a plan for political and economic advancement in Aden.[51] As events would show, however, whatever the

British did or did not do had little effect in preventing the situation in Aden from deteriorating.

Despite the problems facing the Federation, on the eve of the British general election in October 1964, the area remained relatively calm. The Radfan area was largely pacified, with British and Federal troops occupying the strategic heights. Local tribes were offered British aid to resume agricultural operations in return for surrendering guns and hostages. Still, hard-core rebel elements held out against the British.[52] To soften local opposition to the British presence, the Home government pledged independence to the Aden Federation by 1968, while Britain kept the Aden base.[53]

The Home government worked hard to build British influence in Saudi Arabia. The American embassy in London noted in January 1964 that British policy towards Saudi Arabia had hardened in the last nine months, and reflected "a generally more independent posture which has lately characterized HMG foreign policy approaches. Within limits of their capability, Brits are very serious about building their stake in Saudi Arabia." The British had decided at ministerial level, including the prime minister and foreign minister Butler, to challenge the American arms monopoly in Saudi Arabia. The embassy thought it necessary to "impress strongly on HMG great importance we attach to remaining primary arms supplier to Saudi Arabia and close relationship we conceive between this position and US defense commitment to Saudi Arabia".[54] The American ambassador to Saudi Arabia, Parker T. Hart, did not believe that Britain would take over the Saudi arms market, with the exception of the White Army, already a British preserve. King Faisal had expressed a willingness to limit purchases for regular Saudi forces to American sources. Hart had a good working relationship with the British ambassador, but "both UK and US embassies however have been pushed by balance of trade considerations, and by aggressive arms sales salesmanship". It was important for the Saudis to maintain American friendship: "I believe SAG may feel that US govt might lose some of its interest in defense of Saudi integrity if US advice on weaponry were generally disregarded." Saudi Arabia shelved territorial disputes with the British to maintain the friendship of the United Kingdom.

Both Hart and the American embassy in London argued for a delineation of the respective British and American interests in the Saudi arms market. This tug of war continued until the Anglo-American arms deal with Saudi Arabia in October 1965, which was signed not mainly for commercial purposes, but to induce Britain to remain east of Suez (more on this in chapter 6). Hart discounted competition from other arms suppliers: "US and UK emerge as SAG's best friends for different purposes. SAG does not want to lose either and can be counted on to keep both interested."[55] Despite American pressure to avoid the sale of offensive weapons to Saudi Arabia to prevent an arms race in the Middle East, Britain refused to restrict sales to the White Army only. Rusk commented in a telegram to the American embassy in Jidda, that the "British, while acknowledging validity of reasons for excluding offensive and overly sophisticated arms, have emphasized that they see the US as having the responsibility for curbing Saudi appetites".[56]

Aggressive British salesmanship in Saudi Arabia was partly predicated on disagreement within the Home government. Butler admonished his bureaucracy not to alienate the Americans. UK air ministry officials, however, questioned why Britain deferred to the Americans in Saudi Arabia. Head of the Arabian department Frank Brenchley explained:

> that continued U.S. support for and defence of the present Saudi regime was a major British interest. We could not afford to take over these commitments. Moreover, it was important that the U.S. Government should continue to give public support to our position in the Persian Gulf. The Foreign Secretary had ruled that we could not afford to disagree with the United States on too many things at once.[57]

The Foreign Office and the ministry of aviation disagreed on the British assurance to the United States not to make training facilities for the use of fighter aircraft available to Saudi armed forces. Brenchley believed: "We had not thought we were making any concession, since B.A.C. [British Aircraft Corporation] had themselves proposed from the start to employ Airwork Limited for both Thunderbird and Lightning." Besides, a too aggressive posture in Saudi Arabia might lead to an American challenge to the exclusive British arms market in Kuwait.[58] Despite Brenchley's caution, local British company salesmen made an all-out effort to push out American companies Lockheed and Northrop from the lucrative Saudi Air force market.[59] The American response was to express strong concern on September 21, 1964 about the continued British efforts to sell military hardware to Saudi Arabia.[60]

As for the rest of the Middle East, Anglo-Saudi relations and Anglo-American relations concerning Saudi Arabia and the Saudi arms market remained unfinished business when the Conservatives lost the election in mid-October 1964 to Labour. Saudi Arabia of 1964 was a nation of growing importance and confidence. Increasing oil revenues played their part, but Faisal's successful resistance to Nasser in Yemen and his espousal of the Islamic alliance, fostering solidarity among the conservative Arab regimes against the radical challenge, bolstered Saudi prestige in the Arab world. Rhetorically aligning himself with Nasser citing slogans against imperialism and colonialism, Faisal wanted Britain to remain in Aden and the Persian Gulf. The Saudi monarch feared a British withdrawal would open these areas to the influence of Nasserite revolutionaries. British relations with Saudi Arabia had steadily improved since the resumption of diplomatic relations in January 1963, and only Buraimi prevented even closer relations between the two powers.[61]

During its first year, the Johnson administration had, with the exception of the Harib, kept the militant Tories in check and prevented their pacification campaigns in Aden from spilling over into Yemen. Despite the disagreement in emphasis, Anglo-American relations in the Middle East remained good. Relations with Egypt were still on an even keel, and the Soviet Union had little success in expanding its influence in the Middle East. Ironically, after the expenditure of much treasure and effort from Moscow, in Yemen the credit redounded to Egypt. The United States successfully contained the Yemen civil war, Saudi Arabia and American oil supplies remained secure, as did the Aden base. The British complained about infiltration from Yemen into the Aden Federation, but the military problem of containing the guerillas was manageable.

4
Trying to Hold the Line

Lyndon Johnson and the British Role East of Suez

The Johnson administration put great store in a continued British global role, the only significant discord in Anglo-American relations during the presidency of Lyndon Johnson being the British withdrawal east of Suez. For the United States it was a matter of utmost importance, according to the administrative history of the State Department, that they shared "its heavy world-wide security tasks with a responsible ally, particularly as we could not substitute for the British in certain locations East of Suez". The United States worked assiduously to dissuade Britain from cutting its overseas defense commitments. "US efforts involved highest level political persuasion as well as financial improvisations, but they only delayed the ultimate historic British decision." American financial improvisations were considerable and almost continuous in support of the pound, which more or less permanently balanced on the edge of devaluation. Included in the financial persuasion was the joint Anglo-American arms deal with Saudi Arabia, letting the British in on what several American governments had worked to maintain as an exclusive US preserve. But whatever the United States did "the British Government fitfully but faithfully moved toward the decision early in 1968 that would accelerate its military withdrawal from all points East of Suez (South Arabia, Persian Gulf, Southeast Asia), with the exception of Hong Kong, by the end of 1971".[1]

But at the beginning of the new Labour government Anglo-American relations were good. Dispatched to Washington immediately after the election, foreign secretary Patrick Gordon Walker explained to Rusk that:

> he wanted his first act as Foreign Secretary to be to establish a special relationship with the United States. He did not like the phrase 'special relationship', which sounded like protesting too much, but he agreed that the relationship was extremely important and could assure Mr. Rusk that it would certainly be no less warm than under previous the British Government.

Gordon Walker pledged to Rusk that devaluation had been ruled out.[2] As expected, Labour's views on Nasser corresponded closer to the Johnson administration than the Conservatives. Gordon Walker had no objection to continued American wheat supplies to the UAR. Labour intended to retain the base in Aden and hold on to the Aden Federation, which Gordon Walker thought possible as long as the British wished it, without great expense. The United Kingdom wanted to modernize the Persian Gulf sheikhdoms, but retain a military presence "not because of oil, but because of the need not to create a vacuum". Avoidance of a vacuum was hardly a major British national interest. Gordon Walker was, in fact, preparing for the abandonment of the Gulf in 1971. Most importantly, the foreign secretary pledged to coordinate policies with the Americans in the Middle East.[3] In the Middle East, the United States and Great Britain were in basic agreement. Michael Stewart, who replaced Gordon Walker, explained to the cabinet in March 1965: "There is no longer the degree of Anglo-American rivalry in the oil business which caused some friction in the 1950s."[4]

The feeling of mutual good will and public harmony was confirmed during Wilson's American visit in December 1964. Privately, Johnson grumbled about why he had to meet Wilson.[5] Both George Ball, US undersecretary of state, and George Brown, one-time British foreign secretary, argue in their memoirs that the president did not like Harold Wilson much.[6] But despite the missing personal relationship, the United States was an eager and willing underwriter of the pound and the British role east of Suez, until the British devaluation in November 1967. The not so good personal relations at top level, then, had no bearing on Anglo-American relations. During the first Wilson visit, Rusk had taken care to stress in strong terms to Gordon Walker and Denis Healey, British secretary of defense, that the United States "would look with the greatest concern at a diminution of the UK's [world-wide] role, which was of very great importance to US. What the UK did had a considerable bearing on what we ourselves were able to do."[7]

Labour, despite implying otherwise to the Americans, divested Britain rapidly of its still considerable Middle Eastern interest. British influence in the Middle East was basically located in three areas. First, the Aden base enabled Britain to intervene decisively from Kuwait to East Africa. Kuwait was important because of its exceptionally large and accessible oil reserves, of which BP (British Petroleum) had a 50 percent interest. Kuwaiti oil production could be rapidly increased to offset falling production elsewhere due to political complications, as when Iran nationalized the Anglo-Iranian Oil Company in 1951. To prevent Kuwait falling prey to Iraq or to Nasser was an important British interest.[8] Secondly, in Saudi Arabia, British influence had increased so much that Faisal, tired of the American straddling on Yemen and conciliation of Nasser, requested Britain supplant the American security guarantee to his country in August

1964. With limited military resources, and unwilling to challenge the United States and risk further confrontations with Nasser, Britain declined the honor. The Buraimi dispute and Faisal's irredentist claims in the Persian Gulf were added inducements to avoid entanglements with Saudi Arabia.[9] Finally, Britain had special treaty rights with a string of sheikhdoms along the Persian Gulf, being in charge of their defense and foreign affairs. These principalities agreed "not to alienate their territory, enter into relations with foreign powers or grant concessions without the consent of H.M.G.". Britain had air, army and naval bases in Bahrain, and air facilities in the Trucial State of Sharjah and in Masirah in Muscat and Oman. The Trucial Oman Scouts were British officered and financed for internal security functions in the Trucial States (Abu Dhabi, Dubai, Sharjah, Ajman, Umm al Qaiwain, Ras al Khaimah and Fujairah), while the British financed the Sultan's Armed Forces (with British officers on secondment and under contract) in Muscat and Oman. While having no formal responsibility, Britain was fully aware that the sultan looked to Britain for support in foreign affairs and defense. The main British concern was to avoid Soviet penetration of the Gulf, and to secure the oil resources in the area.[10]

Johnson's policies toward the Middle East remained much the same as they had been in 1964. The Soviet Union worked hard to gain influence by exploiting the widening rift between conservative and radical Arab regimes, but with limited success prior to the Six Day War. The United States prevented Moscow from making major inroads in the area, while maintaining satisfactory working relationships with all sides in local disputes. The main USSR interest was to acquire air and naval bases in the Middle East, and its main effort was directed toward Egypt.[11] To increase its influence, the Soviet Union championed the radical Arab states against Israel hoping they would turn against the West as well. But lack of Soviet support during the Six Day War and efforts to achieve a cease-fire while Arab territory was still occupied by Israeli troops, led to a serious loss of Russian prestige in the Middle East.[12] To regain influence, the Soviet Union provided large-scale military assistance to help rebuild the armies of Egypt and Syria. But as long-time Soviet ambassador to the United States Anatoly Dobrynin notes, the reassessment of Soviet policy carried dangers of its own:

> The Soviet Union had to devise a new Middle East policy, since its authority in the region had been considerably damaged by the defeat of its clients. The policy again favored the Arabs because the Soviet leadership wanted to restore its role in the Middle East and prevent the United States from dominating that strategic area. But this policy left us with little flexibility because we often blindly followed our Arab allies, who in turn used us to block many initiatives that were advanced for a peaceful settlement.[13]

By the time of Nasser's death in 1970, the position of the Soviet Union had improved much militarily with air and naval bases in Egypt and port rights in Syria, Sudan, North Yemen, South Yemen, and Iraq. But the risks were considerable, for local Arab allies wanted to involve the USSR in fighting Israel regardless of international consequences. In addition, being the first great power after the British withdrawal to introduce troops in the Middle East, the Soviet Union always ran the risk of possible American counter-measures. For the rights of claiming influence, it required heavy subsidies to its economically weak Arab allies, and, as Dobrynin shows, loss of flexibility in the Middle East from being tied to follow their clients' lead in the area. Apart from its improved military position, there were few other gains the Soviet Union could point to for its expensive Middle East investment.[14] Ironically, while there was a distinct limit to Soviet influence, the view from Washington was much more sinister, as they believed American interests to be in jeopardy from the successful penetration of the area by the Soviet Union and its collaboration with the radical Arab regimes.[15]

The American tilt towards Israel continued without jeopardizing US relations with the Arab governments. The Unites States took care not to alienate the Arab governments over relations with Israel. Johnson's point man on the Middle East, Hal Saunders, explained to the president on June 24, 1966: "With a series of arms sales to both Arabs and Israelis in 1965 and 1966, we have temporarily succeeded in restoring a deterrent balance."[16] American food aid to Egypt continued, but because of Nasser's involvement in Yemen and increasingly strident anti-American rhetoric, Johnson refused to renew the three-year PL480 installment. The president preferred thereafter to provide aid in six-month installments in an attempt to gain some leverage over Nasser. Rusk complains that "Nasser was unpredictable and exceptionally difficult to work with". The United States did not expect Egypt to grovel in gratitude for food, but for Nasser to moderate his criticism of the United States. "Instead, he got up before those big crowds in Cairo and shouted such things as 'Throw your aid into the Red Sea!' Nasser's fiery speeches persuaded Congress to move to do exactly that."[17] In the end, the president became thoroughly alienated from the Egyptian leader, explaining to Israeli ambassador Avraham Harman on February 7, 1968:

> Of Nasser, the President said that he had come into office with the hope of getting along with the Egyptian leadership: He had found, however, that Nasser was unreliable, untrustworthy, and undependable. He had hoped we could achieve some sort of working relationship but did not know exactly what we could work out.[18]

From Cairo, the view was different. Sensing a coolness from the new president and in response to the American threat to suspend economic aid after the destruction of the American Library in Cairo, Nasser burst out in December 1964: "We are not going to accept gangsterism by cowboys."[19] Nasser was convinced that the United States was seeking his overthrow. When fellow leftists and leaders of the nonaligned nations were toppled one after the other in 1965 and 1966, the Egyptian leader was convinced that the CIA engineered the fall of Ben Bella of Algeria, Kwame Nkrumah of Ghana, and Achmad Sukarno of Indonesia. Further evidence, if evidence was needed, was in Faisal's Islamic alliance of conservative Arab regimes against Nasser's leadership in the Middle East. Nasser also believed that the Anglo-American arms deal with Saudi Arabia was part of the Western conspiracy against him, and that Saudi Arabia would assist Britain in crushing the pro-Nasser forces in the Aden Federation.[20]

But despite Labour manifesting a certain ideological affinity with the Egyptian leader and going to some length to conciliate him, Nasser grew less and less important for the Anglo-American Middle East. Being treated as a nuisance by the Western powers was immensely frustrating for Nasser. To compensate he increased the volume of his propaganda campaign but mostly to little effect. His desperate gamble in demanding withdrawal of UN security forces from Sinai in May 1967 was, to some extent, an effort to gain the attention of the West. Unfortunately, the United States and Britain did not listen, but Israel did and inflicted a devastating defeat on Egypt in June 1967. The United States and Britain made only limited and feeble attempts to prevent the war, probably feeling that Nasser would receive a well-deserved comeuppance. Nasser's provocative actions towards Israel in the spring of 1967 were largely in response to taunts from the conservative Islamic powers, Jordan and Saudi Arabia. They accused the Egyptian leader of being too gentle and accommodating towards the Jews while wrapping himself in the mantle of Arab nationalism.[21]

The war was largely of Nasser's own making, even though he was well aware of the dangers of provoking Israel. He admitted in the summer of 1964: "For I would lead you to disaster if I were to proclaim that I would fight at a time when I was unable to do so. I would not lead my country to disaster and would not gamble with its destiny." By ordering Egyptian troops into Sinai after the removal of the United Nations Emergency Force (UNEF), Nasser with one stroke regained his position as leader of the Arab world. The short-term political victory carried the seeds of its own destruction because it meant returning to a state of war with Israel. Even if Israel remained passive, Nasser no longer had an excuse for not acting. The Egyptian army was ordered into Sinai without planning or preparation but in full openness, signaling to Israel that by acting openly Egypt had no aggressive designs but would not suffer any Israeli aggression against Syria. Even though the forward deployment was chaotic, Nasser remained unperturbed, having effectively demonstrated that even with 50,000 men in

Yemen, Egypt was a major power. The problem for Nasser was longer-term outcomes he had not foreseen and could not control. After the closure of the straits of Tiran, the clamor for war from both Egypt's allies and the Arab population left the Egyptian leadership intoxicated with a dream of victory. Nasser's own judgment was probably affected by him feeling that the entire Arab world was behind him, united as never before in their post-colonial history, overcoming the bitter disagreements between them. In Israel the generals, confident of victory, clamored for a first strike against Egypt, whereas the political leaders were more cautious. General Ariel Sharon claimed that "a generation will pass before Egypt threatens us again", to which the prime minister, Levi Eshkol, replied: "Nothing will be settled by military victory, the Arabs will still be there."[22]

While trying to maintain good relations with the major protagonists, Israel and Egypt, the United States was ill rewarded for its efforts during and after the Six Day War. Nasser, for his part, broke off diplomatic relations with the United States and Britain, claiming falsely that their planes were responsible for Israel's stunning success in wiping out the Egyptian air force. Nasser remained deeply suspicious of the United States, exclaiming to the Soviet president Nikolai Podgorny on June 22, 1967 that "the Americans will continue to be our enemies in the future".[23] Israeli planes deliberately and without provocation attacked the spy ship USS *Liberty* in international waters, killing thirty-four and wounding 171 of the crew. Top levels of the Johnson administration were convinced that the Israeli government was behind the attack. Clark Clifford, chair of Johnson's intelligence advisory board, claimed: "The unprovoked attack on the *Liberty* constitutes a flagrant act of gross negligence for which the Israeli government should be held completely responsible, and [the] Israeli military personnel involved should be punished."[24] Secretary of state Dean Rusk "was never satisfied with the Israeli explanation. Their sustained attack to disable and sink *Liberty* precluded an assault by accident or by some triggerhappy local commander. I didn't believe it then, and I don't believe them to this day. The attack was outrageous."[25] Johnson's one-time secretary of state, George Ball, insisted that "the *Liberty*'s presence and function was known to Israel's leaders". For Ball, the costs of the episode were much higher than the injury to the crew:

> Israel's leaders concluded that nothing they might do would offend the Americans to the point of reprisal: if America's leaders did not have the courage to punish Israel for the blatant murder of American citizens, it seemed clear that their American friends would let them get away with almost anything.[26]

When Israel apologized and grudgingly paid compensation to the victims, the president accepted and ordered the incident be kept quiet. Johnson ruled out sanctions against Israel, believing it imprudent to have a falling-out with the Jewish state during the war. Continued good relations offered the only hope of restraining Israel in the middle of the war.[27]

Lyndon Johnson, for all his other worries regarding the Middle East, relied heavily on a continued British presence. Prime minister Wilson assured the president during their first meeting that Britain had every intention of remaining east of Suez. While agreeing to maintain their world-wide role, the British also left the Americans with a clear warning that it was necessary to reduce defense expenditure to get the economy going.[28] The chosen vehicle for defense cuts was the defense reviews. The Labour government gave high priority to social welfare programs, and to secure financing it had to look for savings elsewhere. Defense spending was the only other government area where substantial savings could be made. Healey seemed to be engaged in a never ending series of defense reviews; "as soon as one was completed, another was being called for".[29]

The defense reviews were a concerted Labour plan to divest Britain of its bases east of Suez. Denis Healey admitted as much in an interview with Karl Pieragostini, saying that no move could be made until the whole package was ready, which meant overcoming the resistance of the foreign and defense establishments in the United Kingdom and keeping the Americans quiet. Pieragostini discounts Healey's revelation as a post-withdrawal rationalization, the defense secretary being in a minority in the cabinet at that time.[30] But the defense reviews *in toto* represent a remarkably coherent argument for the British withdrawal east of Suez.[31] "The present Government has inherited defence forces which are seriously overstretched and in some respects dangerously under-equipped," Healey insisted in his first defense review. Furthermore, "There has been no real attempt to match political commitments to military resources, still less to relate the resources made available for defence to the economic circumstances of nation."[32] By setting a ceiling of £2,000 million in annual defense expenditure at 1964 prices[33] and beginning a series of defense studies to match resources to commitments, Healey fired the opening salvo in the campaign to quit British bases east of Suez.

A year later, Healey noted: "Although we have important economic interests in the Middle East, Asia and elsewhere, military force is not the most suitable means of protecting them, and they would not alone justify heavy British defence expenditure."[34] Besides, if Britain were to maintain its current capabilities outside of Europe, the strain would be too heavy on the already overstretched forces, the domestic economy and foreign exchange reserves. Therefore, Healey imposed a number of limitations on continued British military presence outside of Europe:

> First, Britain will not undertake major operations of war except in co-operation with allies. Secondly, we will not accept an obligation to provide another country with military assistance unless it is prepared to provide us with the facilities we

need to make such assistance effective in time. Finally, there will be no attempt to maintain defence facilities in an independent country against its wishes.

The last limitation meant the end of the Aden base. After granting South Arabia independence in 1968, Britain had no intention of keeping the Aden base (more on this below). To fulfill the remainder of British obligations in the Middle East, there would be a small increase of British forces in the Persian Gulf.[35] Healey explained that Britain intended to disengage itself "until we have reached the hard core of our obligations to the States in the Persian Gulf".[36] The limitations spelled out by Healey were used to draw policy conclusions in his next defense statement:

> While the visible presence of even small forces – not necessarily dependent on large and expensive base facilities – may be a good deterrent, it will be more economical to rely mainly on sending forces from Britain in a crisis. We have therefore revised our plans for deployment outside Europe so as to enable major reductions to be made in the size and cost of our forces as whole.[37]

The *coup de grâce* came following the British devaluation in November 1967, which necessitated "a detailed and searching review" of public expenditure. For the Persian Gulf this meant that the hard core of British obligations was more like an onion, that is without a core; the 1968 defense review decreed British withdrawal by the end of 1971 (on this below). Explaining the rationale behind the decision, Healey completed the circle by harking back to his first defense review in 1965, that reductions in defense capabilities would be accompanied by corresponding reductions in British commitments. Healey had no intention of returning to the situation that existed before his tenure, namely a dangerous imbalance between British commitments and capabilities.[38]

The United States had a substantial and vested interest in an overseas British military presence. Britain's contribution to NATO was of course of fundamental importance, as well as British forces in the Far East as support of the United States in the containment of China. According to the State Department: "A substantial British cutback would create a vacuum which would be difficult and costly for the United States to fill."[39] Given the strong American interest in the world-wide role of Britain, how was the British leadership able to keep the Americans quiet until Healey had everything in place?

Clive Ponting has advanced the thesis, much embellished by Philip Ziegler, that there was a secret deal that in return for support of the pound, the British agreed to remain east of Suez. According to Ponting, only the prime minister himself, George Brown and the chancellor of the treasury, James Callaghan, knew about this on the British side.[40] Ziegler takes the secrecy a step further:

> The deal that was in the end done between Wilson and Johnson was not the sort that was enshrined in formal documents. Largely it was a matter of nods, winks and tacit understandings. Its exact details will probably be never known, they were, indeed, hardly known to the negotiators.[41]

Ponting bases much of his evidence on a much-quoted memorandum from McGeorge Bundy to the president, discussing how to shore up the tottering pound sterling:

> My own interests, and those of Bob McNamara and Dean Rusk, are wider. We are concerned with the fact that the British are constantly trying to make narrow bargains on money while they cut back their wider political and military responsibilities. We want to make sure that the British get it into their heads that it makes no sense for us to rescue the Pound in a situation in which there is no British flag in Vietnam, and a threatened British thin-out in both east of Suez and in Germany.[42]

The allegedly secret deal, or 'nods' and 'winks', might well be only a chimera, for there is no hard evidence to substantiate an Anglo-American agreement along those lines.[43] The Johnson government was deeply concerned about the prospect of a British devaluation. McGeorge Bundy advised the cabinet secretary, Burke Trend, on July 30, 1965 that the consequences of a devaluation would be 'disastrous'.[44] The Americans were comforted by calming noises from the prime minister, who disclaimed any intention to devalue. On the contrary, Wilson claimed that the long-term objective of Anglo-American policies ought to be integration of the dollar and sterling.[45] As for the British world-wide role, the Labour government had no intention of turning that into a scuttle: "Such a policy would be contrary to everything he, the Prime Minister, had ever said and would make him eat a great number of his own words."[46] A rather categorical assurance, one would think, but Wilson practiced ambiguity as an art form, often fobbing off the Americans with bland assurances in lieu of concrete pledges to keep maximum freedom of movement. As one commentator noted, "Harold Wilson was adept at concealing his real intentions not only from his colleagues, but also from future scholars."[47] It took several meetings and considerable American pressure before Wilson acknowledged any link between American support of the pound and the maintenance of a British presence east of Suez.[48] The Americans left the talks with Wilson with the clear understanding that the prime minister accepted the connection between the defense of the pound and the British world-wide role.[49]

The Johnson administration was well aware of the fact that Britain's economic problems would remain for years to come. On September 16, 1965, the Labour government published an ambitious national plan aiming at a 25 percent increase in national production and a balance of payments surplus of £250 million by 1970, targets far higher than previous economic performance.[50] The plan exposed the inherent contradictions and perhaps delusions of Labour's economic program. For the plan to succeed it needed a favorable business climate, but to prevent devaluation Labour was forced to pursue restrictive economic policies, particularly when the pound was under pressure and the market needed reassurance.[51]

The British attempts to put their economic house in order carried some important implications for the United States. The American government expected "real consultations" and not to be confronted with established facts in the forthcoming defense reviews: "We are fully cognizant of the fact that British resources are stretched thin. We would not, on the other hand, wish to have the UK abandon any of its commitments for doctrinaire reasons or because of transitory difficulties."[52] As the 1966 defense review wound its way through the British bureaucracy, Healey explained that no decisions would be made before consulting the Americans. By mid July 1965, he hinted that Britain would leave Aden and strengthen its commitment in the Persian Gulf.[53] In fact, by that date the Labour government had already committed itself to major reductions in Britain's overseas role, while at the same time Wilson uttered his famous comment that Britain's "frontiers are on the Himalayas".[54] But as the defense review neared its conclusion, the State Department lamented that the British tended to inform rather than consult the United States on decisions already made.[55]

The State Department and Pentagon coordinated their views to meet the challenges of the upcoming defense review. The administration had repeatedly resisted any British cut-backs, but was now resigned to some readjustments of the British positions. Wilson's assurance that Britain intended to remain a world power despite "certain adjustments in British overseas deployment" sufficed to dull American protests.[56] The British decision to give up the Aden base, despite claims to the contrary,[57] did not elicit much comment from the Americans.[58] The United States had little or no interest in Aden, and not even the prospect of increased Communist influence there caused much concern. After the decision to withdraw had been announced, and Aden slid further toward anarchy, the State Department observed:

> Domination of South Arabia by a leftist oriented group would have an unfavorable psychological impact in Saudi Arabia, the Persian Gulf and Muscat/Oman. It is in our interest to maintain a significant Western presence in the area. However, South Arabia is not of sufficient direct importance to the United States, either economically or strategically, to warrant the massive financial and political effort necessary to pre-empt the area for the West. Accordingly, we must be prepared to accept a certain level of Soviet-Chinese Communist presence in South Arabia following independence.[59]

The process of the British giving up Aden was long in the making. David Holden observes that by the end of 1964, holding on to the base was self-defeating, "as the existence of the base increasingly provoked the unrest it was supposed to prevent or suppress",[60] while for Michael Howard, the Aden base consumed more security than it "could ever produce".[61] The Labour government had long since lost interest in the Aden Federation and base. On October 12, 1965, discussing the forthcoming defense review, the Defence and Oversea Policy Committee concluded: "In the long term, we would have no fundamental objection to the eventual establishment of an Egyptian hegemony over Aden and South Arabia."[62] But Labour was completely cynical not only of the Aden connection, but also over relations with the United States. Successfully browbeating the Americans to accept the January 1966 defense review quitting of Aden,[63] and reaching agreement with the United States on exchange requirements to purchase American F-111A planes, the cabinet noted on February 14 that it "would only maintain commitments as long as in UK interest".[64] To cut costs, Healey cancelled production of the British TSR-2 plane for the much cheaper American F-111A planes. The sale was conditioned on a substantial part of British dollar expenditure being offset by sales of British arms to the United States.[65] For the Johnson administration, the purchase of the F-111 planes was proof that Britain intended to play a major role east of Suez. The F-111 planes long reach capability would enable the United Kingdom to operate from Australia, even after giving up its Far Eastern bases. Thus, even in the absence of bases, Britain could still play an important military role.[66]

While the Ponting thesis is untenable, there was in fact a secret Anglo-American deal: the Americans let the British in on the Saudi Arabian arms market in the wake of the threatened British withdrawal east of Suez. Saudi Arabia made an agreement in December 1965 with a consortium of British and American companies to buy a comprehensive air-defense system, including forty British Lightning jet aircraft; American Hawk ground-to-air missiles; British training and support services; and radar and communications equipment. The deal, worth $400 million, was Britain's most valuable ever with a Middle Eastern state.[67] The Johnson administration did not open the Saudi arms market out of altruism. "In this respect the recently concluded U.S.–U.K. air package for Saudi Arabia," George Moore, officer in charge of the Arabian Peninsula Affairs in the State Department, observed, "should have a salutary effect in ensuring Britain's future role in the Persian Gulf area."[68]

Frank Brenchley, however, downplays the Anglo-American aspects of the Saudi arms deal, believing that opposition from the Jewish lobby forced the Johnson administration to let the British in on the large contract for Saudi air defense. The Jewish lobby feared the sophisticated arms package might be used directly against Israel or transferred to an Arab front line state.[69] While for Nadav Safran, the Anglo-American arms deal was to "offset British purchases of American F-111 aircraft".[70] Ironically, as a result of the devaluation in 1967, Britain cancelled purchase of the F-111A planes. As Anthony Sampson explains: "The Saudis in the end had been persuaded to buy British planes that they did not want, to allow Britain to pay for American planes they could not afford."[71] But the deal was far from a question of money or offsets; the main purpose was to keep British forces east of Suez.[72]

The Anglo-Saudi arms deal was not the only example of American largesse toward Britain. In September 1965, the United States put together a $1 billion credit rescue package for sterling with a consortium that included Austria, Belgium, Canada, West Germany, the Netherlands, Italy, Sweden, Switzerland, Japan and the Bank for International Settlements. The American share of the deal was $400 million.[73] In the long run, the rescue package was barely enough to keep the pound afloat. Soon after the conclusion of the 1966 defense review and the Anglo-American arms deal with Saudi Arabia, Wilson was back for another round of American support for the still wobbling pound. For the American side, the equation was fairly simple: how to translate further financial assistance into a continued British presence east of Suez.[74] The total American financial package was large: the United States arranged financing with the Export–Import bank of up to $1.5 billion for aircraft purchase, an American guarantee of $325 million for defense department purchases in Britain, which came on top of the Saudi air consortium estimated at $400 million in value to Britain. When the British balance of payments worsened again in the first half of 1966, the Johnson administration assisted Britain by increasing their own military purchases in the United Kingdom and pressured Germany for a greater contribution to the British Army on the Rhine. A package of £40–45 million in American aid, plus £72 million extracted from the Germans.[75] But whatever the Americans did, the pound remained unstable. Therefore elements in the Johnson administration – most importantly the secretary of the treasury, Henry Fowler, and George Ball – began to question the rigid American conditions for assistance: no devaluation and Britain to remain in full force east of Suez. In a crisis, they preferred a British pull-out east of Suez to devaluation.[76] The British, of course, continued to fan the flame of a possible withdrawal. In a message to president Johnson on July 20, 1966, introducing further economic stringency measures, Wilson noted:

> But if we are to ask the British public to cooperate willingly over the sacrifices essential to put our economy to rights, they must equally be satisfied that they are not being asked to carry a disproportionate share of the general cost of western defense. We cannot, in imposing these measures at home, avoid also reducing our Government expenditure in Germany as well as elsewhere.

As a concession to Johnson, Wilson added that, in his address to Parliament, he would claim that further defense cuts "should not affect the basic lines of foreign policy on which the defense review was founded".[77] The American reaction to the latest British package was optimistic. If Wilson were successful, "we have the chance, at last", Walt W. Rostow, national security advisor, noted, "to deal with a Britain which can make its commitments stick, even if they are modest, and which will not have an annual sterling crisis".[78] Even this substantial package did not secure a continued British overseas presence or British troops on the Rhine. By 1967, Wilson faced a stagnant British economy, with lots of excess capacity, low investment and a balance of payments close to equilibrium. The Americans were highly skeptical of the prime minister's claim that he could revive the economy if only Britain were left alone by speculators, saved money from a paring down of British forces in Germany and east of Suez, and had international financial assistance.[79] Unable, or unwilling, to take over Britain's military commitments east of Suez, the United States had little choice, therefore, but to continue to support the pound until Britain devalued it. Compounding the problem was Wilson's skill in evading specific commitments and putting off the Johnson administration with bland assurances that Britain had no plans to withdraw.[80] Besides, there was little the Americans could do, since the Labour government had decided as early as November 1964, well ahead of the numerous American rescue packages, significantly to pare down Britain's overseas role.

Nasser's humiliating defeat in the Six Day War forced the Egyptians to withdraw from Yemen. Having gotten rid of the Egyptian threat on the border of the Aden Federation, Britain refused to postpone their date of departure in order to have a chance to shore up the South Arab Federation and defeat the rebels.[81] On the contrary, the British accelerated their withdrawal, while Aden descended into chaos and disorder as the different anti-British groups fought for power, and Britain's former allies and clients were left to face their enemies alone. The withdrawal from Aden alienated Faisal and Saudi Arabia from Britain – a connection both parties in Britain had done so much to cultivate since Saudi Arabia and Great Britain resumed diplomatic relations in January 1963. But as a result of the Aden débâcle these sentiments had largely dissipated by the fall of 1967, evaporating almost five years of conscientious work to improve Anglo-Saudi relations. Not only did the British action create Saudi ill will, but it carried severe financial penalties, when they announced shortly after leaving Aden that they would quit the Persian Gulf as well. The decision to withdraw from the Gulf came in spite of the fact that Britain, only two months earlier, had assured Faisal that it intended to remain in the area. The British defense attaché in Jidda, Colonel C. S. Fitzpatrick, cabled the ministry of defense on January 31, 1968:

> The picture is rather depressing as any saving accruing from our withdrawal from
> the Gulf looks as if it is going to be offset by our immediate loss of some poten-
> tially large scale defence sales here and our possible loss of this wealthy market
> for the foreseeable future.[82]

Britain therefore lost a contract for armored cars worth £40 million to
France, the United Kingdom being no longer considered a trustworthy
partner by Faisal.[83]

All the time, almost up to the announcement of the British withdrawal
from the Persian Gulf, the Labour leadership made suitable soothing noises
to maintain an illusion of a continued British presence in the area.[84] This
included assurances by Wilson to Parliament as late as December 7, 1967,
while in the meantime Goronwy Roberts, now minister of state at the
Foreign Office, went to the Gulf to reassure the rulers of a continued British
presence.[85]

Meanwhile, planning of further reductions in the British defense establishment went full speed ahead. Healey had warned in his July 1967 defense
review that Britain intended to reduce by half its forces in Singapore and
Malaysia by 1970–71.[86] This had the added advantage of lessening the need
for Middle East bases. As we have seen, Healey had given warning in the
same review of further cutbacks; it was preferable to keep forces in Britain
than at local bases. Contemporary commentators questioned the British
commitment to the Persian Gulf. Elisabeth Monroe believed the British
presence to be an embarrassment,[87] while for Michael Howard, the Gulf
bases were "inescapable liabilities rather than Imperial assets".[88] The
Labourites themselves have produced overwhelming and almost uniform
arguments in favor of withdrawing from the Persian Gulf and the Middle
East. One time naval secretary, Christopher Mayhew, argued in a book
published in 1967 that the British bases did not protect the flow of oil from
the Persian Gulf; the oil supply was protected by the need for the producer
countries to market their oil. Besides, the east of Suez role and dependence
on the United States probably prevented British entry into the Common
Market, because of a too close association with the Americans and preoccupation with Britain's overseas role at the expense of Europe.[89] For
Healey, British military bases outside Europe were an "anachronism".[90]
Regrets for the withdrawal were, in the eyes of Michael Stewart, "nostalgia
for the nineteenth century".[91] For George Brown, withdrawal from east of
Suez was "inevitable and essential".[92] Roy Jenkins, chancellor of the exchequer from November 1967, pushed for an early withdrawal.[93] Wilson felt
that clinging to the east of Suez role was one of his worst mistakes as prime
minister.[94]

All this perhaps smacks too much of post-fact rationalization. But there
is little doubt that distaste for empire and anti-colonialism were the chief

factors in the British withdrawal east of Suez.[95] Hostility towards the empire was widespread in the Labour Party.[96] The withdrawal from the Persian Gulf had little to do with saving money, but was necessary to get left-wing acceptance for cuts in social spending to balance the budget after the pound was devalued,[97] a fact accepted by the State Department: "Given the political pressures on the Labour Government, substantial defense cuts were inevitable if the public was also to be asked to accept heavy cuts in social welfare expenditures and steep tax increases."[98] It is hard to explain the decision to leave the Gulf by anything other than domestic exigencies. The British investment in the Gulf was small, compared to the vast British oil interest generating large corporate and government revenues. Britain had stationed 6,000 troops and air support units at an annual non-sterling cost of £12 million.[99] But Labour seized every opportunity to dismantle the empire, and refused to explore any political or economic opportunities to remain. When finally the Egyptian problem disappeared in Yemen, the Labour leadership responded by accelerating the withdrawal from Aden. When the rulers of the Persian Gulf offered to finance the British military presence to prevent withdrawal of British troops, they were brutally and gratuitously shot down by Denis Healey, who in a television interview retorted "that he was not 'sort of a white slaver for Arab shaiks'". British soldiers should not become "mercenaries for people who like to have British troops around". Ironically, Healey willingly accepted contributions from the governments of West Germany and Hong Kong for the presence of British troops.[100]

American acquiescence in Britain terminating its bases in the Gulf was not caused by lack of indications of British intentions. By early 1967, the State Department was well aware that Labour was bent on further reductions east of Suez. When pressured by Rusk to desist, Brown explained on April 10, 1967 that reductions were necessary to satisfy the left wing of the Labour Party and to prepare Britain for membership in the Common Market. Meeting Wilson in June 1967, Johnson protested strongly against British plans, but to little avail. Briefing the president prior to the meeting, Rusk urged Johnson: "Tell him we must have reliable allies. Congress and American people will not permit us to stand alone. Isolationists will demand U.S. withdrawal not only from Far East but also from Europe." At the same time Johnson was urged to warn Wilson that the United States wanted to avoid entanglements in South Arabia, and that American assistance would be in the form of political support in the United Nations and elsewhere.[101] American protests were effectively muted by contradicting British signals; prior to the Johnson and Wilson talks Brown told Rusk that the decision would be held in abeyance until the prime minister returned from Washington, while Healey informed McNamara that Britain was determined to withdraw completely from the Far East by 1975.[102] With the

American hands-off approach towards trouble spots on the Arabian Peninsula, US rejoinders for Britain to remain in the Middle and the Far East must have carried little water for the Labour administration.

A week before the publication of Healey's July 18 defense review, Johnson wrote Wilson, while Rusk wrote Brown, both reiterating deep "American concern about any decisions regarding the reduction of the British presence in Southeast Asia". Labour did not pay much heed, announcing as we have seen a 50 percent reduction of British forces in Malaysia and Singapore.[103] This seemed to have become a recurrent pattern in Anglo-American relations, the United States pleading, sometimes threatening dire consequences, with little or no effect. For instance, Rusk wrote Brown on April 21, 1967 warning against British withdrawal from the Far East. Not only could such a withdrawal increase American isolationism for being left alone in Vietnam, but even result in American withdrawal from Europe.[104] The warning had little or no appreciable affect on Labour policy. As an attempt to mollify Johnson, Wilson, when announcing the withdrawal from the Far East, claimed that Britain would continue to play a part in the area. The Labourites thus planned "to retain a sophisticated military capability for use in the Far East" after the withdrawal.[105]

Phillip Ziegler insists that after learning that Britain intended to leave the Gulf, Johnson threatened financial penalties and the cancellation of orders for British weapons.[106] The president wrote Wilson a blistering letter after learning of the cancellation of the F-111A planes. These planes would have given Britain an overseas capability through rapid deployment in spite of withdrawing from the Far East and the Persian Gulf.

> But if you decide to forego the acquisition of the F-111, everyone here will regard this as a total disengagement from any commitments whatsoever to the security of areas outside Europe and, indeed, to a considerable extent in Europe as well. Moreover, it will be viewed here as a strong indication of British isolation which would be fatal to the chances of cooperation between our countries in the field of defense procurement.

Furthermore, the president expected that recent military contracts awarded to British firms would be cancelled. Far more serious were the political repercussions, because Congress might demand withdrawal of American troops from Europe.[107] On the Persian Gulf, Johnson observed in a communication to Wilson of January 11, 1968, his deep dismay of what was "tantamount to British withdrawal from world affairs". The president wondered "if you and all your associates have taken fully into account the direct and indirect consequences" of leaving the Gulf. "The structure of peacekeeping will be shaken to its foundations."[108]

But as usual, Labour saw little need to placate the Americans to the extent of reversing its policy. Even if applied, the penalties were of insufficient magnitude to alter the British decision. In the end, the United States had little choice but to accept the British withdrawal, a withdrawal that profoundly affected the Anglo-American relationship. Clark Clifford, American secretary of defense after McNamara, summed up the situation in a National Security meeting on June 5, 1968:

> Secretary Clifford said that the British do not have the resources, the backup, or the hardware to deal with any big world problem. He said they are no longer a powerful ally of ours because they cannot afford the cost of an adequate defense effort. . . . Earlier we had the closest working relations with the British. They looked after one part of the world and we looked after another part.[109]

Briefing the foreign minister for meeting the American ambassador on September 12, 1968, the Foreign Office noted that Anglo-American relations were good, but with the British movement away from empire and towards Europe, there was an American tendency to write off Britain "and to leave it to us to find our new rôle in the world".[110] The new British role in the world, according to Labour, was Europe. "Our decision to withdraw British forces from South-East Asia and Persian Gulf by the end of 1971 and to concentrate our defence effort in Europe," Healey notes in his July 1968 defense review, "has made it possible for Britain to offer immediate increases of some of her forces to N.A.T.O."[111] Still, even by sacrificing the empire and downplaying Anglo-American relations, British entry into the Common Market was blocked until 1973.

Given the alleged importance attached to the preservation of the British role east of Suez, American policy is difficult to fathom. At all points where Britain wanted to change policy or diminish its overseas role, American resistance was easily overcome. Apart from financial largesse and a pious wish for Britain to remain, it is difficult to find traces of American policy independent of Great Britain. There were no fall-back positions, no alternative policies, just accommodation to whatever Wilson was doing, and in an earlier age to whatever policies were emanating from London under Butler and Home. With his activist reputation, Johnson's policies, or lack thereof, defy understanding. Perhaps the president's disinterest in all things foreign and his engulfment in the Vietnam war are sufficient explanations. Yet the British withdrawal from the Persian Gulf opened a Pandora's box of competing interests, all the consequences of which we have still to see and measure. Johnson's failure to prevent the Six Day War or take strong countermeasures against Israel in its aftermath, continues to bedevil American relations with the Middle East. Eisenhower, when confronted with Israeli aggression during the Suez crisis, forced Israel to withdraw from its occupation of the Sinai Peninsula in March 1957, ensuring ten years of relative quiet in Arab–Israeli relations; quiet in the sense of avoiding a major war in the Middle East. British policy is easier to fathom, being one-dimensionally ideologically committed to the end of empire.

5
Leaving Aden

October 1964 to November 1967

Aden town had been a British colony since the 1830s, and by the end of the 1950s, excluding New York, it was the busiest harbor in the world. The colony took on new importance after the Suez crisis, being the linchpin of the British military establishment in the Middle East. By 1960, Aden colony was the site of the British Unified Command of the Commander-in-Chief, Middle East, and local headquarters for the army, navy and airforce, with more than 20,000 soldiers of a total of 30,000 British troops in the Middle East. Annual costs for the Middle East Command were estimated at £21 million. The forces in Aden, in addition to internal security and sealing off the Yemen/South Arabian border, provided a reserve for operations in East Africa and the Persian Gulf; a deterrent against aggression against Kuwait; and maintenance of the British position in the Trucial States and Muscat and Oman.[1] Having little interest in the sheikhs, emirs and sharifs in the upcountry, Britain was content to pacify the local rulers with offers of payment and protection. Between 1839 and 1954, Britain signed 90 protectorate treaties with local rulers, gaining control of their foreign and defense policies. The main purpose of the treaties was to give the Aden colony protection from marauding raiders, and the expansionist impulses of neighboring Yemen. To counter the pressure of Arab nationalism, local rulers in the Aden protectorate merged their principalities into the Federation of Arab Emirates of South West Arabia in 1959. The rapidly growing economy in the Aden colony attracted large numbers of migrant workers from Yemen and the protectorates, many of them eager recipients of Nasser's propaganda. The British met this challenge by denying them the vote, the franchise being restricted to native born Adenis or British subjects of long standing there. In September 1962, Britain merged the Aden protectorates and Aden colony into the Aden Federation. Merging the backward hinterland and the comparatively advanced Aden town, with its large disenfranchised immigrant population, was a challenge even in the best of times; it became infinitely more difficult after the Yemen revolution.[2] Excluding both the Aden workers and the tribesmen, the Conservatives had created a system in which neither group had a stake and little to lose if the government disappeared. Labour therefore inherited an explosive situation.[3]

South Arabia was a cauldron of confusing jurisdictions and competing political groups. The South Arabian Federation compromised 16 autonomous tribal areas with approximately 500,000 inhabitants, whose rulers, after much prodding from the British had formed a leaderless confederation. The Aden colony (250,000 inhabitants) was theoretically the 17th member of the Federation, but under direct British emergency rule after the suspension of its constitution on September 25, 1965. A small principality on the Yemen border, Upper Yafi', refused association with the Federation, as well as the three easternmost tribal states of Aden, the Hadramaut with about 500,000 inhabitants and the bulk of South Arabia's territory. Nominally, the South Arabian Federation was under the Federal rulers, who had been given firm support by the Conservative government, but whom Labour distanced itself from. The Aden colony was most receptive to Nasserite propaganda and was the stronghold of competing anti-British organizations. The two main organizations were the Marxist-Leninist NLF (National Liberation Front for Occupied South Yemen) and the Egyptian-supported FLOSY (Front for the Liberation of South Yemen).[4] However honorable their intention to liberate the Aden Federation from British rule, it was an unfortunate fact that most of the victims of their operations were not the British imperialists, but their fellow Arabs.[5]

The Conservative governments tried unsuccessfully to solve the Aden Federation problems with political reforms and military force. The Labour government did not have any interest in either, but wanted to divest Britain of the Aden Federation at the earliest possible opportunity. Although Labourites were determined to rid themselves of the Aden colony, it was not theirs to give away. There were commitments given, promises to keep and preparations to make before another burdensome relic of empire withered away. The Tories' unsuccessful military campaigns in Radfan during the spring of 1964 made the disbandment of empire easier for Labour. The erosion of the British position in Aden began when the Conservatives announced, in July 1964, that South Arabia would be granted independence in 1968, while Britain kept the Aden base. Almost instantly any local loyalty towards the British evaporated, and the Arabs, favoring a continued British presence, fully realized that soon no one would be there to protect them.[6] The independence decision triggered a wave of terrorism in Aden town, so that by the end of 1964 the Aden base caused the unrest it was supposed to suppress.[7] Ideology played a large part in Labour's decision to leave Aden, given its distaste for imperialism and sympathy for the struggling national liberation movements.[8] To pacify nervous Adenis who had cast their lot with Britain, the new Labour government repeatedly assured them that Britain intended to live up to its commitments and defend Aden. When it failed to do so, Labour opened itself to the charge it was abandoning its pledged word.[9]

Anticipating Labour's wish to examine policy towards South Arabia, the Foreign Office expected to be deprived of the use of the Aden base: "In drafting the paper we inevitably came up against the question whether, if we had to leave Aden, we ought to try to stay in Arabia at all." Political stability and continuing the flow of oil at reasonable rates were paramount concerns for the Foreign Office, thereby dictating a continued British presence in the Persian Gulf, regardless of the future of the Aden base. If they decided to leave, the British should do so in good order, handing over power to a government preferably of their own choosing. Being seen to be driven out, or leaving chaos and disorder behind, could jeopardize British influence in the all-important Persian Gulf.[10]

As Britain began its process of disengagement, the guerillas increased their activities. "We are already disturbed," Healey observed on March 31, 1965, "because Aden is sucking in forces of all sorts that we badly need elsewhere."[11] Regardless of Labour's intent of withdrawal, British and Federal forces were engaged in skirmishes and border operations against and along the Aden–Yemeni border.[12] The operations were of a sufficient scale to cause concern in the State Department and Britain was urged to stabilize the border by pulling its troops back.[13] The British military establishment also began questioning the utility of the Aden base.[14] Wheelock, while previously often skeptical towards British policy in Aden, now came round to the conclusion that the British government was following the only sensible policy possible. Still, Wheelock wondered if the base was tenable in the long run: "The time may well come, and possibly sooner than we think, when the political and propaganda cost of maintaining a British military presence here is not worth paying."[15] The situation was bleak; the entire Federal army, the Federal Guard and British units were in the back-country fighting dissidents.

> In Aden combined local and British military security forces totalling several thousand men have been unable to prevent almost nightly grenade, bazooka, and firearm attacks in all sections of the town including heavily guarded military security areas. Nor have the security forces to date succeeded to the Consulate General's knowledge in apprehending a single active leader of the terrorist campaign.[16]

Colonial secretary, Anthony Greenwood, while agreeing on the ultimate goal of withdrawal from Aden, feared that if the umbilical cord to the mother country was cut while the dependency was the victim of aggression, the Federal government could legitimately charge that Britain had broken its treaty obligations. While regrettable, breaching the confidence of the Federal government was in Greenwood's view a lesser evil than remaining in Aden indefinitely.[17] In addition to Labour's anti-colonialist ideology, local reasons abounded for quitting the Aden Federation. The situation in South Arabia was chaotic. On top of fighting in the backcountry, South Arabia was embroiled in a constitutional dispute with Britain, as well as labor disputes in Aden and electoral disputes in the Protectorates. Adding to this volatile mix was Egyptian propaganda contributing to the slide toward extremism and anti-British actions.[18] A dissident campaign operated with impunity, and virtually wiped out the special branch of the local police force in Aden town and assassinated senior British officials. The omnipresence of terrorism led Britain to suspect that the Aden government aided and abetted the campaign.[19] Just a fortnight after reporting increased anti-British activity in Aden, Curtis Jones, the principal officer of the American consulate in Aden, predicted on September 20, 1965: "In Palestine in 1948 the security situation deteriorated to the point that the colonial authorities finally decamped in disgust. This may well be the pattern in South Arabia."[20] As we shall see, Jones' warning was prophetic.

Improving relations with Nasser was the central feature of Labour's policy toward the Middle East. But it was Aden, always Aden, that remained a wedge between Britain and the UAR, because Nasser supported and encouraged Britain's opponents there. Finally, when conditions for improved relations seemed propitious, minister of state George Thompson was dispatched to Cairo. His mission ended in utter failure, because while he was in Egypt the British government suspended the Aden colony constitution on September 25, 1965 and imposed direct British rule. In retaliation, Nasser refused to meet the British envoy. At best, this was a failure of timing, or more likely a failure of policy. Suspending the constitution prior to Thompson's arrival in Cairo would have risked its cancellation; doing so afterwards would have given Nasser grounds for charging Britain with duplicity. However, if agreement with Nasser on Aden was reached, suspension of the constitution would have been unnecessary.[21] Healey, against the wishes of the Foreign Office, insisted on the suspension of the Aden constitution to deal with the turbulent situation in South Arabia, despite his long-standing opposition to Britain retaining the base. It is almost as if he wanted the Thompson visit to fail, preventing a negotiated solution with Egypt over Aden. A calm, quiet Aden was perhaps not the means to induce the rapid withdrawal Healey wanted.[22] Healey's action is even stranger in light of Nasser signaling his willingness to halt terrorism in Aden and to ensure the success of the Thompson visit. Suspending the constitution while Thompson was in Egypt, Nasser believed, was a calculated British snub, which, coming on top of Britain siding with his opponents in the Middle East, convinced him of British perfidy. For Nasser, the suspension was only the last of a series of anti-Egyptian actions in the Middle East, starting with Britain supporting the Royalists in Yemen and siding with Saudi Arabia against Egypt. Egyptian foreign minister Mahoud Riad explained to the State Department on October 8, 1965:

> The British could not be trusted to act in good faith. He went into great detail about the UAR preparations for Mr. Thompson's recent visit to Cairo and what his government considered the insulting duplicity with which the British Government announced the suspension of the Aden State Constitution while Thompson was actually meeting in Cairo with Deputy Prime Minister Fawzi and himself. It was only an hour after these meetings that the British Embassy in Cairo informed the Foreign Ministry of the suspension of the constitution. The Foreign Minister asserted several times that the UAR had already decided before Thompson's arrival that President Nasser would agree to try to halt terrorism in Aden. His government could only interpret British handling of the matter as deliberately calculated.[23]

Thompson, second in command in the Foreign Office and later commonwealth secretary, drew the opposite conclusion. The failure of the Cairo mission was a turning point in his perception of Arab radicalism. But while Thompson's conception of the Middle East changed, it did little to alter British policy in the Middle East. Whatever the realities on the ground, British policy seems to have been withdrawal at almost any price, regardless of leading Labour politicians getting a different or perhaps more realistic appraisal of local conditions. Thompson elaborated his conclusions a year later to George Brown (foreign minister August 1966–March 1968), in response to a request from the foreign minister on how to improve relations with Arab nationalists in general and Nasser in particular. Improving relations with Nasser was a central tenet in Brown's policy toward the Middle East.[24] Contrary to the Egyptian leader's claims, Arab nationalism took various shapes and forms and was not a monolithic movement where Nasser was the natural leader. Furthermore, the more extreme forms of Arab nationalism were anything but progressive, leading often to severe repression of human rights and lack of economic progress, as attested by the experience of Iraq, Syria and Egypt.

> The Labour Party's aim is to encourage the best possibilities of peaceful change. I have come to the paradoxical conclusion that given the Middle Eastern social and economic framework so different from our own, it is autocratic countries like Iran or Saudi Arabia that are pursuing the kind of economic and social reforms that are more likely to result in peaceful change.[25]

This belated recognition of Middle Eastern realities did little to change Labour's policies, and even less to change Brown's singled-minded pursuit of Nasser and abandonment of Aden. The suspension of the Aden constitution received tacit American endorsement.[26] The upshot of the whole episode was, as discussed in chapter 4, the conclusion of the Defence and Oversea Policy Committee on October 12, 1965: "In the long-term, we would have no fundamental objection to the eventual establishment of an Egyptian hegemony over Aden and South Arabia." And, as we have seen, the Johnson administration was equally unconcerned about the future of Aden.[27] Having accepted the conclusions of the 1966 defense review, American policy seemed to be nothing more than the hope that Britain could leave Aden with as little disturbance as possible. The American disillusionment with Nasser took a little longer, but on December 1, 1966 the National Security Council declared that Kennedy's attempted rapprochement with Nasser was officially over. While the United States might have gone a little overboard in courting the Egyptian leader, the results were disappointing, as Nasser did little to moderate his anti-American policies.[28]

Apart from growing disillusionment with Nasser, there were no long-term plans or strategy emerging from London or Washington. Meeting the State Department on October 19, 1965, Greenwood said "he honestly did not know what the next British step should be", aside from pleading with Nasser that Britain was sincere in its pledge to grant independence by 1968. The lack of strategy was equally palpable in Washington, apart from urging the British to keep their options open, and not rushing into a too hasty withdrawal from Aden.[29] Jones suspected that Wilson imposed direct rule as a campaign move in the forthcoming British election to gain votes by being tough on Britain's opponents in Aden.[30] By November 1965, however, whatever doubts were expressed to the Americans and others, the Wilson government had firmly made up its mind to give up Aden.[31] Meeting president Johnson on December 16, 1965, Wilson sweetened the withdrawal from Aden by pledging to strengthen the British military presence in the Persian Gulf.[32] Accepting withdrawal, the Johnson administration pressed for a British security guarantee to the independent South Arabian State.[33] At Britain's request, to facilitate withdrawal, the State Department urged Nasser to desist from encouraging subversion in Aden. With the announced British decision to leave Aden, it would be in the interest of the Egyptian leader, according to Rusk, "that South Arabia enjoy stable independence rather than become another Yemen".[34] Nasser had, in the fall of 1965, when meeting Faisal, agreed to withdraw from Yemen. Following publication of the 1966 defense review, Nasser broke his agreement with Faisal, announcing that Egyptian troops would stay in Yemen for five years if necessary, to ensure the liberation of South Arabia. To put additional pressure on the British in Aden and enhance his revolutionary credentials, the Egyptian dictator intensified his support of the anti-British forces there.[35] It mattered little to Britain, as Labour expected a continued Egyptian presence in Yemen after the withdrawal of British troops. Foreign minister Brown was firmly convinced that withdrawal, the sooner the better, was the only acceptable solution.[36]

With this great power legerdemain, the Johnson administration casually tossed away the very real benefits of the Aden base in return for unspecific promises of increased British military presence in the Gulf. Here, as with the pound, Wilson skillfully gained American support of British policies while at the same time retaining maximum freedom of action. One wonders why Johnson time and again let Wilson wriggle out commitments without even once putting Labour's feet to the fire. After leaving Aden, Britain intended to downgrade their security commitment to Kuwait, a commitment Healey believed to be of little value:

> The growth of nationalism outside Europe made it obvious that in some areas the presence of British troops was becoming an irritant rather then a stabilizing factor. The scales fell from my eyes when I discovered that the Kuwaiti Government, with which Britain had a defence treaty, would not let us keep troops in Kuwait itself for the fear of riots from the local population; we had to keep them hundreds of miles away in Bahrain. But the Kuwaiti Government was financing the Free Bahraini movement, which was trying to get us out of Bahrain as well.[37]

When the Conservative government, in 1964, promised independence to Aden by 1968, it pledged to continue its defense agreement with an independent South Arabian government. Healey, announcing the abandonment of Aden to the House of Commons on February 22, 1966, deliberately confused the government of the Aden State with the government of the Aden Federation, implying that the suspension of the Aden State constitution voided the pledge to the protectorates as well. The Conservatives forced Healey to admit his error in the House and acknowledge continued British obligations to an independent South Arabia.[38] Labour had repeatedly assured the Federal rulers of continued British obligations, only abruptly to renege on them on the eve of announcing the defense review. Labour had dispatched Lord Beswick just three months prior to the defense review to assure the Federal rulers about a continued British presence in Aden. As late as January 1966, Healey, on a visit to Australia, insisted that Britain had "no intention of ratting on her commitments in the Middle East".[39]

One of the Federal ministers observed: "One of my colleagues described that sort of behavior as dishonorable and a betrayal on part of the British Government." So Aden slid into further anarchy as different factions fought for power, a policy making little sense to British Conservatives or to the Federal ministers. Lapping explains that other key players were of a different persuasion:

To ministers in London it made perfect sense: the prime objective of policy was to avoid getting involved in war, more particularly to avoid being accused by Labour Party members of killing socialists and the representatives of the Aden majority in order to bolster the power of feudal sultans.[40]

The defense review was the beginning of the end of the Federal government, as it was given no time to adjust to the new situation. The whole structure rested on British policy, British assurances and British subvention, which were unilaterally taken away. The Federal government was told of the conclusion of the defense review only five days prior to its announcement. They had no opportunity to mend fences with Egypt or seek agreement with their enemies.[41] The defense review, then, destroyed, almost instantly, the basis of British authority in South Arabia.[42]

By now, British and American policies toward Aden were in complete disarray. The ministry of defence pushed for an early withdrawal from Aden, whatever the consequences. The Foreign Office pressured the Americans to cease aid to Nasser and strongly urged them to depose him. The Americans refused to pressure Nasser and dismissed out of hand any thought of deposing him, but pushed for security guarantees for an independent South Arabian Federation. When realizing that the withdrawal was for real they pressed for continued British presence, without being able to change the British withdrawal schedule.[43]

Brown, when foreign minister, had no stomach for countermeasures against the deteriorating situation in South Arabia. Thus when planes, probably of Egyptian origin, bombed a village in Beihan on August 1, 1966, destroying 75 houses and wounding three children, the foreign minister did nothing but protest.[44] But the confusion and vacillation at the top did not prevent energetic local British leaders from taking often vigorous countermeasures against anti-British forces. Political advisor Godfrey Maynell in Dhali showed great energy in pacifying the rebels within his area of jurisdiction. But with British forces to be withdrawn in 1967, there were slim chances of defeating the guerillas. Jones, of the American consulate, thought the Federal Regular Army (FRA) most certainly would fail when replacing British troops.[45] Adding to the problems for the Foreign Office was the request from the chancellor of the exchequer for a £150 million cut in the defense budget, which Brown and Healey saw as an opportunity for further troop reductions in the Middle East.[46]

While Foreign Office civil servants were floundering, the policy of the ministry of defense was withdrawal at any price whatever Nasser and his supporters did in Aden. Continued British military presence would only invite charges of colonialism from Nasser and potentially undermine other areas of British interest on the Arabian Peninsula. Similarly, the Labour leadership argued post-independence defense guarantees to South Arabia were only grist to the mill of Egyptian propaganda.[47] To avoid the appearance of abandoning its clients, Britain committed itself to give $250 million over five years to build up the FRA. Combined with UN membership, Labour argued this sufficed to protect an independent South Arabia from aggression. The American consulate in Aden thought British policies only a smokescreen for withdrawal and believed the chances for establishing an independent state were small.[48] But the point of British policy was to create an illusion of a South Arabian state ready for independence, of which Britain could then wash its hands. "We are forced to conclude that, by terminating the security guarantee, the UK will be throwing the Federation to the wolves."[49] To the Americans, the Foreign Office argued that it was in the best interests of an independent South Arabia, being without a British security guarantee, to avoid "imperialist taint". Complete withdrawal to remove imperialist taint was not only cabinet decision, but also the "long-held personal philosophy" of foreign minister Brown.[50] Still, the United States persisted in pressuring Britain to provide security guarantees to an independent South Arabia.[51] The Foreign Office responded on January 27, 1967 that the main British concern in Aden was "withdrawal in good order", and to avoid future obligations to South Arabia.[52] Brown alerted to the cabinet on March 16, 1967 that the situation in South Arabia was bad and deteriorating. Terrorism was increasing and the Federal government labored under the false impression that a defense agreement with Britain would follow independence; to ensure British withdrawal on schedule "the Federal Government must be kept in being, at least up to the time of our final withdrawal".[53]

Brown was fully aware that the Foreign Office expected the Federal government and the FRA to collapse upon withdrawal, and in the process irretrievably wreck the British position on the Persian Gulf.[54] Brown's indifference to the fate of the Persian Gulf shows the British pledge to beef up forces there for what it really was, a fig leaf for leaving Aden. While Brown informed the cabinet, he dispatched Thompson to Aden to persuade the rulers to advance the date of independence from January 1, 1968 to November 1, 1967. The Federal rulers strongly resented being pushed into an earlier independence date, particularly since they had not even agreed to the 1968 date, and were rushed into meeting Thompson at an hour's notice. Their acceptance of any independence date was on the condition of a satisfactory defense safeguard from Britain. Moreover, announcing an earlier independence date would only encourage the enemies of the Federation and damage the morale of Federal troops. Uncomfortably for the armchair anti-imperialists in London, the Federal government held Britain responsible for its defense and protection until Aden was admitted to the UN.[55] To sweeten his demand, Thompson pledged to station a naval strike force, initially for three months after independence, as a "deterrent force including retaliatory air action against clear external aggressions". But there would be no commitments against internal subversion.[56] It was doubtful that effective liaison and communication between the FRA and the carrier force could be worked out; rather the main purpose was to facilitate the British withdrawal from South Arabia.[57] Whatever their flaws, the Federal leaders, seeing little attraction in the carrier fleet and being abandoned by their protectors, felt betrayed by Labour.[58] In fact, the naval strike force was meaningless. As Richard Crossman recorded in his diary: "George is passionately determined to get out of Aden at all costs and the package is solely designed as a cover for this operation."[59] The Federation refusal to accede to the British request led Labour to push back the date of independence to January 1, 1968 and to offer the naval presence for six months after independence.[60] With the British leaving, the Federal government tried to make the United States take over Britain's security commitments. Unfortunately for the Federation leaders the Americans politely but firmly rebuffed their efforts.[61]

With Thompson in Aden browbeating the Federal government to accept an earlier British withdrawal, Brown, with Wilson's support, sought to open secret negotiations with FLOSY.[62] The whole approach was built on a rather flimsy foundation, the Foreign Office noted: "We want to bring FLOSY into cooperation with others in South Arabia for that country's future welfare. We do not want to give it an additional means of undermining the Federal Government on other terms on behalf of the UAR." Policies and pronouncements were made to smooth the withdrawal process.[63] Courting FLOSY was a way of courting Nasser, but even Brown realized, for all his pro-Nasser proclivities, that it was impossible at present to meet with the Egyptian leader "while the Egyptians were so visibl[y] implicated in terrorism in Southern Arabia".[64] One may wonder, why court Nasser at all under circumstances like this? Britain also approached the NLF, pledging to release their detainees and lift the ban on the party to "discuss things in a reasonable and relaxed atmosphere [*sic*]". In return, Britain only asked for the minor concession that the NLF stop killing British nationals – a concession the NLF was unable or unwilling to give, being in intense competition with FLOSY for the most anti-imperialist credentials. "We have to be seen to drive you out. When we have reached that stage then we can negotiate."[65]

British policy exhibited a curious ambivalence, simultaneously leaving Aden and planning a military search operation in Hauf area of the Eastern Aden protectorate (Hadramut) during early summer 1967. The purpose of the operation was to flush out rebels from the Dhofari region of western Oman who used eastern Aden as a base for operations. The anti-imperialist Brown had approved a similar operation in Hauf in October 1966. While the 1966 operation was temporarily successful, rebel activity was again on the rise in Hauf. The Dhofari rebels had operated for over two years and posed a potentially serious threat to the sultan of Muscat and Oman, and received assistance from the UAR, Iraq and even from Faisal. Saudi Arabian intervention was due to the loss of face Faisal suffered when Britain reoccupied Buraimi in October 1955. Britain hoped to persuade Faisal to desist in aiding the rebels. It was important to subdue the rebels to prevent further erosion of the authority of the sultan of Oman and secure continued oil operations. If the rebels continued to operate freely there was a real danger that they would link up with and encourage former rebel leaders in Oman proper. Dhofari rebels on the rise might ultimately threaten the RAF staging post at Salalah.[66]

Despite Brown's strictures about leaving Aden post-haste, the Foreign Office kept thrashing about for alternatives. One of the more fanciful suggestions was to encourage the FRA to lead an army coup, officially without British knowledge but with acceptance of the *fait accompli*.[67] Of more serious note for Britain was Saudi Arabia expressing strong reservations about the current British policy in South Arabia, reservations augmented by Nasser beginning a bombing campaign against it in early 1967 – a campaign designed to intimidate the Saudis and discourage Saudi support of Yemeni Royalists and Adeni federalists. Saudi frustrations were thoroughly aired when Faisal paid a state visit to London in May 1967. In response to Faisal's concerns about South Arabia, Wilson defended British policy there. A longer defense guarantee would only cause embarrassment for an independent nation and increase subversion:

> South Arabia's real defence would be international acceptance of her as an inde-pendent State. Our naval and naval air offer would simply buy her time to learn to stand on her own feet. It was true that the military help we were giving to the South Arabian forces would not enable these to combat MiG fighters; but the degree of sophisticated defence arrangements required for this would always be beyond South Arabia's capacity to maintain.[68]

The naval presence could not prevent internal subversion; Wilson admitted that only a broad-based government could do that, in this way defending Labour's contacts with FLOSY, UAR and the NLF. To Faisal Aden and the Persian Gulf were interconnected, and any savings gained by withdrawing from Aden would be offset by the loss of the profitable Gulf. Furthermore, it was impossible to include all parties in a government of South Arabia. "If Britain continued her policy of trying to run after crim-inals and secure their approval she would only lose both dignity and control of events." The king urged Britain to extend the same defense commitment to South Arabia as the current commitment to Kuwait, which had done no harm: "Britain should recognise that those who opposed her would never be induced to abate their opposition or their propaganda until British interests had disappeared and Communist influence had probably taken their place in the area." Faisal believed the carrier strike force to have little deterrent value. It was a dangerous illusion to believe that oil would continue to flow if the Soviets increased their influence in the Middle East.[69]

In a later meeting with Faisal, Wilson vigorously defended British policy in Aden: "We genuinely believed that South Arabia would be more secure if she were not bound by a defence agreement with Britain." All experience had shown that British presence increased terrorist attacks. After the British departed, the Federal government would no longer be labeled a British puppet. The new regime was to receive generous aid up to £20 million annually for three years on top of the present aid to the Aden Federation. The carrier force was much more effective than the king believed, being a credible and realistic deterrent against external aggression. Wilson defended British contacts with the insurgents:

> We had no illusions about those men whom king Faisal had described as criminals. However they did represent significant elements in South Arabia. There must be talks sooner or later, and at least we must be shown to have tried. On internal security, so long as we were internationally responsible for Aden we must retain control. Our methods were effective, and would not be made more so by ruthless tactics which hurt the innocent.[70]

Faisal was not impressed: "Britain was still responsible for law and order, but how could we hope to enlist the support of public opinion while people were in a state of fear and intimidation which prevented free expression?" Pressured by Faisal to extend the naval presence beyond the pledged six months, Healey promised to consider such a possibility. Then Wilson gave explicit assurances of a continued British presence in the Persian Gulf: while not intending to stay indefinitely there was no time limit on how long British forces would remain. Indeed, the increase of British forces in the Gulf should clearly "demonstrate our firmness of purpose".[71] In their desperation for Britain to give an extended security guarantee to South Arabia, Saudi officials, during Faisal's visit, offered "to channel orders to the UK to an extent that would help to off-set the Foreign exchange cost to HMG of that support". Healey explained that he would take note of this.[72] There is no indication in the declassified archival record that Healey and the British government ever took this offer seriously.

The American position was one of aloofness and quiet resignation, accepting that Egyptian dominance over South Arabia would be interpreted "as a decision by Washington to play a diminishing role in the Near East". It was at least an American attempt to face reality, as "our significant political influence in the Arab Near East is now confined to the Arabian Peninsula and Jordan". The State Department realized that the Aden débâcle could threaten the very substantial American oil interests in the Middle East. The Joint Chiefs of Staff, in contrast to their 1963 Aden base evaluation, concluded that the base was of some value but not critical to US security: "Its port and airfield, if available to us, would be valuable for various contingency operations but they are not essential." American policy, as far as there was a policy, wanted Britain to remain in the Persian Gulf.[73] However, unable or unwilling to stop the deterioration in Aden or devise policies independent of Britain, the United States seemed reduced to observe and note events only.[74]

On October 2, 1967, while British withdrawal was going full speed ahead in Aden, the Americans (and the Gulf rulers) were assured that Britain "intended to stand by its commitments in the Gulf while there was a need for them".[75] Despite opportunities offered in the aftermath of the Six Day War, when Nasser was forced to withdraw Egyptian forces from Yemen and entreaties from Saudi Arabia and the Federal rulers, Labour refused to be derailed from its schedule of withdrawal. While seemingly trying to pay heed to Faisal's requests when meeting him in May, nothing manifested itself on the ground. As British forces withdrew from the backcountry, the Federal government disintegrated and the NLF rapidly toppled one sheikh after another to Faisal's dismay. But the Saudi monarch did little but grumble and did not render any kind of assistance to the Adeni sheikhs.[76] Greatly fearing Aden in the hands of his enemies, Faisal failed to help his friends. Britain was accused of supporting the NLF at the expense of the Federal rulers. Brown explained to the king that the disappearance of the Federal government gave Britain little option but to negotiate with NLF and FLOSY in an effort to leave a stable government behind. It was the facts on the ground that determined British policy, and Brown therefore welcomed talks with NLF and FLOSY. Even though the situation was 'patchy' it seemed to the foreign minister that NLF was winning the struggle for power. It would therefore "be most unwise" if the Saudis interfered against the NLF; the only result, according to Brown, would be anarchy. Many of the Federal rulers had been absent, pleading their case to Faisal, or in Geneva at Britain's request to meet with the UN mission. It was "nonsensical to suggest", Brown claimed that Britain prevented legitimate rulers from returning to their principalities: "The better federal rulers may still have some part to play though not necessarily in that capacity. But we think it would be disastrous if they tried to return by way of an attempt at counter-attack from outside their states in present circumstances."[77]

Britain thought some of their former clients were somewhat remiss in defending themselves. The sultan of Fadhli, before going to Geneva, opened his prison without consulting British authorities. "Among those he released was the most dangerous NLF multiple killer we had in custody and whom we had transferred to the Sultan's care." This illustrated clearly what the rulers expected Britain to do and what they were willing to do themselves. Sultan Saleh of Audhali refused to unleash his loyal troops against rebellious villages, fearing that it would be the beginning of generations of blood feuds: "King Faisal may think that weak: it is hard however to think that, in the long term interests of unity and peace in South Arabia, it was wrong."[78]

Brown informed the cabinet on September 7, 1967 that the disintegration of the Federal government relieved Britain of its commitments to an independent South Arabia.[79] While on October 30, he observed that the disappearance of the Federal government voided the post-independence naval presence: "We were now in sight of achieving the main objective of our policy, which was to withdraw our forces from South Arabia in an orderly manner."[80] So little did Brown care about the role of the Egyptian leader as instigator of the trouble in Aden, that he proposed to the cabinet the day after resumption of diplomatic relations with the UAR, which Nasser broke off after the Arab–Israeli war. Since Egypt was the most influential Arab state, it was important for the United Kingdom to have "early and regular access at a high level to the UAR Government and hence to influence their policy".[81]

In the end, in their scramble to get out, the British threatened to bomb their long-time ally, the Sharif of Baihan, when he tried to reassert his control over the rebels "who had usurped his power with the aid of a battalion which we were helping to pay and arm and which was nominally still under British command". The British rationale was to support the South Arabian Army as the only remaining authority in the country, even when the army turned against the traditional rulers. The rulers' loyalty to the Crown was ill rewarded. The last high commissioner, Humphrey Trevelyan, claims in his memoirs that to avoid being sucked into a Vietnam situation, support of the South Arabian army was the only option left. But that was when Britain had already opened the gates to anarchy by withdrawing from the hinterland and leaving central parts of Aden town in the hands of the dissidents. Ironically, Britain had ample military might to handle Aden Federation disturbances, but chose not to apply these instruments. That Britain left chaos behind was the fault of the South Arabians, Trevelyan claimed, who "were unable to produce in time a responsible political party having the support of the majority of the people and prepared to negotiate a more civilised approach to independence".[82]

Brown was in complete support of Trevelyan, wanting to avoid situations "where one battalion supports one faction and the next battalion another".[83] Evidently, this policy also had American support. Rusk urged the British ambassador to Washington, Patrick Dean, on November 1, 1967 that Britain continue its support of the South Arabian Army as one of the few stable elements in the country.[84] To the Saudis Brown disclaimed any responsibility for the Beihan incident:[85] "We did not, in fact, betray the South Arabian Rulers: it was they and the Federal Government who ran out on us, not we on them."[86] With little regret, the last British forces left Aden on November 29, 1967 after 128 years of British rule, leaving their federal allies to the NFL wolves.[87] Denis Healey took smug satisfaction from the professional manner in which British forces executed the final withdrawal – all on schedule, in perfect order and without casualties.[88]

Thus ended Britain's long tenure in Aden. No regret and no remorse – just hearty congratulations for a job well done. There was no sense in looking back, at promises broken and allies betrayed. "It is doubtful in the entire history of the British empire," John Kelly observes, "there has been such a shameful end to British rule over a colonial territory as the abandonment of Aden in November 1967."[89] Observing events from his retirement, former prime minister Macmillan remarked that the evacuation of Aden was carried out in a manner "calculated to produce the maximum of trouble and peril . . . our friends were to be abandoned and our enemies comforted".[90] Among many observers, this is also an assessment shared by Michael Carver:

> Since 1963, 57 British servicemen had been killed and 651 wounded, and there was nothing to show for it. . . . There was no doubt that the rulers, their supporters and most of their tribesmen had been left in the lurch, as had the reasonable and law-abiding of the inhabitants of Aden.[91]

Clearly, the British could be faulted for leaving their allies to their enemies. Wilson, Brown and Healey are not the only ones left with little honor. The United States showed little or no interest in the future of South Arabia and its peoples, and even less concern for the increasing influence of Arab radicalism, and potentially Soviet and Chinese Communism. King Faisal, apart from assiduously courting the Western powers, did little to support Adeni rulers in dire straits. The king, having a long history of subverting British interests with arms, money and matériel on the Arabian Peninsula – from Buraimi to Oman proper and Dhofar – declined to help his fellow rulers in Aden. The king's passivity and aloofness, combined with his refusal to establish ties with the winning side in Aden, the NLF, seem particularly inappropriate given the perils to which the new situation exposed the Saudis. Less blame belongs, perhaps, to the Federal rulers, having lived so long sheltered by the British rule. When mercilessly and abruptly exposed to the sun of Arab radicalism, there was little they could do to hide their nakedness, being unable to forge their own destiny. When Britain announced its withdrawal from Aden in February 1966, the Federal government was given no time to adjust. However slim its chances of establishing its independent credentials in the Arab world, the Federal government was declined the opportunity by Britain.

6

Doctrinaire Socialists as Feudal Overlords

Saudi Arabia, 1964–1967

Before the British withdrawal from the Persian Gulf, king Faisal and Saudi Arabia depended on both the United States and Great Britain for its security. The Saudi monarch was willing to go to great lengths to accommodate his main Western benefactors, including placing large orders for military equipment in both countries. The United States' main concerns in Saudi Arabia, in addition to the huge ARAMCO investment, were the American military training mission and the defense guarantee to the country. While the American stake was high, American policy towards Saudi Arabia was somewhat ambiguous. Supporting the regime and cultivating Faisal, the United States at the same time kept Saudi Arabia at arm's length and continued to encourage the process of modernization begun by Kennedy. The United States flatly refused to endorse any Saudi moves against Republican Yemen; the Johnson administration did not want to become involved in military operations against a country it had recognized diplomatically. Besides, any American involvement in the Yemen civil war would greatly complicate the already difficult relations Washington had with Cairo. For Faisal, the reality was simpler. The king was convinced that Nasser was nothing but a Communist stooge; any gain for Egypt in Yemen or elsewhere was therefore a net gain for Moscow. Fortunately for the Saudi monarch, the simmering Yemen civil war itself rarely boiled over. But Nasser's fiery rhetoric threatening dire consequences for the Saudi kingdom, augmented by repeated Egyptian bombing forays into Saudi border areas, kept Faisal well aware that he needed powerful protectors. Britain, likewise the United States, declined to be involved in Yemen, but supported the territorial integrity of Saudi Arabia. Egypt was told time and again of the American support for Saudi Arabia's independence, warnings that may have deterred Nasser from conducting large-scale military operations against Faisal's domain, but not the Egyptian Airforce from bombing across the Yemen frontier.[1]

George Thompson, after being ostracized by Nasser in Cairo following the suspension of the Aden constitution, went to Saudi Arabia in September 1965, explaining to Faisal that the United Kingdom considered "its relationship with SAG most important relationship with any Arab country". The king responded in the same vein, that Saudi relations with Britain were of utmost importance.[2] After years of bickering for arms contracts, the United States included Britain in a major arms deal with Saudi Arabia. Local disagreements were never allowed to disturb an essential Anglo-American harmony in the Middle East at top policymaking levels. While accepting British withdrawal from Aden, the arms deal was to induce a continued British presence in the Persian Gulf and east of Suez generally. In the end, and the end came rapidly, Britain withdrew anyway, and in the process the Lyndon Johnson administration seemed to do little more than hope for a favorable outcome. After decades of intense competition and wrangling in the Middle East, Britain and the United States retreated from their areas of responsibility, and accepted with quiet resignation a corresponding increase of Communist influence on the Arabian Peninsula and among the radical Arab states.

Britain experienced a continued improvement of relations with Saudi Arabia, culminating with king Faisal's visit to London in May 1967. Britain's relations with Faisal were complicated by several border disputes between the British-controlled sheikhdoms on the Persian Gulf and Saudi Arabia, of which disagreement about the Buraimi oasis remained the most important. For all his efforts to improve relations with Great Britain, Faisal had great difficulties in overcoming the loss of face he suffered when Britain reoccupied Buraimi in October 1955. The Labour government was immensely pleased about landing the major Saudi arms deal together with the United States, but complicated contract negotiations and contract fulfillment requirements created difficulties in Anglo-Saudi relations. Introducing a sophisticated weapons system in a backward country caused Britain numerous problems. Despite problems of border areas and the arms consortium, Faisal worked assiduously to maintain good relations with the Wilson government. Only Britain's abandonment of old allies in Aden, and tacit acceptance of the take-over by the Marxist-Leninist NLF, abruptly reversed the Anglo-Saudi rapprochement, leading Faisal to distance Saudi Arabia from Britain. Expressing acute anxieties about a continued British presence in the Persian Gulf, Faisal was assured of this as late as December 1967, only to have the assurance revoked less than two months later. Not unreasonably, Faisal concluded that Britain was not a trustworthy partner. The king cancelled several arms contracts, costing Britain far more in future profits than anticipated savings from the withdrawals from Aden and the Persian Gulf.

But in 1964, this was in the future, and as we have seen, Faisal urged Britain to replace the American security guarantee to Saudi Arabia. In Saudi Arabia, British and American firms competed vigorously with support from their respective governments for valuable contracts to supply the Saudi air force. Reporting to the State Department on November 12, 1964, the American embassy in Jidda warned that even if successful, American companies would find it "exceptionally difficult and exasperating" to implement contracts with Saudi Arabia.[3]

On his first visit to Washington in 1964, British foreign secretary Michael Stewart suggested a joint Anglo-American security guarantee to Saudi Arabia.[4] Stewart may have been overoptimistic, as the UK ministry of defense claimed to have little to contribute in terms of available forces, while the desk officers in the Foreign Office thought Saudi irredentism and claims to Buraimi precluded a security guarantee.[5] The main purpose of any such guarantee was to give warning to Nasser that if successful in subduing Yemen, he would meet Anglo-American opposition if he proceeded to undermine the Saudi monarchy.[6]

Simultaneous to British efforts to coordinate policies towards Saudi Arabia, Britain actively sought to undermine the American arms monopoly in Saudi Arabia. Despite repeated British assurances that it supported the primacy of the American position "with respect [to] training and maintenance facilities in Saudi Arabia" the difficult British balance of payments situation gave Britain little choice other than to pursue arms sales aggressively in Saudi Arabia. The State Department "noted inherent conflict between British assurances for support U.S. primacy in training and maintenance of Saudis and attempts sell British equipment on which U.S. markedly less able provide such training and maintenance".[7] Representatives of American air industries were deeply concerned about British and French competition in Saudi Arabia. John Jernegan, deputy assistant secretary for the Near East, explained that outside Saudi Arabia, the United States, which sought to avoid being the sole arms supplier to the Middle East, had no objections to the sales of French or British planes.[8] At that time, the British Aircraft Corporation (BAC) had negotiated for almost two years with Saudi Arabia to set up a modern air defense system, consisting of Lightning interceptor fighters, Thunderbird A.A. Missiles and early warning radar. BAC consistently pressured the British government for support. Frank Brenchley of the Foreign Office expected that the Saudis would choose American planes for political reasons, but might buy Thunderbirds and radar from Britain:

> From a political point of view, such an outcome would be by no means unsatisfactory to us. It is of great importance to us that British and American policies

in the Middle East should be as closely aligned as possible; the fact that we and the Americans do generally see eye to eye on policy in this area and that the Americans take as much interest in it as they do stems to a considerable extent from American involvement in Saudi Arabia.[9]

In fact, in Saudi Arabia commercial competition was so intense that the traditional Anglo-American rivalry in the country was heating up. Brenchley was well aware that the recent British sales efforts to some extent undermined previous British assurances to the United States of the primacy of the American role in Saudi Arabia.[10] On the American side, plans were underway to warn Britain off Saudi Arabia altogether and even replace Britain as the sole supplier and advisor to the National Guard.[11] An American move against Britain in the National Guard would certainly rankle; British advisors in the White Army persuaded the Saudis to place orders for arms and equipment in Britain.[12] Britain's reluctance to take over American political commitments to Saudi Arabia influenced king Faisal; he informed the British ambassador on July 19, 1965 that "he could not afford to upset [the] Americans" by preferring British to American equipment.[13] In truth, top-level officials in the Johnson administration were only lukewarm about the prospective deal. Komer noted in a memorandum to the president that the United States was not soliciting business, but rather the Saudis approached the Americans. Compared to other Middle East arms deals, this one did little to threaten Israeli security: "Saudi Arabia is too far away and too incompetent."[14]

Then on September 25, 1965 McNamara called off the growing competition between British and American companies for the Saudi arms market. In response to the forthcoming British defense review, McNamara advised the British embassy in Washington that the United States would not be 'upset' if aircraft, missiles and radar contracts went to Britain.[15] The Saudi arms consortium was an American attempt to preempt the consequences of the 1966 defense review and encourage a continued British presence east of Suez. The Johnson administration was very pleased with the Saudi arms package, as George Ball noted in a telegram to Jidda:

> We are at the same time anxious not to create impression among Saudis or other Arabs that there exists US–UK rivalry for their favor which may be exploited by them as they deem advantageous. While it obviously require[s] some adjustment on our part, growth of British interest in Saudi Arabia should be beneficial to overall Western position in Peninsula. We confident we can maintain our position and protect our own interests while cooperating with UK and welcome its participation in solution Peninsula's problems.[16]

Anglo-American relations in Saudi Arabia had certainly come a long way since the difficult and often fiercely competitive days of the 1950s. Evidently, Ball thought it a small price to pay to let Britain in on the United

States' eminent domain, an exclusive relationship with Saudi Arabia it had cost much American treasure and energy to maintain. The chief competitor the United States wanted to keep out of Saudi Arabia from the late 1940s to 1965 was Britain, and now the British were admitted in the interest of American global strategy. Evaluating the package deal in May 1967, the ministry of technology in Britain concluded: "There is no doubt however that without U.S. Government support the joint package could not have succeeded."[17]

While there was high level Anglo-American agreement on the deal, local representatives of both powers seemed to have been deeply ingrained with almost a generation of intense British and American rivalry on the Arabian Peninsula. British and American company representatives, and most importantly British ambassador Morgan Man in Jidda, exhibited considerable suspicion, skepticism and downright hostility to the arms deal.[18] The American press complained that the Johnson administration had given British companies a $500 million-plus contract at the expense of American companies. American business was losing out because of lack of support from their own government. Not only that, but by taking over the Saudi Air Force training mission, British influence would increase further at American expense, allowing Britain a dramatic comeback in the Arab world following the 1956 Suez crisis. Rusk explained in a circular telegram of December 11, 1965 that since 1963 the United States had discussed with Saudi Arabia how to strengthen its air defenses. The Anglo-American arms deal represented the conclusion of these discussions, and was not a ploy to leave Saudi Arabia to the British. The Johnson administration, while accepting the package proposal with Britain, simultaneously pledged its continued support of the all-American air package to avoid the appearance of selling out American interests.[19] When queried by Garry Owen, vice president of ARAMCO, about the arms package, Harrison Symmes, deputy director Near East, State Department, explained that "high-level, world-wide considerations had led the US to go along with the UK initiative to offer the Saudis a joint British–American air defense package". Symmes carefully explained the consistent support provided to the American companies by the Johnson administration. Owen, true to ARAMCO's anti-British posture, proceeded to spin a yarn that Faisal felt abandoned by the United States, and would with proper American handling have preferred American equipment. But in contrast to the 1950s, the oilmen seemed to have little influence in the Kennedy and Johnson administrations.[20] This was in sharp contrast to the crisis in Buraimi in May and June 1954, where the oilmen seemed to have been the instigators and driving force behind US policy on the Arabian Peninsula.

But despite having cleared the arms deals at the highest levels, it took several entreaties to bring ambassador Man into line. While being instructed to cooperate with the American ambassador, Man was extremely sensitive to any perceived or actual American sleight. State Department officials were confident that despite Man's opposition the Foreign Office was solidly behind the deal.[21] Steps were taken on both the British and the American side to coordinate policy on all levels.[22] Complicating the picture was the Saudi request for a British fighter squadron to be transferred immediately to deter Egyptian air attacks on Saudi territory. When the British demurred, the Saudi defense minister prince Sultan strongly hinted that Britain would lose the yet unsigned Lightning contract. Foreign secretary Michael Stewart thought on March 11, 1966 the Saudis were bluffing, but if not there was a real chance that American F-104 aircraft might replace British planes:

> In these circumstances, we might have to accept the serious political risks involved in sending R.A.F. Lightnings to Saudi Arabia, including, in the last resort, the possibility that the "training mission" might have to conduct operations, though for practical reasons this is unlikely. . . . We would not regard this gesture as involving us in any kind of defence commitment to Saudi Arabia such as the United States Government have given. But since the possibility of operations cannot be ruled out, we would like to be assured (for our own information only) that it remained the intention of the United States Government to honour that commitment if Saudi Arabia were attacked.[23]

It is hard to see how Great Britain could have avoided being sucked into a war if British forces were engaged in hostilities. On the other hand, Labour was at the same time busily cutting solemnly pledged defense commitments in neighboring Aden with little or no international discomfort – making, perhaps, questionable the assumption that British soldiers engaged in military operations would entice Labour to war.

Rusk discouraged the British request as it would disturb current negotiations between Saudi Arabia and Egypt over Yemen, besides exposing Faisal to attacks that he was an imperialist stooge. British nationals flying Saudi planes could possibly escalate the Yemen civil war. While concerned about the integrity of Saudi Arabia, Rusk warned that American guarantees were of a limited nature: "It has been clear to king Faisal that our commitment does not extend to providing military cover for Saudi operations of hostilities in Yemen or to any Saudi actions of a provocative nature."[24]

Perhaps to counter increasing British presence on the Arabian Peninsula and to maintain the American position in Saudi Arabia, king Faisal was invited to the United States in June 1966 [25] – an invitation the king, anxious to establish good relations with the new president, had solicited as early as December 1964.[26] Briefing the president Rostow observed:

> Above all, the king is a good friend. He would like to be reassured that his friend-

ship is appreciated. Our ability to continue to influence him constructively in the months ahead, including matters where we reap tangible benefits, will depend in part on whether we can make him feel that, despite certain differences of emphasis, our friendship with Saudi Arabia is real, that we appreciate his problems and, that he can count on us to give appropriate help to try to solve them.

On the other hand, the United States needed to be careful in fussing too much about the Saudi monarch when in the United States since that would only give Faisal an incentive to intensify his struggle with Cairo and in the process damage American relations with Nasser.[27]

Rostow noted with approval the increasing British presence and influence in Saudi Arabia. The arms package was by now an established fact. For Britain it meant a five-year training program in Saudi Arabia with up to 1,400 personnel. In addition, British officers trained the tribally based National Guard loyal to the royal family. The National Guard was of the same size of the army, about 20,000 to 24,000 strong. The king was disturbed by the forthcoming British withdrawal from Aden, but reassured that Britain intended to remain in the Persian Gulf.[28]

For Faisal, the meetings with the president were an overwhelming experience. After returning to Saudi Arabia, Faisal described his American visit a 'complete success', speaking "glowingly both publicly and to his own advisors". American ambassador Herman Eilts reported to Johnson, "of his meeting with you and reiterated that his main reason for coming was to become personally acquainted".[29] Johnson had reaffirmed American interest in Saudi Arabia and the king's personal security. The president agreed with Faisal that Nasser was difficult, but Johnson hewed to the standard American line that it was better to pursue a dialogue with the Egyptian dictator than let him turn to the Kremlin. On Yemen, the president urged Saudi restraint, discounting the probability of an unprovoked Egyptian attack on Saudi Arabia. The king categorically assured Johnson that Saudi Arabia would do nothing provocative whatsoever against Yemen, which could induce further Egyptian hostilities.[30] Faisal was almost overawed by the Johnson treatment. After his *tête-à-tête* with Johnson, the Saudi monarch and the president rejoined their advisors: "The king emphasized that he was fully aware of US good intentions, good will and willingness to support Saudi Arabia. He was so reassured of the US position that he felt he should apologize for having even thought there was a need to mention it."[31] The president worked hard to establish personal relations with Faisal, partly in response to Rostow's urging prior to the meeting:

Your first look may make you feel it will be hard to hit it off with this bearded, robed desert king. But Faisal is a lot more modern than he looks. Under those robes, you will find a sharp mind and deep devotion to educational and social progress. I am sure he will warm to your sincerity and frankness. I would be surprised if you do not find a man you can like and draw out.

According to Rostow, it would be well worth the effort, as Saudi Arabia was the home of the largest American overseas investment of $1.2 billion in the form of ARAMCO: "In addition, all our other Middle East interests – from blocking Communism to preserving Israel – depend heavily on gradual modernization under moderate leaders like Faisal who oppose the revolutionary methods of Nasser and Communism."[32]

While consulting the Saudis and fawning over Faisal, there was an Anglo-American agreement to coordinate policies before involving local officials. This was in order to prevent the Saudis playing the Americans and the British off against each other.[33] The modernization inherent in the acquisition of the air defense scheme carried potential problems of its own. A State Department research paper of September 7, 1966 noted that Saudi Arabia needed to speed up education of military manpower to take control of its own air defense within reasonable time: "It is at present a matter of speculation whether a system of somewhat forced technological education may not lead to a measure of political unreliability." That is, creating a class of Nasserite pro-revolutionary officers.[34]

Compounding the implementation of the arms deal was prince Sultan's request for a smaller and operational system delivered immediately. This system, termed 'Magic Carpet', consisted of 6 Hawker Hunters and 6 Lightnings and a battery of Thunderbird missiles at a cost of £20 million. Magic Carpet delayed the main contract negotiations in addition to, as Man observed, "the problems of operating an integrated air defence system in what is still a primitive and geographically difficult country". At the end of 1966 two contracts for Hawk missiles and Lightnings were unsigned.[35]

British relations with Saudi Arabia were complex and sometimes difficult, despite the apparent success with the arms package. Soon snags developed in the British training mission, problems that remained unsolved until Faisal visited Britain in May 1967. As no Arab regime wanted confrontation with Egypt, Faisal was left in a defensive posture with an expensive weapons system to deter Egypt, if only his soldiers would ever learn to use it.[36] In addition, border problems and Aden caused Anglo-Saudi friction. During the fall of 1966, Saudi Arabia urged foreign minister Brown to slow down the evacuation from Aden, bring the Hadramut states into the Federation, take stronger measures against terrorism, give an extended security guarantee to independent South Arabia and, finally, strengthen Federal forces. Brown rejected all requests apart from increasing Federal forces.[37] When invited to a visit of state in May 1967, the king accepted, provided there was satisfactory progress on Buraimi.

Ambassador Man was bewildered, believing there was little chance of meaningful progress before May.[38] The Foreign Office rejected Faisal's 'bazaar-like tactics' and refused to compromise on Buraimi.[39]

The year 1967 was one of transition in the Middle East. Historians have naturally focused on the Six Day War and its consequences, but for the first half of 1967 the intra-Arab struggle was of greater significance.[40] During this time, Egypt was engaged in a more or less continuous bombing campaign of Saudi border areas – a bombing campaign Nasser could pursue with impunity, the Saudis being unable to respond despite the purchase of the Anglo-American air defense package.[41] Rusk was informed on January 4 that Egyptian planes had overflown Nairan on the border with Yemen on December 27 and January 1, while a small hamlet just over the Saudi border had been bombed on December 26. The State Department assumed the New Year air campaigns were "probably intended as a warning to Saudi Arabia against encouraging any renewed large-scale fighting by Yemeni royalists". The incidents marked an escalation in the war of nerves between Egypt and Saudi Arabia. American officials feared Faisal would retaliate by increasing his efforts in Yemen. The American response, as usual, was mild. Ambassador Herman Eilts was instructed to reaffirm previous American assurances against unprovoked aggression and deflect Saudi retaliation against Yemen.[42] On top of the bombing, there were ample signs that Nasser was stepping up his subversive activities against Saudi Arabia, while the Egyptian dictator was equally convinced that Faisal harbored similar designs against him. Eilts urged a new American initiative to break the deadlock: "But, being Arabs, they seem incapable of constructive action to arrest situation lest it appear as surrender by one or the other. Outside help will be needed if detente is to be effected." But the ambassador offered few remedies other than renewal of Saudi–Egyptian talks.[43] Nasser considered Faisal's Islamic solidarity front to be a direct challenge to his leadership of the Arab world. According to ambassador Man, Faisal was far more concerned about Yemen than Israel: "He has never once mentioned Israel to me since I arrived at this post."[44]

With no troop movements on either side of the Yemen border, Rusk on January 20, 1967 discounted the risk of immediate military operations. Nasser seemed to favor propaganda and harassment to fighting. The secretary refused to involve the United States in military action and believed no useful American initiatives could reduce tensions: "In event situation were to deteriorate to point hostilities appear imminent, we would be willing to consider high level US approach to both sides."[45] Unimpressed by American non-involvement, Egypt continued its bombing raids of Saudi Arabia in January 1967, in spite of the absence of Saudi provocation. American policy moved little from expressing concerns to the Egyptian ambassador about the bombing, explaining that continued bombing might prevent improvement of American relations with Egypt and delay resumption of food aid. The Egyptian ambassador claimed: "Faisal out to humiliate and defeat Egyptians there [Yemen] rather than seek mutually acceptable solution allowing their withdrawal." The Saudis were told that the United States was deeply concerned about the bombing, but being the victim put Saudi Arabia in a "powerful position *vis-à-vis* world press and public opinion". Renewal of assurances, a possible approach to the United Nations and continued dialogue with Faisal substituted for American involvement in the dispute.[46] To soothe fraying Saudi nerves, Rusk authorized the American military training mission "to offer advisory assistance to Saudi air defense units in the border area and agreement in principle was given to providing the Saudis with Sidewinder air-to-air missiles".[47] Privately, the department of defense informed the British embassy in Washington that the United States had no intention of committing fighter planes to Saudi Arabia: "there were almost no circumstances in which the U.S. could contemplate sending planes and forces to the southern border". In addition to avoiding involvement, the British learned that the war in Vietnam absorbed American defense energies, precluding large-scale military measures elsewhere. For Britain this meant that the United States washed its hands of the current imbroglio in Saudi Arabia and South Arabia as well.[48]

Sultan upbraided Man on January 30, complaining about the lack of pilots for operation Magic Carpet and inadequate ground maintenance by the British company Airworks. Only three pilots were on the spot for training. The defense minister demanded combat pilots and, if not forthcoming, threatened cancellation of the British contracts. He pointedly warned Man that France had offered planes with French mercenaries for combat missions. To his shame, Man had to admit that British companies were slow in fulfilling their part of the contract.[49]

Soon alarming noises reached the State Department that Faisal planned to increase aid to the Royalists even at the risk of inviting Egyptian ground attacks. The king believed that an escalation of the border situation might bring Nasser's downfall. In that case, Faisal was willing temporarily to abandon the Saudi border provinces of Najran and Jizan to induce American involvement. To counter Saudi charges of American disinterest Rusk listed, on February 25, 1967, US actions on behalf of Saudi Arabia, including immediate protests to Egypt of recent bombing, active support at the United Nations in spite of the lacklustre Saudi performance there, the American involvement with the air defense package, as well as 235 American advisors in Saudi Arabia. Increasing the number of American advisors would not be in the Saudi interest: "Any further dispatch of US troops Saudi Arabia could mar Saudi case in eyes of world by impression that foreign troops being rushed in to support tottering monarchy." On the basis of this impressive record, Rusk concluded that "one can make case that SAG has been somewhat remiss in helping itself".[50]

Britain had different concerns in Saudi Arabia. Briefing Thompson for a meeting with the Saudi ambassador on February 24, 1967, Weir of the Foreign Office urged a speedy conclusion on the Saudi Arabian Air Defense Consortium. Granted, British companies deficient performance had delayed progress, but the Saudis could expedite matters by rapidly making necessary facilities like customs clearance and workshop accommodation available. As for British nationals flying combat missions for Saudi Arabia as mercenaries, that "is their affair and cannot be given any sort of support by H.M.G.". Wilson and the Labour government deplored Egyptian bombing and praised Faisal's restraint against this act of war: "but we are sure he is right to resist the temptation to retaliate, and to deal with the matter through the United Nations". The Saudis were reluctant to approach the United Nations for the fear of being outvoted. Nasser's use of gas was shocking, and the Labour government would do all it "could to see that it was brought to the attention of the world": in short, the same policy of non-involvement as the United States.[51] In fact, the British attitude was even more cynical. Paul Gore-Booth of the Foreign Office observed: "In regards to things like the bombing, the king must realize that in the noisy and brutal world in which he was operating, the Saudis would not get any help or sympathy unless they handled their own case vigorously."[52] But while the government wanted non-involvement, parts of the press were critical. *The Daily Express* observed on January 31, 1967: "While President Nasser's Russian jets bomb defenceless Saudi villages, a team of his financial experts has arrived in London to ask the Government for permission to delay the payments of debts he owes for British goods." *The Daily Express* believed that Egypt's request would be granted and further credit extended if Nasser asked for it. The newspaper found it rather sickening that Labour appeased the Egyptian dictator while he was actively undermining British interests in the Middle East. Besides, the credits Nasser requested were small – only £5 million, "but Egypt is so broke that Nasser cannot find the cash". The amount was less than the Egyptian dictator spent, *The Daily Express* observed, on training and equipping terrorists that maimed and killed Britons in Aden. The sum was certainly less, the paper went on, than the cost of Radio Cairo, Nasser's chief propaganda outlet, or keeping 60,000 troops in Yemen. With Egypt opposing Britain at every turn in the Middle East, the newspaper was at loss as to why Labour continued to conciliate Nasser:

> There seems to be only one answer. Now that the Government has committed itself irrevocably to leaving Aden, it realises that the whole of Southern Arabia will lie at Nasser's mercy next year. The only way it can withdraw with

any grace is by first securing some agreement that he will not infringe the independence of the new South Arabian State. The Foreign Office may believe that in return for financial aid and other concessions it might secure such a promise.[53]

Despite a strong British wish to downplay the issue, Buraimi remained a festering sore in Anglo-Saudi relations. At the end of 1966, Saudi Arabia protested against oil operations in Buraimi, as well as in Abu Dhabi and Muscat and Oman, which the Saudis claimed as their territory. Faisal's attempt to make his acceptance of an invitation for a state visit conditional on a favorable solution to the Buraimi problem, was successfully deflected by the Wilson government. Also because one concession would lead to another: "On past form the Saudis would almost certainly have used any concession made to them to try and extract more." Britain could not give in on Buraimi, otherwise the confidence of the rulers in the Persian Gulf in Britain might be jeopardized. But Buraimi remained an underlying sore point in Anglo-Saudi relations. Searching for a solution, Britain encouraged bilateral talks between Faisal and the ruler of Abu Dhabi.[54]

After the British reoccupation of Buraimi in October 1955, Britain refused to entertain further discussions on the sovereignty of the oasis. If this position was reversed, Weir noted:

It would also open the way to a repetition of the campaign of bribery and gun-running which the Saudis conducted from 1952 to 1955. If the outcome were then to be some kind of compromise between the excessive Saudi claims, which encompasses two-thirds of Abu Dhabi, and the present frontiers, this would bring the Saudis across the desert barrier which at present virtually cuts them off from contact with and influence in Oman, and would provide them with a bridgehead from which to expand. The Rulers, whose position is now much stronger than in 1952/55, would resist Saudi encroachment, and the risk of conflict would be considerable.[55]

If Britain were to abandon the Gulf sheikhdoms to the tender mercies of the Saudis, it would mean jeopardizing the British position on the Gulf and precluding the maintenance of stability and orderly evolution, as well as the possibility of an orderly withdrawal. The last thing Labour needed was a repeat of the Aden situation in the Persian Gulf. In addition, British oil interests in the Gulf might be endangered. The stumbling block for a solution on Buraimi, from the British point of view, was Faisal's insistence on territorial concessions, despite repeated claims that he was only interested in his 'honour'. The king's 'honour', unfortunately, could only be satisfied by territorial concessions. The situation was far from hopeless, the Foreign Office argued: Egyptian pressure against Saudi Arabia and the unsettled conditions in South Arabia necessitated Anglo-Saudi cooperation. Needing British support and cooperation from the Gulf rulers gave Faisal an incentive to overcome the question of Buraimi. Britain considered giving the Saudis a special role on a par with Britain's in the Persian Gulf, but shelved the idea as premature given that cooperation among the rulers had just been initiated. Despite Faisal's obvious need to seek accommodation with Britain and the rulers, Buraimi remained a difficult point for the king: "Faisal has very strong feelings about Buraimi and has not forgiven us for the loss of face he suffered in the 1955 débâcle." Brenchley agreed about the importance of Britain standing firm on Buraimi, but noted with the wry and cynical comment so often reflected in the archives by him: "My guess is that it will be a typical Arab solution which totally evades the real issue, e.g. a joint declaration by Faisal and Said [ruler of Abu Dhabi] that they are Arab brothers and as such have no boundary between them."[56] British firmness paid off; during his state visit in May 1967 Faisal refrained from raising the Buraimi issue.

In addition to Buraimi and British withdrawal from Aden, the still unsigned air consortium package was the main problem in Anglo-Saudi relations. The British part of the air consortium was extensive. The British Aircraft Corporation (BAC) was to supply 34 Mark 53 Lightnings and 25 Jet Provosts for a total value of £55.5 million. Associated Electrical Industries (AEI) was to provide radar and communications equipment for a total value of £22 million. Airwork Services Limited offered training and maintenance for the planes and accommodation and training facilities, a contract estimated at almost £50 million. A letter of intent for the air consortium was signed on December 20, 1965, but on the eve of Faisal's visit, AEI and Airwork's contracts were still unsigned. AEI could not begin ground surveys before the conclusion of the contract and the Saudi request for additional equipment was settled. Even with local difficulties arising, the American military mission had been uniformly helpful to the British companies. Complicating the arms package, Magic Carpet revealed many snags in Anglo-Saudi cooperation, among them two planes destroyed in accidents. British company representatives and Saudi authorities were reduced to haggling about who should pay for the lost aircraft. British ministers closely supervised the negotiations and conclusion of the arms deal, but refused any financial responsibility for the arms package. After obtaining final Saudi signatures, Britain expected to be involved with Saudi air defense for a long time to come. The British companies needed Saudi assistance on the ground: "With the best will in the world the Consortium cannot carry out its programme effectively if the Saudis fail to perform their part."[57] Ambassador Man believed Airwork more to blame than the Saudis: "Airwork's negotiations have been bedeviled by bad relations between the Company and the Saudis, thanks mainly to the poor calibre of the Airwork representative on the spot and inept bargaining tactics."[58] King Faisal's visit of state provided the occasion to sign the outstanding contracts.

After his first meeting with Faisal, Wilson noted in his memoirs that the king was passionately anti-Egyptian and solicited a post-independence British presence in South Arabia to deter further Nasserite adventures. Wilson believed their second meeting was to discuss British Middle East policy, but the growing Arab–Israeli crisis had dramatically changed the situation. Faisal, according to Wilson, claimed that all bets were off:

> He told me that whatever he might have said about President Nasser before the weekend was of no account now. An Arab brother was in immediate peril from an attack by the common enemy and he would join his brethren in resisting such an attack to the utmost.[59]

This is correct as far as it goes, but by leaving out part of what Faisal replied Wilson gives an incorrect impression and downplays the king's critique of British policies in South Arabia. The memorandum of the Wilson and Faisal talks rounds out this part of the conversation in the following manner:

> King Faisal said that it must be understood that the Arab countries stood together against Israel without exception. If President Nasser's moves were directed against Israel only, he would be joined by all the other Arab states. It was important however that these moves should not be directed against another Arab country, as Saudi Arabia feared they might be.[60]

Between Faisal's talk with Wilson, Nasser took advantage of the occasion of the state visit to continue the bombing campaign, for the first time raising concerns in the whole of Saudi Arabia and questions why the air package did not work to deter the Egyptians.[61] Rusk was "prepared to register our deep concern at these new reported raids", believing the bombings to be only an attempt by Nasser to intrude into the Anglo-Saudi talks.[62] In that case, Rusk hoped, "further unwarranted intrusions Saudi air space will not occur".[63] The Egyptian dictator escalated the tension by using gas against a northern Yemeni village near the Saudi border on May 20, 1967, killing 75 people.[64] Unknown to Faisal, the Johnson administration was backing away from the president's assurances of American support of the territorial integrity of Saudi Arabia and the personal safety of Faisal from June 1966. The conclusions of an inter-regional group (IRG) meeting of April 12, 1967 attempted to restrict the American security guarantee to Saudi Arabia. Johnson had told Faisal that he would not let Nasser "gobble you up". Now the American commitment was limited to a regime friendly to the United States; there was no commitment to the monarchy, nor Faisal as an individual, or "to the geographical area of Saudi Arabia".[65] The Egyptian bombing campaign proved to all and sundry that the main Anglo-American concern on the Arabian Peninsula was to stay aloof from the hostilities.

Other interested parties also tried to get into play in the interval of the Anglo-Saudi talks. Oil company representatives conveyed the idea that the king was unhappy with the talks, and with Britain for insisting on leaving Aden and refusing to support Saudi Arabia with military measures against Egyptian bombing.[66] The oilmen had less influence on British policy, than they did on American. Awareness of the tremendous oil resources in the Middle East did little to change American policy. A State Department paper of February 8, 1967 explained: "Simple statistics on Middle Eastern oil can only be defined as staggering." The area contained two-thirds of the free world's oil reserves, and more than one-third of its production, costing less than 10 percent of the American oil production. American companies had invested $2.75 billion in the area (of which 93 percent was in oil), with an annual profit of $750 million.[67] Part of the reason for the hands-off approach may simply lie in the fact that central elements of the Johnson administration questioned, in the words of Harold Saunders of the NSC, "Why should the President care about the Middle East?"[68] Saunders posed the same question after the Six Day War: "Is the Middle East–North Africa an area of real significance to the United States?" Saunders met strong opposition from the state and defense departments, listing the usual litany of American concerns: oil and opposition to increased Soviet influence.[69]

At a second meeting between Faisal and the British leadership on May 22, 1967, Brown explained that Britain took a more serious view of the situation than only the week before. Nasser had made a substantial build-up of his forces in the Sinai desert, including an armored brigade from Yemen. The British government wanted a meeting of the UN Security Council and a declaration from the maritime powers to keep the Straits of Tiran open.[70] Faisal's meetings with the British leadership ended on a very positive note, with Wilson praising king Faisal to the skies. The Saudi monarch returned the compliment: "In all he had said he had been thinking only of the interests of his country and his people. The friendship between the two countries transcended any differences between them."[71] In the interest of Anglo-Saudi harmony, Faisal put aside his pet projects of Buraimi and Dhofar. But by the late 1960s, the Dhofari rebellion had acquired a life of its own, growing independent of Saudi coffers, and being highjacked by hardcore Marxist-Leninists. Furthermore, the outstanding contracts of the arms consortium were signed during the king's visit, and Faisal accepted, albeit grudgingly, British policy in Aden, even to the extent of offering additional arms contracts to finance a continued British security guarantee to South Arabia. In return for the king's generosity, Labour adjusted its position, but mostly verbally and not in genuine changes of policy. Wilson offered increased British naval presence and aid to Aden, pushing the date of independence back to January 1, 1968 (a concession pre-dating the king's visit). The prime minister unequivocally guaranteed a continued British presence in the Persian Gulf for the foreseeable future, and certainly far longer than the January 17, 1968 withdrawal announcement proclaimed. Healey promised to consider further Saudi arms contracts against an extended security guarantee to South Arabia. But as soon as the glow of Faisal's visit faded away, Labour's pledges evaporated by the force of dismantling the empire. Perhaps this was because king Faisal and the Saudis were lacking in the sophistication of Western ways, as Paul Gore-Booth puts it: "It is only too easy to assume that the Saudis understand more of the outside world than they really do."[72] Whatever the case, even if the king was not as worldly wise as his British interlocutors, he did not take kindly to them reneging on their pledges.

Nasser falsely claimed that Egypt suffered such a dramatic defeat in the Six Day War because British and American planes materially assisted Israel in destroying the Egyptian air force. Faisal, easily seeing through Nasser's transparent lies, refused to sever relations with Great Britain and the United States in despite of his strong views on Israel and pressure from other Arab countries to do so. Fearing that the outcome of the Six Day War could upset all calculations in the Middle East, Brown observed: "I believe that we can already count it as a gain that Saudi Arabia has not allowed her relations with Britain and the United States to be affected beyond the minimum requirements of Arab solidarity and is clearly anxious to see them restored as soon as possible."[73] Faisal expressed his hostility towards Israel to Man, but was still distrustful of Nasser "the man he considers to be an arch-intriguer and his inveterate enemy". On the Six Day War the king explained:

> Nasser had embarked on a gigantic bluff. Unfortunately for Nasser and the rest of the Arab world – the Jews had called his bluff and he had been decisively beaten. The king said that if he had been in Israel's place he would have done exactly the same and struck first rather than risk being attacked and over-whelmed. If Nasser had not tried to be too clever and waste time by seeking to bargain with the Americans from what he believed to be his new position of strength, he could have launched a decisive attack on the Israelis.

Faisal fully expected Nasser to turn against the conservative Arab regimes as soon as the question of the Palestinians was solved.[74]

The Six Day War was to Faisal's advantage in that he forced Nasser to withdraw his forces from Yemen in return for Saudi financial assistance, Egypt being bankrupt as the result of its defeat. But while pleased by the situation in Yemen, Faisal was shocked by developments in South Arabia. Meeting Man on September 4, 1967, the king accused Britain of handing the country over to the NLF. Man countered by arguing, whether the king liked it or not, that the NLF in fact represented a large part of the population:

The NLF were better than FLOSY because they had more of a national feeling for South Arabia and could well mature when they assumed responsibility for running the country. We had to move with the times and the NLF had now become a basic fact of life which could not be ignored.[75]

The Foreign Office instructed Man to approach Faisal to set the record straight on South Arabia. It was meaningless to accuse Britain of favoring the NLF "which after all has killed far more British, usually in a cowardly fashion, than any other group". Also, the king downplayed the extent of British aid, including the offshore carrier fleet which the Foreign Office termed "an unprecedented and burdensome form of external reassurance".[76]

In exile in Saudi Arabia, the sharif Hussain of Beihan expressed great bitterness towards British policy and told British representatives that he had completely disassociated himself from Britain. There were no longer any legal obligations binding the parties. The sharif accused Britain of plotting with the NLF against him. The whole Arab world knew that Britain was in cahoots with the NLF and the British air threat was "an act of sheer treachery".[77] Britain pleaded with Saudi Arabia that the Saudis do their utmost to prevent the sharif from returning to Beihan. The Foreign Office wanted at all costs to avoid a Saudi invasion of South Arabia. If not "there will be disaster and we shall be involved, and unable to come out for a very long time. If we can come out before the Saudis move the onus will not be on us".[78]

Faisal's great fear was that the British would cut and run prematurely in the Persian Gulf, handing over power to revolutionaries bent on undermining Saudi Arabia. Meeting with the king, Man explained to Faisal in October 1967 that the withdrawal from the Gulf "would not occur for some time", but was not allowed to tell the monarch that Britain expected to stay at least until 1970. At this point, plans were underway in the Labour government to abandon the Gulf, making Man's assurance disingenuous at best. To the American embassy Man expressed his personal reservations on continued British presence in the Gulf to 1971.[79] Rusk was puzzled about the new time limit for the British presence in the Persian Gulf:

It has been impression here that British fully intend to remain in Gulf to protect interests there in foreseeable future. While Department had no specific time frame in mind, would have thought this extended well beyond 1970 . . . British should be aware of USG views regarding UK presence in Gulf, to which we continue to adhere.[80]

The Persian Gulf was by now the only remaining fixture of the formerly extensive British presence in the Middle East. Labour, having successfully whittled away the British position in the area, was poised for the next step, to topple the crumbling edifice of empire in the Gulf. By abandoning Aden and downgrading its security commitment to Kuwait, much of the former rationale for the British position had already disappeared. It would then take but little effort to leave the Persian Gulf. As Labour had already ascertained, American opposition to British withdrawal was far from overwhelming, as seen by Rusk's rather mild reaction when learning of the changed British schedule in the Persian Gulf.

7

The Withdrawal from the Persian Gulf

Given its large oil reserves, strategic location and repeatedly expressed policy of keeping the Soviet Union out, one would think the Persian Gulf was more important to Labour than the last act in dismantling the empire. It is useful perhaps, again, to outline the extent of British interests and commitments in the Persian Gulf at the time of Labour's ascension to power. Kuwait was the largest and most important Gulf state, with a population of about 400,000. Being independent and a member of the United Nations, the United Kingdom had no formal obligations to Kuwait, apart from an expressed readiness since its independence in 1961 to assist the sheikhdom upon request. On the other hand, Britain had treaty relationships with the Trucial States, the largest being Bahrain, with a population of about 160,000, and Qatar with about 50,000–60,000 inhabitants. There were in addition seven lesser principalities also called the Trucial States, with about 100,000 inhabitants. Britain's annual economic assistance was increased to £200,000 for the fiscal year 1964/1965.[1] Certainly more was at stake than just balancing budget cuts after the devaluation. Britain had time and again pledged to the United States, king Faisal and local rulers in the Gulf that it intended to remain. Local rulers, as in Aden, relied on British support and protection. Ironically, the extended British commitment did not outlast the final evacuation of Aden on November 29, as the pound was devalued on November 16, 1967, spelling the end to the British presence in the Gulf. Labour ministers seemed to care little for broken promises, and for British credibility as a great power. Only the brave or the foolish could thereafter attach much faith to Britain's solemnly pledged word or security guarantees.

But there were wider repercussions relating to Aden and the decision to withdraw from the Gulf. Supported from the People's Republic of South Yemen PRSY, as the re-christened Aden was called, the Dhofar rebels stepped up their activities in western Oman.[2] Dhofar's border with the PRSY was demarcated at only four points, with local tribesmen crossing the border at will. Crisscrossed by mountains (jebels) and densely forested valleys (wadis) facing the coastline, travelling was extremely difficult and time consuming. In the north, the terrain gave way to desert, where the rebels easily spotted troop movements miles away from their jebel lookouts. Numerous tribes occupied Dhofar, the largest being the Qarra, which furnished the largest number of rebels. According to a British military intelligence report, the Qarra were "cattle or camel-owners, and live in caves or grass huts. They cover their bodies in dark blue indigo dye, and wear only loin cloths." Dhofar had only the most rudimentary of administrative systems, one not very qualified doctor, no private vehicles and no telephone system. The sultan of Muscat and Oman lived permanently in the Salalah village of Dhofar, but rarely left the palace, being of ill health. His son Sayyid Qaboos, educated in the United Kingdom and trained at Sandhurst, was under house arrest and excluded from the government. The sultan's government paid little attention to its subjects as long as taxes were paid. "Tribal feuds with accompanying murders are common. The Government usually leaves the tribes to sort out such feuds and killings amongst themselves."[3] The rebellion continued to spread and, given the sultan's lackluster response, the new Conservative British government authorized his deposal in 1970. The Sultan was replaced by Qaboos, who, with support of British officers and Jordan and Iran, took energetic countermeasures against the rebels, finally overcoming their resistance in 1975.[4] Faisal kept his hands off, letting the British-led forces of the sultan deal with the Dhofari rebels as they saw fit. The king's position was a little awkward because of the long-time rivalry with Britain over Buraimi, Saudi Arabia having originally encouraged and supported the rebels.[5] However much Labour wanted it, the withdrawal from Aden and the Persian Gulf did not end British involvement in the Middle East. The Dhofar campaign was in fact a continuation of the anti-British campaign in Aden.[6]

The Johnson administration was unwilling or unable to prevent the British withdrawal and refused to take over British commitments in the Gulf. To prevent the Kremlin from exploiting the power vacuum left by the British, the United States appointed Saudi Arabia and Iran as replacements for the British in the Persian Gulf. With its limited population and military capability, Saudi Arabia was reluctant to project its military forces outside the homeland. The shah of Iran was willing and, with the rise in oil prices and concomitant prodigious military spending, eager to take Britain's place. The Americans, for a decade, relied on an Iranian security blanket in the Gulf of the most tenuous kind, which easily collapsed when challenged by Ayatollah Khomenei.

Meeting his officials on December 3, 1964, foreign secretary Michael Stewart explained that Britain should maintain a military presence in the Gulf, but doubted if it was necessary in order to protect British oil interests there. Key to development was modernization, throwing about one of the catch phrases of which Labour was so fond, without defining the term: "He was keen that we should give a public impression that changes were taking place: this would improve our general image in the world, and we could make an important story out of it."[7] Pious wishes aside, nothing much seemed to happen thereafter. From then on until the final British withdrawal, Labour seemed content to let the Gulf languish in its usual torpor. Although there were storms on other parts of the Arabian Peninsula, there were only mild breezes in the Gulf. The only rumbling of discontent was the embryonic guerilla campaign in Dhofar.

The Johnson administration was well aware that Labour's enthusiasm for a continued British presence in the Gulf was tenuous at best. The CIA warned, as early as June 7, 1965, that while the UK earned almost $500 million annually from investments east of Suez, including $300 million in oil revenue from the Middle East, many felt the income did not justify the cost:

> Their opinion is that the income would by and large still flow to Britain even if drastic economies were made in expenditures. The possible saving of some hundred millions in the balance of payments is large enough to engage the grim attention of a government anxious to restore the international confidence in the pound.[8]

For the Labour leadership it was of little importance that British forces in the Gulf guarded oil reserves of immense value. Patrick Gordon Walker, Wilson's first foreign minister, was unimpressed by the argument that Britain should keep bases to maintain the flow of oil: "Why should we not, like other European countries, obtain oil from the Persian Gulf by paying for it instead of maintaining forces there."[9] For Healey the main concern was cutting costs, a principle he had clearly enunciated in his February 1966 defense review. While the first defense review had already achieved a major cut in expenditure without jeopardizing military efficiency, it had done "nothing to reduce the excessive cost of defence in foreign exchange".[10] The British political resident in the Gulf, Stewart Crawford, warned Brown in a dispatch of December 1966, that dissidence and terrorism would probably increase in the Gulf when Britain withdrew from South Arabia. The risk would rise correspondingly if the Eastern Aden Protectorate became a terrorist base after the British departure. In this precarious position, the Gulf rulers would only with great reluctance accept Britain transferring responsibilities to them, anxious as they were for a continued British presence.

> Taken all in all, the rulers do not in my view compare at all badly with the average of political figures in the Arab world as a whole; nor do I think that the shaikhly system of government is likely to be put under intolerable strain in the next few years, provided Saudi Arabia remains on its present course. I do not, in any case,

see any possible alternative to this system of government in the period ahead. I
am quite sure that we must accept it and work with and not against the rulers,
while exerting steady pressure to modernise and improve the efficiency of their
Governments and find ways to increase their peoples' acceptance of them.

The decision to leave Aden without any post-independence security guarantee was a severe shock to the rulers. All of them wanted Britain to remain
in the Gulf and continue in charge of their defense and foreign policy.
Crawford expected post-Aden reinforcements in the Gulf to "have a
calming effect on the ruler's nerves", but thought it wise to avoid further
upheavals.[11]

Jeffrey Pickering and David Reynolds argue that the Labour government had every intention of remaining in the Persian Gulf, but was forced
to liquidate its final holdings given the emergencies caused by the pound's
devaluation in November 1967.[12] To many observers, the withdrawal was
of little consequence. Ben Pimlott airily dismisses the final act: "'East of
Suez' lingered, and then faded. Over the next two years the issue ceased to
be whether Britain should withdraw, but at what rate."[13] Alan P. Dobson
correctly observes that the end was proclaimed in Healey's July 1967
defense review which announced British withdrawal from the Far East by
the mid-1970s: "Britain's east-of-Suez defence policy was finally buried by
the devaluation of sterling in November, but the writing was clearly on the
wall before then."[14] Outside Europe, Healey explained that Britain planned
for major reductions in the size and cost of forces – reductions to be carried
out "either more slowly or more quickly according to political and
economic need". Ending the British presence in the Far East reduced the
rationale for Persian Gulf bases as a point of transition to Singapore and
Malaysia.[15] The secretary of defense and foreign minister Michael Stewart
had, well ahead of the 1967 review, and in response to left-wing criticism
of the role east of Suez, explained to the Parliamentary Labour Party that
Britain was in a 'posture of withdrawal'.[16] The 1967 defense review, then,
was a policy in search of an opportunity, to be realized following the devaluation in November. In the 1968 defense review, Healey wrote: "The
Government has carried out a detailed and searching review of the whole
range of public expenditure as one of the measures necessary for a radical
solution of the country's balance of payments problems." For Healey the
basis of British security was in Europe, not overseas. But as recent wars on
the Arabian Peninsula had provided British forces with "more recent and
varied fighting experience than any other European army", Britain's
contribution to NATO was formidable.[17]

Healey's claims makes it hard to avoid the conclusion that the withdrawal from the Persian Gulf was the end of a planned and conscientious
process. Frank Brenchley, head of the Arabian department of the Foreign

Office in the era of the defense reviews, explains that his role was to point out the risks involved in a withdrawal from Aden and the Persian Gulf. "The 1961 Kuwait crisis was a telling argument, but the economic imperatives resulting from the over-valuation of sterling were so strong as to prevail eventually over any arguments for maintaining commitments."[18] Brenchley, a central participant in this period, tries unconvincingly to hide behind the fig leaf of economic crisis for ending the British presence east of Suez. Still, given the importance of the Gulf there should have been room for alternative solutions. The British withdrawal left a potentially dangerous power vacuum in an area that supplied 32 percent of the free world's oil and contained 58 percent of its proven reserves.[19] King Faisal was incredulous that Britain contemplated leaving the Gulf given the very large British stake there. In London in May 1967, the king gave Wilson a document outlining the scale of British economic interests in the Gulf. British companies had a 50 percent interest in Kuwait oil, which produced 114 million tons of oil in 1966. In Iraq, Britain had 23 percent of the oil production, or 76 million tons, while for Iran the figures were 55 percent and 101 million tons respectively, and 100 percent in the Gulf Sheikhdoms. In addition profits came from transporting, refining and marketing of oil, as well as jobs for British oil experts and workers. The Saudis estimated British annual profits from oil and related enterprises to be between £1,250 million and £1,400 million, while total British investments were in the £1,000–£1,350 million range.[20]

Despite repeated assurances to Faisal and the Gulf rulers about a continued British presence in the Persian Gulf, the Labour government's policy seems like a holding operation until the defense reviews were rammed through, the Americans pacified, and the withdrawal from Aden successfully completed. British allies and dependencies probably did not comprehend the scale of the deception perpetrated by Labour. Healey piously noted in his first defense review of 1965: "It would be politically irresponsible and economically wasteful if our bases were abandoned while they were needed to promote peace in the areas concerned."[21] A steady stream of reassurance emanated from the Wilson government to placate allies and clients alike.

In a post-mortem of American policy during the Johnson presidency, the State Department noted that maintenance of peace and security in the strategic Persian Gulf was a major American interest. "Our general desire to see the Arab world get its house in order, and to see Soviet opportunities for expanding in that direction blocked, lay behind this interest in the Gulf."[22] Despite discouraging signs, the Johnson team was convinced that Britain would stick to its historic role in the Gulf for "a considerable period". According to the State Department, the closure of the Suez Canal in June 1967, and the devaluation of sterling in November, on top of

Labour's increasing distaste of empire, "combined in the winter of 1967–68 to produce a sudden British decision to accelerate the UK withdrawal from the Gulf". The United States received its first clear information of the impending British withdrawal on January 4, 1968, being somewhat surprised at the abrupt change of British policies.[23]

While the State Department, in its post-mortem of the Johnson administration, affirmed belief in a continued British presence, in real life it requested reaffirmation of British intentions in late October 1967. The American embassy in London continually received reports predicting an earlier withdrawal, many of which originated from the British ministry of defense. So much so that the Foreign Office suspected defense of waging a sub-rosa campaign to push forward the final departure date from the Gulf. Labour's open-ended formulas – 'foreseeable future', 'while the need is there', and 'not for ever' – encouraged press speculations when the British presence in the Gulf would be terminated, thereby creating insecurity of British policy and thus opening the way for the final withdrawal. Brenchley believed the campaign to be orchestrated at ministerial level, disliking the interference with Foreign Office turf. The ministry of defense flatly rejected that it participated in a 'quit the Gulf' campaign. Unable to prove defense involvement, the Foreign Office let the matter rest.[24] When finally deciding to devalue the pound, Wilson continued his ambiguous statements to Johnson. In a note to the president on November 16, 1967, the prime minister explained that the new pound rate was carefully chosen to "to cause the minimum disturbance to the dollar". Furthermore:

> The package we have decided on will include a substantial saving on defence which I feared at one stage might require us, in particular, to withdraw earlier than planned from Singapore or even possibly make savage troop reductions in Europe. I am happy to say this is not the case and I can answer you that, provided, as we confidently believe, the pound can now be held and our economy forge ahead. In the new circumstances, we shall be able to maintain, both in Europe and East of Suez, the policies set out in our Defence White Paper as I explained to you at our last meeting.[25]

Whatever Wilson said, the engine of withdrawal inexorably hummed forward. While the evidence is inconclusive on the ministry of defense waging an undercover campaign, it certainly fits Healey's policy of ending the British presence east of Suez. Healey took early advantage of the pound's devaluation to push for withdrawal. Meeting Wilson on December 20, 1967, he argued:

> Healey said that he thought it would be essential that no attempt should be made to disguise the fact that if there were to be large defence cuts arising out of the Government's current review, these were bound to effect the speed of our withdrawal from present positions and commitments outside Europe.

He felt that Britain's allies should therefore receive advance warning as soon as possible, since there would be little time for consultations once the decision to withdraw had been made. As usual, Wilson wanted to keep his options open: "he would of course make it clear that no firm decisions whatever had yet been taken", but "nothing in any field of Government expenditure was to be regarded as sacrosanct". The prime minister noted that he would inform president Johnson on what may lie in store, without expressing any undue concern that this would be unacceptable to the Americans.[26] Whatever doubt there may have been about Britain's world-wide role was dispelled when the new chancellor of the exchequer, Roy Jenkins, on January 3, 1968, demanded a budget improvement of up to £1,000 million – an improvement he thought impossible to raise from taxes. For Jenkins, the only realistic option was to cut defense commitments east of Suez. The chancellor demanded withdrawal from the Persian Gulf in 1968 or 1969 at the very latest.[27] Brown and George Thompson, then commonwealth secretary, warned about the consequences of Jenkins' demanded cutback on January 3, 1968. "Given the present situation, we accept that the Government's defence expenditure has to be cut, in line with home civil expenditure, if the new economic measures as a whole are to be regarded as fair and sufficient." The secretaries agreed with Healey that if defense expenditure were cut, there must also be a corresponding cut in commitments to avoid damaging the morale of the armed forces. But after four defense reviews the price was heavy. Domestic cuts could be easily restored once the economy revived, "but our position and influence overseas, once lost, will be irretrievable". Britain would be "breaking our obligations and our pledged word". Britain's huge oil investments in the Persian Gulf could be lost by a precipitate withdrawal that could well end in an Aden situation. The warnings went unheeded, and no further action seemed to have been taken by the concerned ministers. Their memorandum may well have been an attempt to cover their backs if things went terribly wrong after the British withdrawal.[28] Incidentally, Roy Jenkins describes in his memoirs how Healey and Brown put up a mock fight for the benefit of the service chiefs and Foreign Office officials to prove they had resisted the treasury's chopping of the empire to the bitter end. But, as Jenkins freely admits, he had worked out the details of the withdrawal with Healey prior to the meeting.[29]

The United States received its first clear indication of a premature British withdrawal on January 4, 1968.[30] Rusk was annoyed, urging Brown on January 6, 1968 to refrain from any irrevocable decisions before they met the week after. A rash British withdrawal would only "feed instability in the region". Rusk wanted a British presence for the indefinite future.[31] Rusk cabled Brown to tell him he was "deeply disturbed" to learn of British plans to withdraw from the Gulf.[32] Brown was noncommittal, replying on the same day that the Gulf was an issue he hoped to discuss with Rusk when in Washington.[33] Prior to talks with Brown, assistant secretary of state Lucius Battle recommended to Rusk that he press for a continued British presence, or at the very least for the British not to announce a specific departure date.[34]

State Department officials were dismayed by the way Brown handled the visit. "Foreign Secretary Brown came to Washington, not to consult but to inform us" that Britain would completely withdraw from the Gulf and the Far East. Leaving the Gulf was a breach of another British promise: "they had previously intended to maintain and perhaps increase their forces in that area indefinitely".[35] Rusk's initial reaction was so sharp as to shock Brown: "I had a bloody unpleasant meeting in Washington this morning with Rusk. His courtesy and moderate Southern manner did not disguise the depth of feeling and at times even contempt which he expressed."[36] Rusk believed that leaving the Middle East was "tantamount to British withdrawal from world affairs", and warned that the United States had no intention of filling the vacuum left by the United Kingdom.[37]

The secretary of state feared that the British decision would have a profound effect on the world situation, dismissing Labour's fig leaf that British forces would have a 'general capability' to act outside of Europe. Rusk feared Britain's withdrawal into a 'Little England' would lead to increased isolationism in the United States. The American public, on learning the United States was alone without responsible allies to share its burdens, would force a reduction in the US worldwide commitments. Alleged British savings, Rusk believed, would be offset by damage to British commercial interests in the Middle and the Far East. Brown dismissed Rusk's fear of turmoil in the Middle East, arguing that the "situation in the Gulf was better now than it had been for some time". Urging Britain to reconsider, and not to subordinate their worldwide role to temporary political considerations, Rusk concluded by voicing his dislike of the "acrid aroma of the fait accompli", urging that Brown "for God's sake be British".[38]

According to the State Department, Rusk's presentation was eloquent but had little effect on his British counterpart: "Brown said that he would report the Secretary's views to the Cabinet but gave no indication that the UK decision would be modified." Johnson again wrote Wilson, wanting Britain to reconsider. Evidently, American views were of little concern, as Brown announced the decision to withdraw from the Gulf in the House of Commons on January 16, 1968.[39] How little the Labour government valued American views is indicated by the fact that British representatives arrived in the Gulf on January 7, 1968, a day after Rusk urged Brown to reconsider and four days prior to their meeting on January 11, to inform Gulf rulers of the pending British withdrawal.[40] In the end there was just quiet resignation from the Americans concerning the British withdrawal. A briefing paper of February 2, 1968, prepared for the president for the upcoming Wilson visit, pointed out:

> While the basic British decision to withdraw UK forces by 1971 probably cannot be reversed, we think we should urge the British maintain certain elements of their position beyond 1971 – particularly in providing leadership and assistance for indigenous security forces.[41]

In discussions with Wilson, the president at no point deigned to talk about the Persian Gulf.[42] In fact, for such an important British decision as dismantling the empire, the American reactions were surprisingly low key (apart from the letters sent by Rusk and Johnson to Brown to Wilson).[43]

From there on things unraveled rapidly in the Gulf. Only two months after he had assured the Gulf rulers and king Faisal of a continued British presence, minister of state Goronwy Roberts was dispatched again to announce a March 31, 1971 withdrawal date for British forces in the Gulf. To prevent Faisal from stirring up the sheikhs, Roberts had assured them in November 1967 that Britain would not abandon them to the same fate as Aden. The king claimed that, as Britain had abandoned Aden, it would repeat the performance in the Persian Gulf.

> Mr. Roberts said that he could give an official assurance on behalf of Her Majesty's Government that the British Government would maintain their political and military presence in the Gulf to enable them to carry out their obligations to the Gulf States, for so long as this was necessary, and that there was no time-limit set upon the British presence in the Gulf.[44]

A rather firm assurance one would think, but carefully phrased to leave an opening to opt out of the pledged word.

Only two months later, Roberts was back in the Gulf to announce the reversal of British policy. To king Faisal, Roberts explained on January 10, 1968, the decision was based on Britain's grave balance of payments difficulties. Well aware that a precipitate withdrawal could cause local problems, the Labour government proposed an alternative system of security to replace British troops: "We had therefore provided for a period over three years during which we would want to work out a strong and secure system for the future, managed led and organized by the countries of area themselves." As an ally of longstanding, Roberts claimed, Faisal's views in setting up the organization were of special importance. The king was anxious to avoid another Aden. Roberts insisted Labour wanted to do everything possible to prevent revolutionary activity in the Gulf. Needless to say, Roberts failed to convince the Saudi monarch.[45] For the rulers, Roberts' second visit was a very unpleasant experience:

> All the Rulers were deeply shocked by the reversal of Her Majesty's

Government's policy, by comparison with what they had been assured by the Minister in November. They were also stunned by being confronted with a decision by Her Majesty's Government, which would make it impossible for us to carry out our protection obligations to them (renewed in Bahrain as recently in 1961 and in Abu Dhabi on Shaikh Zaid's accession in 1966), but about which they had not been consulted, yet it was still far from clear what kind of alternative security arrangements would be possible after our withdrawal.

To induce Britain to remain the rulers of Bahrain, Quatar and Abu Dhabi offered to contribute to the costs of keeping British forces in the Gulf, but were arrogantly dismissed by Healey who declared he was not a 'white slaver' to Arab sheiks.[46] On a more serious note, Healey explained to Parliament on February 13, 1968 that the cabinet rejected subsidies from the Gulf rulers because the object was not only to reduce foreign exchange costs but also public expenditure as a whole. To the cost of the actual British military presence in the Gulf, Healey claimed, must be added the cost of a general capability to maintain forces overseas.[47] Whatever his reasons, Healey offended the rulers and British Gulf officials. "Grave exception is being taken to the term 'white slaver' which is seen as an intrusion of the colour problem in an area where it does not exist," *The Daily Telegraph* observed on January 25, 1968. "The use of the term mercenary, with its Congo connotation is even more resented." Besides, British officers had long served in the Trucial Oman Scouts, the Abu Dhabi Defence Force and the Sultan of Muscat and Oman's forces.

Mr. Healey, presumably, had forgotten their existence when he rejected the concept of British soldiers serving the Gulf State rulers, with whom Britain has treaties. His language was ready-made for pro-Nasser propaganda and an encouragement to terrorist organisations.[48]

Michael Palmer observes that an American president preoccupied with the Tet offensive in Vietnam (which began on January 31, 1968), and who would announce his refusal to accept nomination as democratic presidential candidate two months later, had little time and energy to devote to the Persian Gulf.[49] In fact, a suitable low-key American policy emerged in the wake of the British decision. The United States did not contemplate a direct American role, but wished for the regional powers to safeguard Gulf stability. For this purpose, the United States advocated greater economic and political cooperation among the Gulf states, also to prevent a local arms race. The American contribution to Gulf stability was an American naval presence to "avoid any impression that the United States was withdrawing from the region". While avoiding involvement, the United States was well aware that the situation in the Gulf was, at best, "fragile". Increased Soviet interest, including the first Russian ships to visit the Gulf since 1903, was cause for concern but not undue alarm.[50] Undersecretary of state Nicholas Katzenbach, observed to the National Security Council on February 21, 1968 that "there is no blinking the fact" that American influence in the Middle East was decreasing, while Soviet influence was increasing, citing the consequences of the Six Day War and the growth of Arab nationalism.[51]

American protests, pleading from the Gulf rulers and requests from local British representatives were to little avail. Nothing seemed to dissuade Labour from the liquidation of empire. There was no question of prolonging the stay, regardless from where the entreaties came, rather the Government could not withdraw fast enough. At the cabinet meeting on January 4, 1968, regarding withdrawal from the Persian Gulf, Wilson concluded that ending British commitments in the Gulf would hopefully be sooner than the announced deadline of the end of 1971. Shades of Aden all over again. Nothing deflected Wilson from this course, whoever pleaded for an extension. The prime minister refused to budge on the date "since this gave us the flexibility to withdraw earlier should the opportunity arise".[52] Labour was little concerned about the consequences of withdrawal. Nadav Safran points out that while Britain wished for an orderly transfer of responsibility in the Gulf, "the announcement itself unleashed dynastic animosities, tribal feuds, and territorial disputes".[53] Paying lip service to peace and stability, the main British concern was withdrawal of British forces. Soon thereafter, the Persian Gulf faded away as an Anglo-American concern. During Anglo-American discussions on the Persian Gulf on March 27, 1968, neither of the parties expressed great concern or anxieties at the turn of events. Denis Allen of the Foreign Office explained: "We had of course to recognise that our influence in the area has declined from the time that the withdrawal decision was announced and would continue to decline progressively."[54]

The Conservative party in Britain raised a great fuss about the decision to withdraw, charging betrayal of Britain's long-time allies, and pledging to undo the damage when returned to power. But this turned out to be a largely empty gesture. When they failed to live up to their promise after the 1970 election victory, the excuse was changing circumstances in the Gulf.[55] The Foreign Office initially fought the withdrawal, but came to regard it as the correct decision.[56] Frank Brenchley insists, "On balance, it can be argued in retrospect that the decision to withdraw was justified."[57] Soon, the Foreign Office took it upon itself privately to warn leading Conservatives that their statements about a continued British presence in the Gulf was misleading and damaging to the national interest. By 1971, British capability in the Gulf would be so run down that it would be impossible to reverse. This, again, would change the political climate in the Gulf, making a return of the British very difficult indeed: "The danger is that such statements may lull the Shaiks into complacency and inactivity: and that they will find by 1971 that they have been deluding themselves." While the Conservatives certainly were entitled to their own policy, it did not matter much in the real world. "What can hardly be disputed is that we would, sooner or later, have had to relinquish our special position in the Gulf." In 1971, this process would be almost irreversible irrespective of Conservative policy.[58] And so, unceremoniously, the fixed British presence in the Middle East ended, with the Americans doing next to nothing to prevent the withdrawals.

Filing his annual review on Saudi Arabia on January 15, 1968, Man noted that Faisal was still deeply suspicious of Nasser, despite the maintenance of a common Saudi–Egyptian front against Israel for public consumption. Anglo-Saudi relations had deteriorated sharply since Faisal's visit to London. Britain handing over power to the NLF, the king felt, was a betrayal of the pledges the Wilson government made at the London summit. "To Faisal's mind these developments held sinister implications for the future stability of the Gulf shaikhdoms as well as creating a potential threat to his own Kingdom."[59] Brenchley dismissed Faisal's refusal to buy armored cars, to penalize the British, as an example of Saudi irrationality:

> I am afraid that this is just the kind of childish Saudi reaction to our policy that we had to expect, and the fact that they damage their own defence capability by buying inferior equipment will not deter them. There is a very vivid Arabic equivalent of our proverb about cutting off the nose to spite the face.[60]

While showing his displeasure by awarding the arms contract to France, British policy bewildered Faisal. It was inconceivable to the king that Britain would break its pledges only two months after Roberts was dispatched to the Gulf in November 1967 to give assurances of a continued British presence. By announcing their departure, the Saudis believed Britain implicitly encouraged anti-Saudi forces in the Gulf.[61] But there were more penalties to come, Saudi Arabia refused to renew Magic Carpet and turned over training and maintenance to Pakistan. Ministry of defense officials responded by threatening to refuse Lightning training for the Pakistani pilots, while Sultan, minister of defense in Saudi Arabia, warned that in that case the Saudis would cancel the entire contract with Britain.[62]

Excessive favoritism of the new regime in Aden, in Saudi opinion, served further to alienate Faisal from Britain. When aid negotiations with the PRSY were close to breaking down, Lord Shackleton, minister in charge of handing power over to the NLF, minuted his concern to the prime minister. The objectives of Labour's South Arabian policy, Shackleton observed, was most importantly "to effect a peaceful withdrawal and secondly to leave, if possible, a stable government behind". The successful withdrawal meant considerable economies to the treasury. Britain offered the Federal government £60 million in aid over three years to sweeten the withdrawal. The collapse of the Federal government released Labour from this pledge, and the NLF was given only £12 million. The new government in Aden was offered £1.75 million for the next year:

> The sum we are now offering is nicely calculated to ensure that we have made some gesture while totally failing to make it possible for the Government of South Yemen to survive economically and therefore politically, on the grounds that it is doomed anyway and we do not particularly want it to survive.[63]

While Britain no longer had a national interest in the PRSY, Shackleton argued, it had a moral obligation to the people living there. "I know South Yemen is not popular with anyone; it is a far off country of which we know little and, furthermore, they have shot and killed some of our people." But the killings were mainly to rid themselves of the sheikhs that Britain supported 'willy nilly'. Now peace had descended and even Europeans walked the streets without fear. If aid was not forthcoming, the regime might in desperation nationalize British business interests.

> We were, in the past, prepared to support a right wing government of limited merit, at least until we could find a better alternative. We now virtually wash our hands of a government which clearly has objectionable features, but whose principal leaders are, to my mind, a great improvement on past rulers.

Shackleton wanted to avoid a breakdown in the talks and the Labour government to reconsider its position, and offer substantially more aid.[64] The Saudis did not take kindly to the continuation of aid to revolutionary Yemen. Saudi officials warned "that king Faisal would nevertheless be very disturbed: it appeared that we and the Russians were jointly supplying the NLF with arms". Faisal again rattled the threat of canceling air defense contracts.[65] American policy towards the new regime in southern Yemen was one of non-involvement; there was certainly no intention of replacing Britain as the major donor of aid. Besides, there was little the United States could do. Reporting a power struggle in the Republic on March 21, John W. Foster, assistant to Rostow, observed that the moderates seemed to be winning, indicating a potential swing away from the Communist bloc. But the moderates were only moderates in a South Arabian context, and were still Arab nationalists with an anti-Western ideology.[66] When the confusion in Yemen persisted, Foster reported to Rostow on May 21, 1968: "We just don't have the money – or the interest – to buy in, and the Saudis are still too skeptical of even this latest shift to pick up the burden themselves, though that would be ideal from our viewpoint."[67]

American concerns for Saudi Arabia were equally limited. Briefing the president before a meeting with Saudi crown prince Khalid on June 22, 1968, Walt Rostow wanted Johnson to convey "a sense of continuing US interest in, and friendship for, Saudi Arabia". There was much to be concerned about; almost 7,000 Americans worked for ARAMCO in Saudi Arabia. Faisal believed the United States was increasingly disinterested in the Middle East and was "hyper-sensitive to any signs which he might see as evidence of a diminishing regard for Saudi Arabia". But the United States had little to offer other than sympathy for the Saudis' 'legitimate aspirations' to be the leading power on the Arab Peninsula.[68] President Johnson did little to prevent further erosion of American influence in the Middle East, leaving a policy in disarray to his successor Richard Nixon. Meeting the Saudi minister of state for foreign affairs, Omar Saqqaf, on October 16, 1969, Nixon explained that he was well aware that Saudi Arabia's extremist neighbors criticized its friendship with the United States. "The President hoped that our policies will be such as not to be a liability for our friends but an asset." This was the ignoble end of the Anglo-American Middle East; at the end of the 1960s decade that had started so optimistically, the president wished American friendship to be an asset not a liability. With the British leaving the Persian Gulf, the United States, with Saudi advice, hoped to play a stabilizing role in the area.

> Sometimes, the President said, rhetoric and news stories make it seem as if the US, to be blunt, had written off the Arab world. The President said he had a very strong conviction that the US must work with the moderates so that there could be a peace in which all could work and live together.

Faisal sent along his pledge of good relations with the United States, and asked for reciprocity from the president. Nixon responded: "His Majesty has that assurance absolutely."[69] This conversation, symbolically, marks the end of the British presence in the Persian Gulf also on the American side. The president and the Saudis take note of the British decision to withdraw, but no longer make any attempt to prolong British presence in the area. The United States, while seeking continued friendship with Saudi Arabia, is reluctant to pick up any further commitments in the Middle East. After Britain pulled out of the Persian Gulf, Saudi Arabia and Iran became 'pillars' of American policy in the Gulf.[70]

During 1964 and after, the United States and Great Britain searched for alternatives to land-based facilities to project their forces in the Indian Ocean littoral. Butler commented in April 1964: "we should look for points where the local political scene has no anti-colonialist or anti-Western complexes, or, preferably, where there are no inhabitants at all".[71] In addition to Diego Garcia in the Indian Ocean as a joint Anglo-American base, Britain wanted to develop Aldabra (an uninhabited Crown island 500 miles off Tanganyika) as an airbase. This was in anticipation of refusal of over-flying rights in the Middle East and Africa, and to stage operations against East Africa from this point.[72] An additional motivation for the United

States, by agreeing to a joint base with the United Kingdom, was to encourage the British to remain east of Suez. The agreement called for Britain to acquire the land, resettling and compensating the local population, while the United States paid for construction and maintenance. The prospective base was carefully chosen because only 100 to 200 of the locals would be affected.[73]

To sweeten the withdrawal from Aden, Labour offered the possibility of developing Aldabra. The United States accepted the option, shouldering the costs but refusing major involvement in the base apart from having the facilities available in an emergency. The hope was that making Britain responsible for constructing and running the base would encourage a continued British presence east of Suez.[74] Aldabra developed incrementally, but on August 4, 1966, McNamara approved joint financing of Aldabra and a joint survey of Diego Garcia.[75] Progress was painfully slow both for the Aldabra and Diego Garcia concepts, but officially Britain remained a serious partner in the venture as late as spring of 1967.[76] During the summer of 1967, Labour indicated it was unable or unwilling to shoulder its share of development costs. The United States pressed ahead with planning, still thinking an established facility at Diego Garcia was an additional inducement for Britain to remain east of Suez.[77] But the idea of British participation was already dead. Officially, Aldabra (and Diego Garcia as well) was axed as a result of the British devaluation, as Healey explains in his memoirs: "But I had already decided that it did not make military sense."[78] In reality, the minister of defense was far more blunt. "When we got rid of Aden," Healey admitted in a later interview, "the Air Force tried desperately to get an agreement to building a base at Aldabra . . . I went along with it for a bit then chopped it – it would have been an absolutely ludicrous idea."[79] Even after the British opted out, the United States proceeded with plans to develop naval facilities at Diego Garcia, the Labour government having no objections to its development. The Johnson administration realized that chances of British participation were slim. Still, the State Department hoped for some British involvement, at a bare minimum that the "British flag should fly over facility and that UK liaison officer would need be appointed in order to establish necessary relations with other HMG officials and local inhabitants".[80] The United States received British approval in principle on September 4, 1968, generously allowing the British flag to fly over the base and providing one or more liaison officers.[81] This marks the melancholy end of the Anglo-American Middle East – an agreement in principle to let the British flag fly in the middle of nowhere in the Indian Ocean.

8

The End of the Anglo-American Middle East?

As long as the United States and Great Britain cooperated in preserving their influence in the Middle East, the area was a relatively tranquil place from their point of view. The first half of the 1960s, then, was the heyday of the Anglo-American Middle East. Even with different policies and approaches, when supporting each other, both powers easily maintained their influence. Sometimes their policies were fundamentally different, like Kennedy's attempt at rapprochement with Nasser and the more militant Conservative approach to challenges to British authority. But with essential Anglo-American agreement in support of their respective positions, they could afford the luxury of pursuing different priorities without jeopardizing their influence. The Middle East nations were militarily insignificant, particularly compared to the superior power of the Anglo-Americans. As long as the potential for applying military force remained credible, the West was not seriously challenged by unfriendly regimes in the region. While the Middle East was never quiescent, there was no need for undue concern. Even the Labour government thought it possible to retain the Aden base and hold on to the Aden Federation as long as Britain wished and without great expense. From the Anglo-American point of view, Nasser's strident rhetoric and confrontational politics, which made him more a nuisance than a threat eased tensions. With the United States and the United Kingdom in basic harmony, and generally in support of each other's policies, they succeeded, with relative ease, in containing Arab nationalism and limiting Soviet influence in the Middle East. All this began to change dramatically with Labour's electoral victory in October 1964. The United States remained very supportive of its main ally, and Labour, too, claimed to be in fundamental agreement with the Johnson administration in maintaining the British role east of Suez. But as we have seen, Labour's hidden ideological agenda was withdrawal at almost any price. As the British dismantling of empire gathered momentum, American disinterest toward the Middle East grew. American policy seemed to be in support of the British position in the Middle East at all costs, making no attempt at exploring or developing alternative approaches to the area. It is a significant comment on American Middle East policy that the United States was unwilling or unable for the most part to pursue policies independent of Britain. The British withdrawal from Aden and the Six Day War were a turning point: from then on, the Anglo-American Middle East declined rapidly. America's failure to restrain a militant Israel led to dramatically increased Soviet influence among the radical Arab regimes in an effort to compensate for their devastating defeat. Having said that, Nasser's unwillingness to accommodate the United States gave president Johnson little incentive to prevent Israel from attacking. In Aden, the war provided Britain with a golden opportunity to crush the revolutionaries in order to leave political stability behind, as Egypt was forced to withdraw from Yemen after the Six Day War. But the local scene was of little concern to Labour. Rather than exploit the possibilities resulting from Nasser's defeat, Britain accelerated its withdrawal from Aden. The decline of the Anglo-American Middle East, then, was not due to lack of power but lack of will. It was a willed retreat.

Ironically, with its announcement to leave the Persian Gulf by the end of 1971, Labour found itself in a position of heavy responsibility combined with steadily decreasing influence. Problems in the Gulf abounded, requiring continued British attention and work if they were to leave the area in good order and avoid another Aden-type situation. There were numerous border claims to sort out, as well as opportunistic new ones emerging in the wake of British withdrawal. Iran claimed Bahrain by virtue of temporary occupation in the eighteenth century, the Abu Musa Island from the sheikhdom of Sharjah and the Tunbs Islands from the sheikhdom of Ras al Khaimah. The Foreign Office feared this dispute between Iranians and Arabs could result in military confrontation, complicating British efforts to leave on schedule. If the shah occupied the islands, Britain might have to use force in accordance with its treaty obligations. Faisal renewed his dormant claim to Buraimi, but the Foreign Office discounted the king using military force to press his case. While challenging the declining imperial authority, Britain at the same time needed the assistance of the shah and king Faisal to press Qatar, Bahrain, Abu Dhabi, Dubai, Sharjah, 'Ajman, Umm al-Qaiwain, Ras al-Khaimah and Fujairah to federate into the United Arab Emirates (UAE). Then, all good things could happen: Britain would help create a union force incorporating the Trucial Oman Scouts (TOS). The TOS were a mercenary force commanded by British officers, controlled by the British government and not owing allegiance to any ruler. By local standards it was well trained, experienced and effective. Progress toward the UAE was painfully slow, both because of internal squabbles among the potential members of the union and Irani and

Saudi territorial claims. Following the British announcement to leave, the rebellion in Dhofar deepened. The Foreign and Commonwealth Office believed the substantial British investment in the Sultan's Armed Forces could successfully contain the uprising, making it possible to withdraw British forces according to the established timetable.[1]

For all their bluster about reversing Labour's withdrawal decision of January 1968, the Conservatives adhered to Labour's policy after their surprise victory in the election of June 1970. But in contrast to Labour's wish to cut the umbilical cord of empire, the Conservatives wanted to retain as much influence as possible in the Persian Gulf. During the Anglo-American talks on the Gulf in June 26, 1972 the Foreign Office explained the new British role in the area:

> Britain intended to play as active and prominent a role in Gulf affairs as was possible in existing political circumstances. The modernisation of British relations with the Gulf States had proceeded smoothly, and instead of the low profile usually adopted by Britain in such post-independence or post-colonial situations, British influence remained strong and visible throughout the area.[2]

Sir Alec Douglas-Home, now foreign minister, began a series of consultations with the Gulf rulers to see whether Labour's policies could be reversed. The major powers of the Gulf, Iran, Iraq, Saudi Arabia and Kuwait opposed continued British presence after 1971, while the lesser sheikhdoms favored Britain to remain, although only Dubai was prepared to say so publicly. Remaining under such circumstances would have opened Britain to charges of imperialism and supplied grist to the propaganda mills of Iraq and PLOAG, making a continued presence exceedingly difficult.[3] The new prime minister, Edward Heath, explained to the cabinet on July 23, 1970 that Britain's objective in the Gulf was "to secure a progressive reduction in expenditure while encouraging and assisting the local Rulers to shoulder their own responsibilities within the framework of an effective federal organization".[4] The shah was persuaded to drop his claim to Bahrain, in return for Britain's tacit acceptance of Iran occupying the Persian Gulf islands to which he had laid claim. The UAE was proclaimed on December 2, 1971, but was the most fragile of creations having been patched together rather hurriedly by the departing British. Bahrain and Qatar opted out of the new federation. Sharjah's ruler was murdered two months after the inauguration of the UAE in an attempted coup, while Sharjah and Fujairah fought a small war over local territorial issues in 1972.[5] Still, even after 1971 vestiges of the British position remained in the Persian Gulf. According to James H. Noyes, US deputy assistant secretary of defense, Britain still had important political, commercial and military ties to the area. The military ties, in addition to air facilities on the Masirah island off the coast of Oman, included regular air and naval visits, joint exercises with the local states and military forces assigned to Oman, UAE, Bahrain, Abu Dhabi and Qatar. The Americans were well pleased with the residual British influence in the Gulf. "So while small in number and without direct operational functions as British military per se," Noyes observed, "their importance is considerable."[6] Britain's treaty of friendship with the UAE provided for the provision of British military advisory teams.[7] In fact, as one authority notes, the British withdrawal from the UAE was more apparent than real. British nationals still dominated the commercial and banking life of the sheikhdom, while British officers ran its military forces.[8] The whole point of Tory policy, Home explained to his American counterpart, was to establish an indirect British presence "so that we could exercise the maximum political influence with the minimum British presence".[9]

Edward Heath continued Labour's policy of liberating Britain from the American embrace and completed the turn towards Europe. The United Kingdom joined the European Union in 1973. Nixon and Kissinger nostalgically longed for the 'special relationship', but there were no suitors in London. Heath's experience as the chief whip during the Suez crisis had implanted a deep skepticism against the Americans in him. Kissinger laments: "Of all British political leaders, Heath was the most indifferent to the American connection and perhaps even to Americans individually."[10]

While Britain wanted Faisal's assistance in leaving a peaceful Gulf behind, Britain's relations with Saudi Arabia were complicated. Aside from Buraimi, the king was still upset with Britain for leaving Aden and the Gulf. The king only reluctantly agreed to cooperate for a stable transition in the Gulf. Suspecting that the main British concern was orderly withdrawal, it lessened Faisal's need to continue his special relations with Britain.[11] Furthermore, problems with the Anglo-Saudi air package continued to bedevil relations.[12] The king's attitude changed when Airwork, one of the partners of the Anglo-American arms consortium, provided important assistance in beating back a PRSY invasion of Saudi Arabia in late November 1969. One Airwork pilot, ex-wing commander Winship, led the successful air counterattack, while the whole Airwork organization worked very hard to assist the Saudis in defeating the invasion force, improving Airwork–Saudi relations and Anglo-Saudi relations.[13]

Distancing himself from Britain, Faisal could not afford to alienate the Americans. Attempting an independent posture in the Middle East, Faisal had created an 'Islamic Alliance' in 1964 to counter Nasser's appeals to Arab nationalism and maintain a certain distance from the great powers. As the king grew older, he put more and more store in his Islamic credentials, not only as a guardian of the holy places, but also as an instrument for gaining support of Saudi policies in the Arab and Muslim world. Faisal viewed American policies in Yemen, support of Israel, and failure to counter the growing Soviet influence after the Six Day War with distaste. The king, however, was realist enough to know that ties with the United States were so substantial that the links could not be broken without endangering the survival of his regime. Several American presidents had guaranteed Saudi security against unprovoked aggression, and the United States was the leading arms supplier to the kingdom. American companies and technicians were closely interwoven with the Saudi administrative and economic fabric, while ARAMCO supplied 80 percent of Saudi revenue.[14] The United States, therefore, had little cause for concern when designating Saudi Arabia as one of its pillars in the Persian Gulf, the other pillar being Iran, as a substitute for Britain in the Persian Gulf.[15]

Faisal was deeply upset by Israel's victory in the Six Day War, but the war worked to his advantage. In return for a substantial subvention to Egypt, the Saudi Arabian monarch forced Nasser to withdraw Egyptian forces from Yemen. Ostentatiously united in the fight against Israel, there was a deep undercurrent of Egyptian and Saudi mistrust and rivalry.[16] Having broken relations with the United States, Nasser was forced to turn to the Kremlin in an effort to recoup his losses after the Six Day War. With the aid of massive Soviet military assistance, Egyptian artillery bombarded Israeli positions along the Suez canal in early 1969, in what Nasser termed a 'war of attrition'. When Israel responded with air raids deep into Egyptian territory, Moscow eagerly supplied Nasser with surface to air missiles and even Soviet pilots. Ironically, having seemingly secured a strong foothold in the eastern Mediterranean, the Soviet Union was unceremoniously evicted from Egypt by Nasser's successor Anwar Sadat in 1972 in an attempt to seek American goodwill. American relations with Egypt were still broken when Nasser died of a heart attack in September 1970. He had always been committed to Arab nationalism, telling Nixon's envoy plainly that he did not trust the United States.[17] Nasser hinted to the United States he might be willing to restore relations if the Americans pressured Israel to return to its pre-1967 borders. The new realist team in the White House, president Nixon and national security advisor Henry Kissinger, saw little reason to placate a supplicant Nasser, who was requesting favors while offering nothing in return. "Why we should pay a price," Kissinger condescendingly sniffs in his memoirs, "for the restoration of relations which he had cut off under a totally false pretext was never made clear." As long as the Egyptian leader harbored large numbers of Soviets and championed radical Arab nationalism with its concomitant anti-American rhetoric, he offered Kissinger and Nixon little incentive to restore American relations with Egypt.[18] In reality, Nixon continued the traditional American policy of conciliating Nasser: "We are prepared for a restoration of relations on the basis of mutual respect whenever conditions are appropriate."[19]

To cover the withdrawal of American troops from Vietnam, the president introduced the Nixon doctrine, which also had global implications. The United States would still honor its treaty obligations and provide nuclear cover to its allies and economic and military assistance in lieu of American troops, but the threatened country (read Vietnam) had to do the fighting. Cynical commentators claim that, in Vietnam, the bodies changed color, reduced American losses and covered American troop withdrawals. Reducing American commitments, the Nixon doctrine called for close American allies to substitute for the United States. In Asia the close ally was Japan, while in Africa Zaire, Angola (then a Portuguese colony) and South Africa divided the honor. In the Middle East, Nixon believed the shah fitted the job description as regional policeman.[20] Much has been made by scholars of Iran being called, in the context of the Nixon doctrine, to fill the power vacuum in the Persian Gulf for the Americans, arguing the president and Kissinger tilted towards Iran to counter growing Soviet influence in Iraq. But regional issues were also of importance: Iraq supported revolutionary movements on the Arabian Peninsula to counter the growing influence of Saudi Arabia and Iran.

Nixon wanted to build up Iran as one of the strongest powers in the Middle East. When Nixon and Kissinger flew directly to Tehran from the Moscow summit in May 1972, it was for the shah a flattering confirmation of his importance. In Tehran, Nixon and Kissinger permitted the monarch to purchase any conventional weapons he desired from the American arsenal, and the shah bought in a grand style. Walter LaFeber notes "the shah responded by ordering planes and other equipment" as if he was going through the Sears, Roebuck catalog, "in the words of one [American] official". To pay for all this military hardware, Nixon and Kissinger encouraged the Iranian monarch to increase oil prices. Finally, the shah had the means to make Iran a great power, and, combined with rapidly rising oil prices, his dream of making Iran into one of the five leading industrialized powers in the world seemed possible.[21]

The resulting Iranian military expansion was of gigantic proportions; arms were purchased on a scale never seen before. Between 1972 and 1977, Iran bought weapons and weapons systems for $16.2 billion, while the Iranian defense budget increased by 680 percent. At the same time, oil prices increased drastically, but most of the profits went to the United States to pay for all this military hardware. The Iranian army was on paper much stronger than the British army, but the reality was different. Lacking the infrastructure and educated personnel to service the sophisticated military machinery, the shah imported large numbers of Americans to run his armed forces. Americans brought with them the best and the worst from the United States, having little understanding, respect or knowledge of Iranian society. There were numerous unfortunate episodes, which fuelled the enormous hatred of America that later came to the surface during the Iranian revolution of 1979. Episodes included a lightly dressed American woman strolling through a mosque and American teenagers on motorbikes riding through the Shah mosque, while Iranians were often referred to as 'sand-niggers' and 'ragheads'.[22]

Iraq was the only obstacle to the shah's dream of dominating the region. Iran and Iraq had been mutually antagonistic since the Iraqi revolution in 1958, but this came only on top of centuries of ethnic and religious rivalries. The Iraqis are in the main Arabs and the Iraqi elite are Sunni muslims, while most Iranians are non-Arabs and Shia muslims. In the wake of its revolution, and deeply conscious of being Iran's inferior in population, wealth and economic growth, Iraq signed a treaty of friendship and cooperation with the Soviet Union in April 1972, just a month prior to Nixon and Kissinger's visit to Tehran. Both the United States and Iran had a common interest in breaking up the Iraqi–Soviet coalition, as standard scholarly accounts go, and when the shah proposed that Iran and the United States jointly support the Kurdish rebellion in Iraq, he found an eager audience in Nixon and Kissinger. Great Britain and Israel, each for its own reasons joined in supporting the Kurds.[23] Overlooked by most accounts, additional motivation for destabilizing Iraq was its strong support of revolutionary movements on the Arabian Peninsula.[24]

The Central Intelligence Agency (CIA) secretly transferred $16 million to the Kurds between 1972 and 1975. While the amount was insignificant, its symbolic value was great, since the leader of the Kurdish rebellion, Musta Mustafa Barzani, believed that this meant an American commitment to aid his cause, or at the very least to protect his people. For Barzani this was important, since he never trusted the shah. Israel also supported the Kurds, because it feared a militant Iraq (a fear that was confirmed when Israel bombed Iraqi nuclear reactors in 1981). The combined American, British, Iranian and Israeli assistance enabled the Kurds to fight Iraq to a stalemate, at a heavy cost to the regime, since the bulk of the Iraqi army was engaged against the Kurds.[25] American relations with Saudi Arabia were important too in the policy of pressuring Iraq. Henry Kissinger admits as much in his memoirs, pledging in March 1974 to coordinate American policy with Saudi Arabia on the Arabian Peninsula "to assuage the growing Saudi uneasiness about being squeezed in a radical pincer movement between Iraq in the north and South Yemen in the south". Kissinger assured Faisal that the enemies of Saudi Arabia were the enemies of the United States.[26]

Neither the United States nor Iran wanted the Kurds to succeed, but rather to force Iraq to expend manpower, matériel and revenue to punish it for the agreement with the Soviet Union and support of guerillas on the Arabian Peninsula. The shah was well aware that if the Iraqi Kurds succeeded, his own Kurds might rebel. The United States did not believe that Barzani was a reliable partner, given his strong Soviet connections, his exile in the Soviet Union in the 1950s, and USSR arms supplies to him and the Kurds. The United States began to limit its aid in 1973, and when the shah gained territorial concessions from Iraq in 1975, he immediately cut off aid to the Kurds as his part of the bargain. When the shah turned off the aid spigot, the United States followed suit. In addition, the shah closed his borders to the Kurds. Iraq then finally managed to crush the fifteen-year-long Kurdish rebellion.[27]

To manage the new relationship with Iran and Saudi Arabia (and later Egypt) the US State Department and treasury set up Joint Commissions with these countries. Under the umbrella of the Joint Commissions, thousands of American civil servants and employees from the private sector took part in multidollar development schemes in the areas of defense, economic and agricultural development, technology transfer and nuclear energy. But mostly the Joint Commissions "acted as arms salesmen supreme".[28] Britain too joined in the arms bonanza.[29] Selling large quantities of military hardware hardly constitutes a policy, nor is it an effective substitute for policy. Nixon and Kissinger's attempt at managing the Arabian Peninsula and the Persian Gulf ended in dismal failure. As did Johnson, Richard Nixon left the presidency in a shambles. Nixon did little to prevent the oil crisis. In fact, the Nixon administration seems to have encouraged its allies to raise oil prices in order to pay for large amounts of American military hardware. In announcing the Nixon doctrine, Nixon anointed Iran, Israel and Saudi Arabia as flag-bearers for the United States. The United States hid under the Iranian security blanket for almost a decade. Given the weakness of the regime and the shah's nonsensical dreams of turning Iran into one of the top five industrial and military powers in the world, the policy was cavalierly irresponsible. However, every president since 1967 shares the responsibility for Israel's mushrooming settlements in the occupied territories. Israel's value as a strategic asset to the United States is exceedingly limited: apart from driving back a Syrian invasion of Jordan in 1970, Israel has done little to help the United States in the Middle East. Instead its militancy and aggression have caused the United States much grief. Similarly, leaving Saudi Arabia wallowing in oil money and medieval stupor, a seedbed for Islamic fundamentalists, has created a huge future problem for the United States. It is difficult to point to a single occasion on which Saudi Arabia has served as a strategic asset.

The decision to leave the Persian Gulf was the end of fixed British positions (with the exception of Masirah Island) in the Middle East. In that sense, Labour succeeded in cutting the umbilical cord of empire; in another sense, the British never left. On the eve of the British withdrawal from the Persian Gulf, they deposed the sultan of Oman in 1970 because of his lackluster response to the growing insurgency in his country. Thereafter, Britain with Jordan and Iran conducted a sustained anti-guerilla campaign in Dhofar, culminating in victory in 1975. Critics alleged that Britain deliberately allowed the rebellion to fester in order to prolong British influence in Oman.[30] As events have shown, the United States is finding that there are few if any realistic substitutes for the special relationship in the Middle East and elsewhere. Henry Kissinger observes that, with the exception of the Edward Heath (1970–74) interregnum, the special relationship is alive and well. The United States appreciates the British contribution to the common enterprise, Kissinger notes, "both in the sophistication of British diplomacy and the seriousness of the British military effort". Aside from the United States, Britain's was the largest and most effective allied contribution to the Gulf war in 1991, while Britain in 1993 was the first NATO country to dispatch forces to Bosnia.[31] Even before the tragic events of September 11, 2001, George Bush insisted that Britain was America's staunchest ally. During the current campaigns in Afghanistan and Iraq, Britain has again proved to be the most reliable American partner. But Afghanistan today also proves that the Middle Eastern and Islamic world cannot be safely ignored, as Anglo-American policy makers falsely believed in the 1960s.

Notes

Introduction *The Anglo-American Middle East, 1961–1969*

1   Johnson to Wilson, January 11, 1968, National Security File, Special Head of State Correspondence, United Kingdom [2 of 4], Lyndon Baines Johnson Library, Austin, Texas.

2   Michael Middeke, "Britain's Global Military Role, Conventional Defence and Anglo-American Interdependence after Nassau", *Journal of Strategic Studies* 24, 1 (March, 2001): 143–64.

3   David Reynolds, *Britannia Overruled: British Policy and World Power in the 20th Century* (London: Longman, 1991), 208–9.

4   Reynolds, *Britannia Overruled*, 228.

5   Denis Healey, *The Time of My Life* (London: Michael Joseph, 1989), 280–1.

6   Saki Dockrill, *Britain's Retreat from East of Suez: The Choice between Europe and the World?* (New York: Palgrave, Macmillan, 2002), 114, 116.

7   Ben Pimlott, *Harold Wilson* (London: HarperCollins Publishers, 1992), 433.

8   Dean Rusk, *As I Saw It: A Secretary of State's Memoirs* (London: I. B. Tauris, 1991), 323–4.

9   Assistant secretary of state Benjamin Read to McGeorge Bundy, May 24, 1962, 611.86B/5-2462, State Department Decimal File, United States National Archives, Record Group 59 (hereafter cited as NARG 59), College Park, Maryland.

10   Yaacov Bar-Siman-Tov, "The United States and Israel since 1948: a 'Special Relationship'?", *Diplomatic History* 22, 2 (Spring, 1998): 231–62.

11   Abraham Ben-Zvi, *John F. Kennedy and the Politics of Arms Sales to Israel* (London: Frank Cass, 2002), 1, 50, 89; see also David Tal, "Symbol Not Substance?: Israel's Campaign to Acquire Hawk Missiles, 1960–1962", *International History Review* XXII, 2 (June, 2000): 304–17.

12   Moshe Gat, *Britain and the Conflict in the Middle East, 1964–1967: The Coming of the Six-Day War* (London: Praeger, 2003); Robert McNamara, "Britain, Nasser and the Outbreak of the Six Day War", *Journal of Contemporary History* 35, 4 (October, 2000): 619–39.

13   Robert McNamara, *Britain, Nasser and the Balance of Power in the Middle East 1952–1967: From the Egyptian Revolution to the Six Day War* (London: Frank Cass, 2003), 242.

14   Douglas Little, *American Orientalism: The United States and the Middle East since 1945* (London: University of North Carolina Press, 2002), 97–8.

15 Saunders to Walt Rostow, June 24, 1966, memorandums to the president, Walt W. Rostow, volume 7 [1 of 2], June 21–30, 1966, Lyndon Baines Johnson Library, Austin, TX.

16 Douglas Little, "A Fool's Errand: America and the Middle East, 1961–1969", in Diane B. Kunz (ed.), *The Diplomacy of the Crucial Decade: American Foreign Relations During the 1960s* (New York: Columbia University, 1994): 283–319.

17 Alan P. Dobson, *Anglo-American Relations in the Twentieth Century: Of Friendship, Conflict and the Rise and Decline of Superpowers* (London: Routledge, 1995); Warren I. Cohen, "Balancing American Interests in the Middle East: Lyndon Baines Johnson vs. Gamal Abdul Nasser," in Warren I. Cohen and Nancy Bernkopf Tucker (eds), *Lyndon Johnson Confronts the World: American Foreign Policy 1963–1968* (New York: Cambridge University Press, 1994) 279–309, quote from p. 281.

18 Rusk, *As I Saw it*, 322. Rusk's most recent biographer pays scant attention to the Middle East, and when he does, he is preoccupied with the Six Day War: Thomas W. Zeiler, *Dean Rusk: Defending the American Mission Abroad* (Wilmington, DE: Scholarly Resources, Inc. imprint, 2000); see also Thomas J. Schoenbaum, *Waging Peace and War: Dean Rusk in the Truman, Kennedy and Johnson Years* (New York: Simon Schuster, 1988).

19 Richard Austin Butler, *The Art of the Possible: The Memoirs of Lord Butler* (London: Hamish Hamilton, 1971), 256–7 (although Butler places his meeting with Johnson in May, not April as the archival record shows); the British records of the memorandum of conversation (hereafter cited as mc) are in Butler to Home, April 29, 1964, Prime Ministers' Records 11/4680 (hereafter cited as PREM with appropriate filing designations). Butler's biographer is inattentive to RAB's policies toward the Middle East during his tenure as foreign minister. See Anthony Howard, *RAB: The Life of R. A. Butler* (London: Jonathan Cape, 1987).

20 Alexander Frederick Douglas-Home, *The Way the Wind Blows: An Autobiography* (London: Collins, 1975); see also John Dickie, *The Uncommon Commoner: A Study of Sir Alec Douglas-Home* (London: Pall Mall Press, 1964); D. R. Thorpe, *Alec Douglas-Home* (London: Sinclair-Stevenson, 1996); Lyndon Johnson, *The Vantage Point: Perspectives of the Presidency, 1963–1969* (New York: Holt, Rinehart & Winston, 1971); Irving Bernstein, *Guns or Butter: The Presidency of Lyndon Johnson* (New York: Oxford University Press, 1996); Robert Dalleck, *Flawed Giant: Lyndon Johnson and His Times* (New York: Oxford University Press, 1998). Dalleck's study has been criticized for giving less than full treatment of Johnson's foreign policy; see Melvin Small reviewing the book in the *International History Review* XXI, 2 (June, 1999): 549–50.

21 Karl Pieragostini, *Britain, Aden and South Arabia: Abandoning Empire* (London: Macmillan Academic and Professional Ltd, 1991), 77.

22 Philip Ziegler, *Wilson: The Authorized Life of Lord Wilson of Rievaulx* (London: Weidenfeld & Nicolson, 1993), 206; Phillip Darby, *British Defence Policy East of Suez* (London: Oxford University Press, 1973); Jeremy Fielding,

"Coping with Decline: US Policy toward the British Defense Reviews of 1966", *Diplomatic History* XXIII, 4 (Fall, 1999): 633–56.

23 Ben Pimlott, *Harold Wilson* (London: HarperCollins, 1992), 350.

24 Austen Morgan, *Harold Wilson* (London: Pluto Press, 1992), 263; the same point is also made by Peter Paterson, *Tired and Emotional: The Life of Lord George-Brown* (London: Chatto & Windus, 1993), 167: "In fact, the government itself was instrumental in heightening the sterling crisis over the next few weeks by insisting on dramatising the 'mess' bequeathed them by the Tories."

25 Crossman's diary from Chris Wrigley, "Now You See it, Now You Don't: Harold Wilson and Labour's Foreign Policy 1964–70", in R. Coopey, S. Fielding and N. Tiratsoo (eds), *The Wilson Governments 1964–1970* (London: Pinter, 1993), 123–35, quote on p. 132.

26 Clive Ponting, *Breach of Promise: Labour in Power* (London: Hamish Hamilton, 1989), 52.

27 Henry Kissinger, *Diplomacy* (New York: Simon & Schuster, 1994), 531.

28 Michael Thornhill, "Britain and the Politics of the Arab League, 1943–50", in Michael J. Cohen and Martin Kolinsky (eds), *The Demise of the British Empire in the Middle East: Britain's Response to the Nationalist Movements, 1943–1955* (London: Frank Cass, 1998), 41–63.

29 Nigel John Ashton, *Eisenhower, Macmillan and the Problem of Nasser: Anglo-American Relations and Arab Nationalism, 1955–59* (London: Macmillan Press, 1996), 21.

30 Malcolm H. Kerr, *The Arab Cold War: Gamal 'Abd Al-Nasir and His Rivals, 1958–1970* (London: Oxford University Press, 1977), 3–7, 23.

31 Cohen, "Balancing American Interests in the Middle East", 279, 287.

32 Burton I. Kaufman, *The Arab Middle East: Inter-Arab Rivalry and Superpower Diplomacy* (New York: Twayne, 1996), 46.

33 *Ibid.*, 45; Ethan Nadelmann, "Setting the Stage: American Policy toward the Middle East, 1961–1966", *International Journal of Middle East Studies* XIV (November, 1982): 435–57; William Burns, *Economic Aid and American Foreign Policy toward Egypt, 1955–1981* (New York: State University Press of New York, 1985), 151–2.

34 Little, "A Fool's Errand: America and the Middle East, 1961–1969", 292; *idem*, "Gideon's Band: America and the Middle East since 1945", *Diplomatic History* 18, 4 (Fall, 1994): 513–40. In this historiographic essay on US relations with the Middle East after World War II, Little is not overly concerned with events in 1964. *Idem*, "Choosing Sides: Lyndon Johnson and the Middle East", in Robert A. Divine, *The Johnson Years, vol. 3, LBJ at Home and Abroad* (Lawrence: University Press of Kansas, 1994), 150–97, notes British pressure on the United States to support British policy in the Middle East without outlining the full extent of this policy (see p. 158).

35 Kaufman, *The Arab Middle East*, 50.

36 Burns, *American Policy toward Egypt, 1955–1981*, 172 (for quote), 168.

37 Robert W. Stookey, *America and the Arab States: An Uneasy Encounter* (New York: John Wiley & Sons, Inc., 1975), 172.

38 Kerr, *The Arab Cold War: Gamal Ábd Al-Nasir and His Rivals, 1958–1970*, 154:

"What had he really accomplished in his endless involvements with other Arab states? The Union with Syria had collapsed, the Ba'th had defied him, the Yemen war had cost him much and gained him nothing, the Iraqis had given him nothing but trouble, and Husayn [king of Jordan] and Faisal were still in power. What successes he had enjoyed had come by promising, threatening, pretending, juggling, borrowing on the resources lent him by the Russians and Americans. He had posed as a great power, but without possessing a great power's means. The successes, which were mainly in the 1950's, kept him going for an extraordinary long time, even beyond the Six Day War, but left him saddled with problems that were eventually fatal."

39 Bundy memorandum to the president, January 12, 1965, National Security File, Bundy memorandums, VIII, 1/1-2/28/65, Lyndon B. Johnson Library, Austin, Texas (hereafter cited as NSF, LBJL).

40 For an early assessment of the recently declassified record, see Tore T. Petersen, "Crossing the Rubicon? Britain's Withdrawal from the Middle East, 1964–1968: A Bibliographical Review", *International History Review* XXX, 2 (June, 2000): 318–40.

41 Travaskis to Sandy, February 20, 1964, PREM 11/4678.

42 Eilts to State Department, January 17, 1967, POL 27 Saud-UAR.

43 Memorandum of conversation, J. A. N. Graham (Foreign Office) and the Saudi Arabian ambassador, February 16, 1967, Foreign and Commonwealth Office, 8/59/B4/2, Public Record Office, Kew, England.

Prologue   *The Great Powers and the Middle East, 1952–1961*

1 Edward Ingram, *The British Empire as a World Power* (London: Frank Cass, 2001), 7.

2 Paul Kennedy, *The Rise and Fall of the Great Powers: Economic Change and Military Conflict from 1500 to 2000* (New York: Random House, 1987); Gordon Martel, "The Meaning of Power: Rethinking the Decline and Fall of Great Britain", *International History Review* XIII, 4 (November, 1991): 662–94.

3 Evelyn Shuckburgh, *Descent to Suez* (London: Weidenfeld & Nicolson, 1986), 207–10.

4 Tore T. Petersen, "Transfer of Power in the Middle East", *International History Review* XIX, 4 (November, 1997): 852–65.

5 Briefing paper to the President, "Relative US–UK Roles in the Middle East", November 27, 1953, Ann Whitman File, international series, Bermuda misc., Dwight D. Eisenhower Library, Abilene, Kansas (hereafter cited as DDEL).

6 Robert O. Freedman, *Soviet Policy toward the Middle East since 1970* (New York: Praeger, 1982), 40–1.

7 John Lewis Gaddis, *We Now Know: Rethinking Cold War History* (Oxford: Clarendon Press, 1998), 163–4.

8 Freedman, *Soviet Policy*, 1, 15; see also George W. Breslauer, *Soviet Strategy in the Middle East* (Boston: Unwin Hyman, 1990); Galia Golan, *Soviet Policies in the Middle East from World War Two to Gorbachev* (New York: Cambridge University Press, 1990).

9 Wm. Roger Louis, "The Tragedy of the Anglo-Egyptian Agreement of 1954",

in Louis, Wm. Roger and Roger Owen (eds), *Suez 1956: the Crisis and Its Consequences* (New York: Clarendon Press, 1989), 43–71.

10 Mary Ann Heiss, "The United States, Great Britain, and the Creation of the Iranian Oil Consortium, 1953–1954", *International History Review* XVI, 3 (August, 1994): 511–35.

11 Geoffrey Warner, "The United States and the Suez Crisis", *International Affairs* 67 (April, 1991), 307 n. 16.

12 Eden to cabinet, October 4, 1955, Cabinet papers (hereafter cited CAB and filing designations), CAB 128/29, CM (55), Public Record Office, Kew, England.

13 Michael B. Oren, "A Winter of Discontent: Britain's Crisis in Jordan, December 1955–March 1956", *International Journal of Middle East Studies* 22 (May, 1990): 174–84.

14 Tore T. Petersen, *The Middle East between the Great Powers: Anglo-American Conflict and Cooperation, 1952–7* (London: Macmillan Press, 2000).

15 Memorandum of conversation (hereafter cited as mc), Dulles and journalist Don Cook, February 28, 1957, the political correspondence of the Foreign Office (hereafter cited as FO with appropriate filing designations), FO 371/12692/EA 1081/15, Public Record Office, Kew, England; mc Hoover and Australian ambassador Casey, November 20, 1956, FO 371/1189916/JE 1094/309; mc Hoover and Caccia, November 23, 1956, FO 371/121274/V 1045/138.

16 National Security Council Paper 5801, "Long Range US Policy toward the Near East", January 10, 1958, and staff study of same, White House, Office of Special Assistant, National Security Affairs, DDEL.

17 Malcolm H. Kerr, *The Arab Cold War: Gamal 'Abd al-Nasir and His Rivals, 1958–1970* (London: Oxford University Press, 1977), 1–23.

18 Briefing paper for the President, "Macmillan Talks, March 19–23, 1959", n.d., Briefing book for the President, Ann Whitman File, International Series, Macmillan visit, March 1959 (5), DDEL; Marion Farouk-Sluglett and Peter Sluglett, *Iraq since 1958: From Revolution to Dictatorship* (London: I. B. Tauris, 1990), 56–7.

19 Michael B. Oren, *Six Days of War: June 1967 and the Making of the Modern Middle East* (Oxford University Press, 2002), 38.

20 Memorandum by Francis Russell, secretary of state, John Foster Dulles' special assistant; "U.S. Policies toward Nasser", August 4, 1956, United States Department of State, *Papers Relating to the Foreign Relations of the United States* (hereafter cited as FRUS, with year and volume), 1955–1957, vol. XVI, *Suez Crisis, July 26–December 31, 1956* (Government Printing Office, Washington, 1990), 140–1.

21 Nasser's book from Anthony Nutting, *Nasser* (New York: Dutton, 1972), 76, 77; Ritchie Ovendale, "Great Britain and the Anglo-American Invasion of Jordan and Lebanon in 1958", *International History Review* XVI, 2 (May, 1994): 284–303; Douglas Little, "Ike, Lebanon, and the 1958 Middle East Crisis", *Diplomatic History* 20, 1 (Winter, 1996): 27–54; Nigel John Ashton, "'A Great New Venture'? – Anglo-American Cooperation in the Middle East

and the Response to the Iraqi Revolution July 1958", *Diplomacy and Statecraft* 4, 1 (March, 1993): 59–89.

22 Douglas Little, "Gideon's Band: America and the Middle East since 1945", *Diplomatic History* 18, 4 (Fall, 1994): 513–40; William J. Burns, *Economic Aid and American Policy toward Egypt, 1955–1981* (New York: State University Press of New York, 1985), 113.

23 Jeffrey A. Lefebvre, "The United States and Egypt: Confrontation and Accommodation in Northeast Africa, 1956–60", *Middle Eastern Studies* 29, 2 (April, 1993): 321–38.

24 Henry William Brands, "What Eisenhower and Dulles Saw in Nasser: Personalities and Interest in U.S.–Egyptian Relations", *American–Arab Affairs* 17 (Summer, 1986): 44–54, the quote is from page 53.

25 Briefing memorandum for the president by undersecretary of state Douglas Dillon, "The President's Conversation with President Nasser", September 25, 1960, DDE diary series, Staff Notes – September 1960 (2), DDEL.

26 American embassy to State Department, December 24, 1960, FRUS 1958–60, XIII: 609–11.

27 Kerr, *The Arab Cold War*, 26.

28 Oren, *Six Days of War*, 38.

I John F. Kennedy Confronts the Middle East: A New Beginning?

1 Fawaz A. Gerges, *The Superpowers and the Middle East: Regional and International Policies, 1955–1967* (Boulder, CO: Westview Press, 1994), 148.

2 Ernest R. May and Philip D. Zelikow, *The Kennedy Tapes: Inside the White House During the Cuban Missile Crisis* (London: Belknap Press of Harvard University Press, 1997), 670; see also William Taubman, *Khrushchev: The Man and His Era* (New York: W. W. Norton & Company, 2003).

3 Vladislav Zubok and Constantine Pleshakov, *Inside Kremlin's Cold War: From Stalin to Khrushchev* (Cambridge, MA: Harvard University Press, 1996), 175–94; James G. Richter, *Khrushchev's Double Bind: International Pressures and Domestic Coalition Politics* (Baltimore: Johns Hopkins University Press, 1994).

4 Burton I. Kaufman, "John F. Kennedy as World Leader: A Perspective on the Literature", in Michael J. Hogan (ed.), *America in the World: The Historiography of American Foreign Relations since 1941* (Cambridge: Cambridge University Press, 1995): 326–57.

5 Arthur M. Schlesinger, *A Thousand Days: John F. Kennedy in the White House* (New York: Fawcett Premier, 1992), 64, 200.

6 Douglas Little, "The New Frontier on the Nile: JFK, Nasser, and Arab Nationalism", *Journal of American History* 75, 2 (September, 1988), 504.

7 Komer to JFK, December 8, 1961, FRUS 1961–3, XVII: 362.

8 Malcolm H. Kerr, *The Arab Cold War: Gamal 'Abd al-Nasir and His Rivals, 1958–1970* (London: Oxford University Press, 1971), 26, 96.

9 Walworth Barbour (US embassy London) to State Department, "Principal Problems Presently Outstanding between Britain and the United States", January 11, 1960, United States National Archives, College Park, Maryland,

Record Group 59, State Department Decimal File, 611.41/1-1160 (hereafter cited as NARG 59 with appropriate filing designations).

10 See memorandum R. S. Crawford (Foreign Office), "Talking Points on Persian Gulf" to United Kingdom embassy Iran, January 4, 1963, Political Correspondence of the Foreign Office, FO 371/168632/B 1052/4 (hereafter cited as FO 371 with appropriate filing designations), Public Record Office (hereafter cited as PRO), Kew, England.

11 Karl Pieragostini, *Britain, Aden and South Arabia: Abandoning Empire* (London: Macmillan, 1991), 20–40.

12 Brian Lapping, *End of Empire* (London: Granada Publishing, 1985), 287; Glen Balfour-Paul, *The End of Empire: Britain's Relinquishment of Power in Her Last Three Arab Dependencies* (Cambridge: Cambridge University Press, 1991); David Holden, *Farewell to Arabia* (London: Faber & Faber, 1966), 71–2; R. J. Gavin, *Aden under British Rule, 1839–1967* (London: C. Hurst & Company, 1975); Kennedy Trevaskis, *Shades of Amber: A South Arabian Episode* (London: Hutchinson, 1968); James Lunt, *The Barren Rocks of Aden* (London: Jenkins, 1966); for Yemen, see State Department to American Legation, Taiz, Yemen, December 28, 1960, 641. 86H/12-2460; on Omani rebels, see for instance Barbour to State Department, January 18, 1961, 641.86E/1-1861, NARG 59; for the importance of Buraimi, see: John C. Wilkinson, *Arabia's Frontiers: The Story of Britain's Boundary Drawing in the Desert* (London: I. B. Tauris, 1991); for an American assessment of British defense policy in the Gulf, see David Bruce (American ambassador United Kingdom) to State Department, April 8, 1963, Political Affairs and Relations, 7 UK-US, State Department Central Foreign Policy Files, NARG 59 (hereafter cited as POL with appropriate filing designations).

13 Mc Robert Strong, State Department and Henry Moses and Christian Herter, Socony Mobil, March 2, 1963, POL NR. EAST-US.

14 Yergin, *The Prize*, 524, 555–8.

15 James A. Bill, *The Eagle and the Lion: The Tragedy of American–Iranian Relations* (London: Yale University Press, 1988), 137.

16 Eden to cabinet, February 16, 1953, quoted from Norman Brook to Eden, April 14, 1956, PREM 11/1457.

17 Alistair Horne, *Macmillan, 1957–1986* (London: Macmillan, 1989), the quote is from p. 579; see also 279–97; memorandum by Home to Macmillan, February 24, 1961, Prime Minister's papers, PREM 11/3326, PRO, Kew, England (hereafter cited as PREM with appropriate filing designations); Harold Macmillan, *Pointing the Way, 1959–1961* (London: Macmillan, 1972), 308. [For the quotes: "I must somehow convince him . . .", and "Apart from a formal telegram . . ."]

18 Schlesinger, *A Thousand Days*, 350; Theodore C. Sorensen, *Kennedy* (New York: Smithmark, 1995), 558–9.

19 For examples of Macmillan's pleading, see: memorandum of conversation (hereafter cited as mc) by Macmillan and Harriman, February 27, 1961, FO 371/156455/Au 1054/2; mc Macmillan and Kennedy, April 28, 1962, PREM 11/3783; mc Home and Rusk, January 16, 1962, FO 371/162591/Au 1051/1/G ["how much the United States Government valued . . . "]; for an example of

United States being concerned about British official and public opinion, see for instance: mc Rusk and David Ormsby Gore (United Kingdom ambassador United States), January 11, 1963, 611.41/1-1163, NARG 59 ["The Secretary asked the Ambassador whether he would comment on the general malaise of the press in the United Kingdom".]; for an American assessment of Macmillan, see Bruce to State Department, December 13, 1961, 611. 41/12-1261, NARG 59 ["He is a political animal, shrewd, subtle in maneuver, undisputed master in his Cabinet house. . . . But this is no mean man".]

20 Mc Macmillan and Kennedy, April 28, 1962, PREM 11/3783.
21 John Darwin, *The End of the British Empire: The Historical Debate* (Oxford: Blackwell, 1991), 60–1.
22 Miriam Joyce, *Kuwait 1945–1996: An Anglo-American Perspective* (London: Frank Cass, 1998); Kennedy's approval in memorandum of NSC meeting, June 29, 1961; see also; mc lord Hood and Kohler *et al.* February 2, 1961; memorandum by Robert B. Elwood (Bureau of Intelligence and Research) to Robert Strong (director Office Near Eastern Affairs), June 26, 1961; Home to Rusk, June 29, 1961; all in FRUS, 1961–1963, XVII, *Near East, 1962–1963*, 20, 21, 25, 160, 170, 172; John B. Kelly, *Arabia, the Gulf and the West* (New York: Basic Books, 1980), 277; memorandum by Lord Privy Seal (Edward Heath) to cabinet, October 2, 1961, Cabinet Records (hereafter cited as CAB with appropriate filing designations), 129/106, C. (61), 140, PRO.
23 American consul Kuwait to secretary of state, July 1, 1961, 686D. 87/7-161, NARG 59.
24 American embassy London to department of state, September 11, 1961, 641. 86D/9-1161, NARG 59.
25 For an example of Britain attempting to involve the United States in concrete practical cooperation, see Tore T. Petersen, "Anglo-American Rivalry in the Middle East: The Struggle for the Buraimi Oasis, 1952–1957", *International History Review* XIV, 1 (February, 1992): 78–9.
26 Home to Rusk, July 2, 1961, and Rusk to Harold Caccia (United Kingdom ambassador United States), July 3, 1961; both in FRUS, 1961–1963: XVII: 177, 178; Kelly, *Arabia*, 277; Caccia to Foreign Office, July 4, 1961, FO 371/156848/BM 1083/72.
27 Mc Greenhill and Talbot *et al.* January 11, 1962, 611.41/1-1162, NARG 59.
28 Little, "The New Frontier", 510, 511.
29 Abraham Ben-Zvi, *John F. Kennedy and the Politics of Arms Sales to Israel* (London: Frank Cass, 2002), 50.
30 Kennedy to Nasser, May 27, 1963, POL 15 – 1 UAR.
31 Yaacov Bar-Siman-Tov, "The United States and Israel since 1948: 'A Special Relationship'?", *Diplomatic History* 22, 2 (Spring, 1998): 231–72.
32 Badeau to secretary of state, March 7, 1963, POL 1 UAR-US, NARG 59.
33 Assistant secretary of state Benjamin Read to McGeorge Bundy, May 24, 1962, 611.86B/5-2462, NARG 59.
34 Little, "The New Frontier", 510, 511; Burns, *Economic Aid*, 3, 121, 122, 134; for the rationale behind the American approach to Nasser, see Rusk to Kennedy, January 10, 1962; FRUS, 1961–1963, XVII: 384–95; memorandum Talbot to Chester Bowles (undersecretary of state), March 21, 1962,

611.86B/3-2162; for United States private view on the importance of aid to Egypt, see memorandum Robert Komer to Kennedy: "Though all this seems impressive, it is in fact just enough to keep Nasser afloat economically", May 28, 1962; memorandum by Robert Strong, "Whither United States–United Arab Republic Relations", May 24, 1962; both in FRUS, 1961–1963, XVII: 677–82; 686–7; mc Talbot and Stevens, May 3, 1962, FO 371/165357/VG 103145/9; memorandum by Caccia, November 11, 1963, FO 371/168479/Au 16375/3.

2 Kennedy, Nasser, Macmillan and the War in Yemen, 1962–1963

1 Dana Adams Schmidt, *Yemen: The Unknown War* (New York: Holt, Rinehart & Winston, 1968); Edgar O'Ballance, *The War in Yemen* (Hamden, CT: Archon Books, 1971).
2 Nadav Safran, *Saudi Arabia: The Ceaseless Quest for Security* (London: Cornell University Press, 1991) pp 93–4, argues: "The speed and scope of the Egyptian intervention clearly indicated Nasser's prior knowledge of and preparation for the coup"; see also mc David Ormsby-Gore (United Kingdom ambassador to Washington) and Kennedy, February 27, 1963, PREM 11/4357 ["It was sickening to have to listen to Egyptian complaints about interference from outside into the affairs of Yemen. We all knew that the revolt had been to a considerable extent engineered by Nasser who had had all ready to fly in on the first day of the rising"]; F. Gregory Gause III, *Saudi–Yemeni Relations: Domestic Structures and Foreign Influence* (New York: Columbia University Press, 1990), p. 59, argues: "There is now no disputing the fact of Egyptian foreknowledge of and support for the coup which overthrew Iman Muhammed al-Badr".
3 Memorandum by Komer, October 5, 1962, FRUS, 1961–3, XVIII: 161.
4 Christopher J. Mullen, *Resolution of the Yemen Crisis, 1963: A Case Study in Mediation* (Washington: Institute for the Study of Diplomacy, School of Foreign Service, Georgetown University, 1980), 2; Fred Halliday, *Arabia without Sultans* (Middlesex: Penguin Books, 1979); David Ledger, *Shifting Sands: The British in South Arabia* (London: Peninsula Publishing, 1983); State Department to Rusk, September 27, 1962 ["We wish UAR understand, however, USG has vital interest in maintenance security in Persian Gulf area, which dependent UK position in Aden area. USG could not accept campaign mounted from Yemen against this position"]; Badeau to State Department, October 1, 1962; both in FRUS, 1961–1963, XVIII, *Near East, 1962–1963*, 141, 150.
5 Chargé d'Affaires, James N. Cortada, American embassy Taiz, Yemen to State Department, April 22, 1964, POL 2-3 Yemn.
6 Parker T. Hart, *Saudi Arabia and the United States: Birth of a Security Partnership* (Bloomington: Indiana University Press, 1998), 119, 121 (for quote).
7 Administrative history of the department of state, Chapter 4: "The Near East and South Asia", Section G. Yemen, p. 1, Box 2 [1 of 2], Lyndon Baines Johnson Library, Austin, TX (hereafter cited as LBJL).

8 Gerges, "The Kennedy Administration and the Egyptian–Saudi Conflict in Yemen", 292–311.

9 Komer, memorandum for the president, October 4, 1962, National Security Files, Saudi Arabia, Faysal briefing book, 10/3/62-10/5/62, John F. Kennedy Library, Boston, MA.

10 Hart, *Saudi Arabia and the United States*, 114.

11 Rusk to American embassy Saudi Arabia, November 7, 1962, FRUS, 1961–3, XVIII: 203–5.

12 Robert W. Stookey, *America and the Arab States: An Uneasy Encounter* (New York: John Wiley & Sons, 1975), 183.

13 Kennedy's letter in Rusk to American embassy, Saudi Arabia, November 2, 1962, FRUS, 1961–3, XVIII: 198–9.

14 Talbot to Rusk October 9, 1962; Nasser's request, see Badeau to State Department, October 10, 1962; Rusk to American embassy Saudi Arabia, November 7, 1962; and to American embassy UAR, November 10, 1962; Rusk to Kennedy, November 12, 1962; Talbot memorandum to Rusk, January 2, 1963; all in FRUS, 1961–1963, XVIII: 172–3, 174–5, [on the bombing, see editorial note pp. 199–200], 203, 209, 210, 218, 219, 292, 293–4; memorandum Robert C. Strong to Talbot, December 11, 1962, 786H.00/12-1162, NARG 59.

15 Burns, *American Policy toward Egypt*, 137.

16 Kennedy to Nasser, January 19, 1963, FRUS 1961–3, XVIII: 309–10.

17 Komer to JFK, July 2, 1963, FRUS, 1961–3, XVIII: 621–2; administrative history, Yemen, 4–5.

18 Hart, *Saudi Arabia and the United States*, 157–61.

19 Little, "The New Frontier", 521; Talbot to United States embassy Paris, January 7, 1963, 786H.00/1-763; for an assessment of Saudi and Egyptian motives, see American embassy Dahran to secretary of state, February 13, 1963, POL 26 Yemen; both in NARG 59; McGeorge Bundy, president's special assistant for national security affairs to Rusk and Robert McNamara, secretary of defense, February 27, 1963; memorandum by Komer, "The Next Round in Yemen", September 20, 1963; both in FRUS, XVIII: 366, 367, 710; mc Walmsley (United Kingdom) and Eilts (United States), November 23, 1962, FO 371/162960/BM 1015/345.

20 Kennedy to Faisal, February 22, 1963, FRUS 1961–3, XVIII: 355–7.

21 Administrative history, Yemen, 3.

22 David Ormsby-Gore (United Kingdom ambassador Washington) to FO, October 13, 1962 and October 22, 1962; FO 371/163949/BM 1015/125/G and FO 371/162950/BM 1015/148; Macmillan to Kennedy, November 15, 1962, Kennedy to Macmillan, November 16, 1962; both in FO 371/162957/BM 1015/294G and 300G; Wamsley "Talking Points on Yemen" for cabinet, November 21, 1962, FO 371/162960/BM 1015/357/G; oral message Kennedy to Nasser, December 24, 1962, FRUS, 1961–1963, XVIII: 275–6.

23 Mc Macmillan, Home *et al.*, January 10, 1963, PREM 11/4446; for documentation of the White Army see the following folders in FO 371/168871-74; for arms supplies to Saudi Arabia, see: FO 371/168885-89; for an American view of British arms sales to Saudi Arabia, see American embassy London to secretary of state, May 21, 1963, and December 16, 1963 ["British Aircraft

Corporation representatives are currently in Saudi Arabia attempting to sell Thunderbird surface to air missiles, radar warning systems, anti-tank missiles and supersonic fighters".]; both in DEF[ense] 12-5-Saud, NARG 59; Maxwell D. Taylor, chairman joint chiefs of staff, March 6, 1963, FRUS, 1961–1963, XVIII: 394–6.

24 Robert McNamara, *Britain, Nasser and the Balance of Power in the Middle East, 1952–1967* (London: Frank Cass, 2003), 181.

25 Kennedy to Macmillan, January 26, 1963, PREM 11/4357; see also Rusk to American embassy London, January 23, 1963, 786H.02/1-2463, NARG 59.

26 Harold Macmillan, *At the End of the Day* (London: Macmillan, 1973), 274; for the Foreign Office view, see: Walmsley brief on Yemen, December 12, 1962, FO 371/162963/BM 1015/410; Johnston to FO, February 8, 1963, PREM 11/4357.

27 Macmillan to Kennedy, February 14, 1963, PREM 11/4357.

28 For continued American efforts to press for British recognition of Yemen, see: Rusk to American embassy London, February 28, 1963, POL 26 Yemen, NARG 59; Johnston downplays these differences in his memoirs, see Charles Hepburn Johnston, *The View from the Steamer Point: Being an Account of Three Years in Aden* (New York: Frederick A. Praeger, 1964), 161–2; see also David Ledger, *Shifting Sands: The British in South Arabia* (Peninsular Publishing, 1983).

29 Johnston to secretary of state for Colonies, February 20, 1963, FO 371/168824/BM 1051/72 (E); Rusk to American embassy United Kingdom, February 28, 1963, FRUS, 1961–1963, XVIII: 379.

30 For examples of American suspicions of British gun-running in Yemen, see Rusk to American embassy London, December 19, 1962, 786H.00/12-1962; American embassy to Rusk, December 29, 1962, 786H00/12-2962; Wheelock to Rusk, January 2, 1963, 786H.00/1-263; for examples of British attitudes Aden, see Wheelock to Rusk, January 14, 1963, 786H.00/1-1463; and Wheelock to department of state, April 8, 1963, POL 26 Yemen; all in NARG 59.

31 Cf. W. Taylor Fain, "'Unfortunate Arabia': The United States, Great Britain and Yemen, 1955–63", *Diplomacy and Statecraft* 12, 2 (June, 2001): 125–52.

32 Bruce to State Department, April 4, 1963, POL 7, UK-US.

33 American embassy, London to State Department, May 31, 1963, POL UK-US.

34 Eilts to State Department, March 16, 1963, POL 17 UK-Yemen.

35 American embassy London to State Department, May 31, 1963, POL UK-US.

36 Mc Kermit Roosevelt and James Grant, deputy assistant secretary Near East, January 28, 1963, 611.86/1-2863; mc Strong and Henry Moses et al., Socony Mobil, February 21, 1963, PET 6, Near East; both in NARG 59.

37 Little, "JFK, Nasser, and Arab Nationalism", 520; for Egyptian pressure to recognize Yemen, see Badeau to State Department, October 10, 1962; and memorandum by Komer, October 12, 1962, State Department to Cairo, March 2, 1963; Nasser to Kennedy, March 10, 1963; all in FRUS, 1961–1963, XVIII: 174–5, 177–8, 390, 391, 411; for brandishing the aid weapon, Rusk to

American embassy Cairo, March 3, 1963, POL 26 Yemen; Badeau to Rusk, March 7, 1963, POL 1 UAR-US; both in NARG 59.

38   Robert Strong to Talbot, March 13, 1963, POL 17, UAR-US.

39   United Kingdom embassy Washington to Foreign Office, May 18, 1963, FO 371/168832/BM 1071/66; mc Eilts (United States) and Brenchley (United Kingdom), June 21, 1963, FO 371/1688343/BM 1071/66.

40   Brenchley (Saudi Arabia) to Foreign Office, March 7, 1963, FO 371/172877/VG 1091/5; *ibid.*, June 26, 1963, FO 371/168798/BM 1015/246/G.

41   Badeau to State Department, July 11, 1963; Komer to Kennedy, July 15, 1963, FRUS 1961–3, XVIII, 640, 643.

42   Memorandum by Komer, "The Next Round in Yemen", September 20, 1963, FRUS, 1961–1963, XVIII: 710–13.

43   Rusk to Cairo, October 19, 1963, FRUS, 1961–1963, XVIII: 752, 753, mc Eilts (United States) and Higgins (United Kingdom), October 3, 1963, FO 371/168838/BM 1071/143; Little, "JFK, Nasser, and Arab Nationalism", 524–5; on Rusk warning the Egyptians, see Rusk to Ormsby Gore, October 19, 1963; mc Kamel and Davies (United States), October 29, 1963; both in POL 23-10 Yemen, NARG 59.

44   McGeorge Bundy to Senator J. William Fulbright, November 11, 1963, FRUS 1961–63 XVIII: 775–6.

45   Memorandum by Harold Caccia, November 11, 1963, FO 371/168479/Au 16375/3.

3   *The Flickering Embers of Empire: Douglas-Home, Lyndon Johnson and the Middle East*

1   Talbot to Rusk, November 23, 1963, FRUS, 1961–3, XVIII: 804.

2   Robert A. Caro, *The Years of Lyndon Johnson: Means of Ascent* (London: Bodley Head, 1990).

3   George C. Herring, *LBJ and Vietnam: A Different Kind of War* (Austin: University of Texas Press, 1994), 17.

4   Rusk to Johnson, February 7, 1964, United Kingdom 2/12-13/64, PM Home Visit, Briefing Book [1of 2], Country File, National Security File (hereafter cited as CFNSF), Lyndon Baines Johnson Library, Austin, Texas (hereafter cited as LBJL). According to Rusk, Home succeeded in establishing personal relations with the president, in a circular telegram of February 14, 1964, the secretary of state noted: "the warm atmosphere of the talks . . . cannot be over-stated", FRUS 1964–8, XII: 454–5.

5   D. R. Thorpe, *Alec Douglas-Home* (London: Sinclair-Stevenson, 1996), 340.

6   W. T. Beale, minister for economic affairs, London to State Department, November 21, 1963, POL 2-3 UK.

7   Peter Henessy, *Muddling Through: Power, Politics and the Quality of Government in Postwar Britain* (London: Victor Gollancz, 1996), 239.

8   James N. Corteda, US Chargé d'Affaires, Yemen to State Department, April 22, 1964, POL 2-3 Yemen.

9   Robert O. Freedman, *Soviet Policy toward the Middle East since 1970* (New York: Praeger Publishers, 1982), 20.

10   Komer to Bundy, April 2, 1964, Yemen vol. I. Memos 11/63-6/64, CFNSF, LBJL.

11 Butler to Home, March 30, 1964, PREM 11/4678.

12 Eilts to State Department, December 19, 1963, POL 27 Yemen.

13 Komer to Bundy, April 21, 1964, United Kingdom, Meetings with Butler, 4/64, CFNSF, LBJL; see also mc Rusk and Butler, April 27 in *ibid.*

14 Hart to State Department, November 30, 1963, FRUS 1961–3, XVIII: 808-11.

15 Bundy and Komer, memorandum for the president, April 29, 1964, memos to the president, McGeorge Bundy, vol. 6 [1 of 2], 7/1-9/30/64, NSF, LBJL. In fact, Komer bombarded the president with memorandums urging him to avoid alignment with Britain, see for instance, Komer to Bundy, April 28, 1964, FRUS 1964–8, XXI: 632–4.

16 Mc Rusk and Butler, April 27, 1964, United Kingdom, Meetings with Butler, 4/6, CFNSF, LBJL.

17 Mc Rusk and Butler, April 27, 1964, PREM 11/4787.

18 Butler to Home, April 29, 1964, PREM 11/4680.

19 Mc Rusk and Greenhill in State Department circular telegram, August 22, 1964, POL 1 Saud-UAR, NARG.

20 *Ibid.*

21 Rusk to Butler, August 28, 1964, POL 1 Saud-UAR, NARG.

22 Butler's reaction in Rusk to American embassy London, September 2, 1964; see also David Bruce (US ambassador United Kingdom) to State Department, August 29, 1964; both in POL 1 Saud-UAR, NARG.

23 Komer to Johnson, memorandum for the president, September 12, 1964, memos to the president, McGeorge Bundy, Vol. 6 [1 of 2], 7/1-9/30/64, NSF, LBJL.

24 Little, "Lyndon Johnson and the Middle East", 160.

25 Julian Paget, *Last Post: Aden 1964–1967* (London: Faber & Faber, 1969), 49, 51; Michael Dewar, *Brush Fire Wars: Minor Campaigns of the British Army since 1945* (London: Robert Hale, 1990), 119; Air Chief Marshall Sir David Lee, *Flight from the Middle East* (London: HMSO, 1980), 205; Bruce Hoffman, "British Air Power in Peripheral Conflict, 1919–1976", United States Air Force/Rand Publication Series (Santa Monica, 1989), 87–96.

26 Sam Belk to Bundy, "'Postmortem' on the Yemen and the Role of the U.S. in the Security Council", May 29, 1964, CFNSF, Middle East, Yemen Cables, Vol. I, 11/63–6/64, LBJL.

27 United Kingdom mission to UN, March 28, 1964, PREM 11/4679.

28 Quoted from Paget, *Last Post Aden*, 52.

29 Trevaskis to colonial secretary, March 30, 1964, PREM 11/4679.

30 Kennedy Trevaskis, *Shades of Amber: A South Arabian Episode* (London: Hutchinson, 1968), 210.

31 Rusk to American consul, Aden, March 27, 1964, CFNSF, Yemen – Cables, Vol. I 11/63 – 6/64, LBJL.

32 Komer to Bundy, April 2, 1964, CFNSF Middle East, Yemen memos, vol. I 11/63- 6/64, LBJL.

33 Bundy memorandum to the president, April 9, 1964, McGeorge Bundy, vol. 3 4/1-30/64, LBJL.

34 Mc Rusk and Stevenson, April 9, 1964, FRUS 1964–8, XXI: 623, note 4.

35 Belk to Bundy, May 29, 1964.

36 Home to LBJ, April 10, 1964, PREM 11/4679.
37 LBJ to Home, n.d., *ibid.*
38 Mc LBJ and Butler, in Butler to Home, April 29, 1964, PREM 11/4680; see also Burke Trend to Prime Minister, April 22, 1964, PREM 11/4680.
39 Mc Butler and Rusk, April 27, 1964, PREM 11/4798.
40 Wheelock to State Department, April 27, 1964, POL 2 Aden.
41 Paget, *Last Post Aden*, 53–5.
42 Foreign office paper, "UAR Subversion of the South Arabian Federation", n.d. in Eilts to State Department, May 8, 1964, POL 2, Aden.
43 *Ibid.*
44 Lee, *Flight from the Middle East*, 39.
45 Briefing from ministry of defence, "Operations in the Radfan Area", to prime minister, May 2, 1964; see also Home in House of Commons, May 4, 1964, both in PREM 11/4680; Wheelock to State Department, May 4, Yemen, Vol. I, Cables 11/63-6/64, CFNSF, LBJL.
46 Wheelock to State Department, August 1, 1964, POL 2 Aden, NARG 59; Paget, *Last Post Aden,* 109.
47 Butler to Home, April 20, 1964, PREM 11/4718.
48 Trevaskis to Sandys, February 20, 1964, PREM 11/4678.
49 *Ibid.*
50 Burke Trend to prime minister, April 22, 1964, PREM 11/4680.
51 Home to Butler, prime minister personal minute, 49/64, May 5, 1964, PREM 11/4680.
52 Wheelock to State Department, October 3, 1964, POL 14 Aden; Donald Bergus, United States embassy Cairo to State Department, August 29, 1964, POL 19 Aden.
53 Balfour-Paul, *End of Empire*, 82.
54 American embassy London to Department of State, January 13, 1964, DEF 12-5 Saud.
55 Rusk to American embassy, London, January 9, 1964; Hart to department of state, January 12, 1964 DEF 12 Saud, NA.
56 Rusk to American embassy Jidda, February 5, 1964, DEF 12-5 Saud.
57 'Supplement of Record of Meeting March 6 to Discuss Lightnings for Saudi Arabia', March 6, 1964, F0 371/174683/Bs 1192/14G.
58 *Ibid.*; see also 'Draft of a Meeting March 6 to Discuss Lightnings for Saudi Arabia', March 6, 1964, FO 371/174683/Bs 1192/14G.
59 John Evarts Horner, consul general Jidda, to State Department, April 1, 1964, POL 2 Saud.
60 Ball to American embassy, London, September 21, 1964, FRUS 1964–8, XXI: 449–50.
61 Crowe to Butler, October 14, 1964, FO 371/174676/BS 1051/2.

4 *Trying to Hold the Line: Lyndon Johnson and the British Role East of Suez*

1 Administrative history of the State Department, D. Bilateral Relations with Western Europe: Great Britain, Box 1, pp. 3–4, LBJL.
2 Mc Gordon Walker and Rusk, October 26, 1964, PREM 13/109.
3 Mc Gordon Walker and Rusk, October 26, 1964, FO 371/178584/ VG 1023/38.

4 Stewart to cabinet, March 24, 1965, CAB 129/120 part 2.

5 Bundy to Johnson, December 10, 1964, MPMGB, vol. 7 [1of 2], 10/1-12/31/64, NSF, LBJL.

6 George W. Ball, *The Past Has Another Pattern* (New York: Norton & Company, 1972), 336; George Brown, *In My Way: The Political Memoirs of Lord George-Brown* (London: Victor Gollanz, Ltd., 1971), 146.

7 Mc Rusk, McNamara, Gordon Walker and Healey, December 7, 1964, United Kingdom, 12/7-8/64, PM Wilson visit (1), CFNSF, LBJL.

8 R. S. Crawford to George Harrison, November 4, 1964, FO 371/179751/B 1052/26.

9 Memorandum by T. F. Brenchley, November 23, 1964, FO 371/174676/BS 1051/11.

10 W. Morris, "H. M. G's Policy in the Persian Gulf", November 2, 1964, FO 371/174489/B 1052/27; see also G. G. Arthur, "Defence Arrangements in the Persian Gulf", December 2, 1964, FO 371/174505/B 1190/i G.

11 Galia Golan, *Soviet Policies in the Middle East from World War Two to Gorbachev* (New York: Cambridge University Press, 1990), 58.

12 Robert O. Freedman, *Soviet Policy toward the Middle East since 1970* (New York: Praeger, 1970), 27, 29.

13 Anatoly Dobrynin, *In Confidence: Moscow's Ambassador to America's Six Cold War Presidents* (New York: Times Books, 1995), 161.

14 Freedman, *Soviet Policy toward the Middle East*, 40–1.

15 Robert W. Stookey, *America and the Arab States: An Uneasy Encounter* (New York: John Wiley & Sons, 1975), 215.

16 Saunders to Walt W. Rostow, June 24, 1966, Memorandums to the president, Walt W. Rostow (hereafter cited as MPWWR), volume 7 [1 of 2], June 21– 30, 1966, NSF, LBJL.

17 Dean Rusk, *As I Saw It: A Secretary of State's Memoirs* (London: I. B. Tauris, 1991), 323, 324.

18 Mc Johnson and Harman, February 7, 1968, FRUS, 1964–1968, XX: *Arab–Israeli Dispute 1967–1968*, 150.

19 Douglas Little, *American Orientalism: The United States and the Middle East since 1945* (London: University of North Carolina Press, 2002), 31.

20 Burton I. Kaufman, *The Arab Middle East and the United States: Inter-Arab Rivalry and Superpower Diplomacy* (New York: Twayne Publishers, 1996), 47, 50.

21 William B. Quandt, *Peace Process: American Diplomacy and the Arab–Israeli Conflict since 1967* (Los Angeles: University of California Press, 1993), 27. Undersecretary of state George Ball noted after the war: "Few, either at the State Department, the White House, or on Capitol Hill would have been sorry to see Nasser humiliated or even overthrown. In addition, elements in the Pentagon saw a potential Arab–Israeli war as a heaven sent opportunity not only to test American vs. Soviet weapons under combat conditions, but also destroy Soviet influence in the Arab world by demonstrating that nation's inability to protect its Middle East clients." The United States was partly motivated in addition:
      "Many people felt that Nasser had been guilty of monumental ingratitude

toward America" [George W. Ball and Douglas B. Ball, *The Passionate Attachment: America's Involvement with Israel 1947 to the Present* (New York: W. W. Norton & Company, 1992), 55.

22 Michael B. Oren, *Six Days of War: June 1967 and the Making of the Modern Middle East* (New York: Oxford University Press, 2002), 19, 58–9, 92, 151–2, 163.

23 Abdel Magid Farid, *Nasser: The Final Years* (Reading: Ithaca Press, 1996), 4.

24 Clifford to Rostow, July 18, 1967, memorandums to the president, W. W. Rostow, vol. 35 [2 of 2], 16–24 July, 1967, LBJL.

25 Dean Rusk, *As I Saw it: A Secretary of State's Memoirs* (New York: I. B. Tauris, 1990), 332. For an alternative view, see Oren, *Six Days of War*, 263–71.

26 Ball and Ball, *The Passionate Attachment*, 57–8.

27 Mc Rusk and Israeli deputy prime minister Yigal Allon, September 11, 1968, FRUS 1964–1968, XX: 490, 492, for Israel's tardiness in paying victims compensation; see also H. W. Brands, *The Wages of Globalism: Lyndon Johnson and the Limits of American Power* (New York: Oxford University Press, 1995), 212.

28 Burke Trend, "North American Visit: Notes for Cabinet", December 11, 1964, PREM 13/104.

29 Frank Brenchley, *Britain and the Middle East: An Economic History, 1945–87* (London: Lester Crook Academic Publishing, 1989), 166.

30 Karl Pieragostini, *Britain, Aden and South Arabia: Abandoning Empire* (London: Macmillan, 1991), 114–15. Incidentally, Healey freely admitted the same in a later interview that when he accepted a defense department budget ceiling of £2,000 million annually as early as November 1964, it meant a substantial reduction in the British world-wide role. See Saki Dockrill, *Britain's Retreat from East of Suez: The Choice between Europe and the World* (London: Palgrave Macmillan, 2002), 210.

31 Secretary of state for defence, *Statement on the Defence Estimates, 1965* (Her Majesty's Stationery Office, London, 1965), Cmnd. 2592 [hereafter cited as HMSO]; *idem, Statement on the Defence Estimates, 1966: The Defence Review*, part I, Cmnd. 2901 and part II, Cmnd. 2902; both in HMSO, 1966; *idem, Supplementary Statement on Defence Policy, 1967* (HMSO, 1967), Cmnd. 3357; *idem, Statement on the Defence Estimates, 1968* (HMSO, 1968), Cmnd. 3540.

32 Cmnd. 2592, 5.

33 Cmnd. 2901, 1.

34 *Ibid.*, 6.

35 *Ibid.*, 7, 8.

36 *Ibid.*, 14.

37 Cmnd. 3357, 4.

38 Cmnd. 3540, 2.

39 "Administrative History", United Kingdom, pp. 4–5.

40 Clive Ponting, *Breach of Promise: Labour in Power* (London: Hamish Hamilton, 1989), 48–52.

41 Philip Ziegler, *Wilson: The Authorized Life of Lord Wilson of Rievaulx*

(London: Weidenfeld & Nicolson, 1993), 205; John Dumbrell, "The Johnson Administration and the British Labour Government: Vietnam, the Pound and East of Suez", *Journal of American Studies* 30: 2 (1996): 211–31.

42 Bundy to Johnson, July 28, 1965, MPMGB, vol. 12 [1 of 2], July 1965, NSF, LBJL.

43 Dobson, *Anglo-American Relations in the Twentieth Century*, 132.

44 Mc Bundy and Trend, July 30, 1965, PREM 13/672.

45 Mc Wilson and Ball, September 9, 1965, PREM 13/674.

46 Mc Wilson and Ball, September 8, 1965, PREM 13/2450.

47 Dockrill, *Britain's Retreat from East of Suez*, 215.

48 Mc Ball and Wilson, September 9, 1965, United Kingdom, vol. VI, Cables [1 of 2], 7/65-9/65, CFNSF, LBJL.

49 Bundy to Johnson, September 10, 1965, MPMGB, vol. 14, [2 of 2], 9/1 – 22/65, NSF, LBJL: "You will notice that it took two talks for Wilson to agree to the association between our defense of the pound and their overseas commitments"; for a British assessment, see memorandum by T.W. Garvey, "Sterling and Strings", September 21, 1965, FO 371/179587/AU 1159/4: "The Prime Minister turned the argument by asserting as axiomatic the fact that we have 'world-wide responsibilities' like the U.S., that we want to carry them out, but cannot of course do so unless we are freed from the pressure of economic stringency."

50 State Department, briefing paper, "Visit of Foreign Secretary Michael Stewart: UK Economic Situation", October 7, 1965, Conference Files, Box 387, National Archives, Record Group 59 [hereafter cited as NARG 59].

51 Pimlott, *Wilson*, 362–3.

52 "Visit of Foreign Secretary Michael Stewart"; "British Defense Review".

53 Henry Rowen to Bundy, July 14, 1965, FRUS 1964–8, XII: 497–9.

54 Dockrill, *Britain's Retreat from East of Suez*, 105.

55 United States department of state and defense, "UK Defense Review: Joint State-Defense Scope Paper", January 21, 1966, Conference Files, box 399, NARG 59.

56 Administrative history, United Kingdom, 6.

57 Pieragostini, *Britain, Aden and South Arabia*, 167.

58 United States department of state and defense, "UK Defense Review: Joint State-Defense Scope Paper", January 21, 1966, Conference Files, box 399, NARG 59.

59 Roger Morris, background paper, Visit of U.K. foreign secretary George Brown, "South Arabia", October 10, 1966, United Kingdom 10/14/66, Visit of Foreign Sec. Brown, [2 of 2], CFNSF, LBJL.

60 David Holden, *Farewell to Arabia* (London: Faber & Faber, 1966), 64.

61 Michael Howard, "Britain's Strategic Problem East of Suez", *International Affairs* 42, 2 (April, 1966): 179–83, the quote is on p. 181; see also Glen Balfour-Paul, *The End of the British Empire in the Middle East: Britain's Relinquishment of Power in Her Last Three Arab Dependencies* (Cambridge: Cambridge University Press, 1991), 85–6.

62 Defence and Oversea Policy Committee, Defence Review Working Party, 12 October , 1965, CAB 148. O.P:D. (O) (D.R.)(W.P)(65) 15th mtg.

63 Healey and Stewart to Wilson, January 28, 1966, PREM 13/801: Rusk and McNamara "were in general agreement with our presentation of broad policy objectives and congratulated us on the skill which we had shown in working towards the solutions and in maximizing our military and financing capabilities". This success was owed in part Stewart's to assurance to Rusk, that despite certain retrenchment, he believed that in the Indian Ocean and Pacific area it was imperative for the United Kingdom "to continue a large and indeed expensive military program in that region". Also to augment American efforts in the area. [Mc Rusk, McNamara, Stewart, Healey *et al.*, January 27, 1966, FRUS 1964–8, XII: 516–28].

64 Cabinet conclusions, February 14, 1966, CC (66), 9th Conclusions, CAB 128/41, pt.1.

65 Healey and Stewart to Wilson.

66 Bator to Johnson, February 16, 1966, FRUS 1964–8, XII: 529.

67 Rusk circular telegram, December 21, 1965, DEF 12-5, Saud.

68 George C. Moore, "British Defense Interests: Persian Gulf, Trucial States and Aden", January 25, 1966, Conference Files, box 399, NARG 59.

69 Brenchley, *Britain and the Middle East*, 140–1.

70 Nadav Safran, *Saudi Arabia: The Ceaseless Quest for Security* (London: Cornell University Press, 1988), 201.

71 Anthony Sampson, *The Arms Bazaar: The Companies, the Dealers, the Bribes: from Vickers to Lockheed* (London: Hodder & Stoughton, 1977), 164.

72 Briefing paper, "Visit of Prime Minister Wilson December 15–19, 1965, Middle East Arms Sales", December 11, 1965, Conference Files, box 392, NARG 59.

73 Diane B. Kunz, "'Somewhat Mixed Up Together': Anglo-American Defence and Financial Policy during the 1960s", *Journal of Imperial and Commonwealth History* 27, 2 (1999): 213–32.

74 Walt Rostow, memorandum to the president, April 3, 1966, Walt W. Rostow [hereafter cited as WWR], Volume 1, [3 of 3], April 1–30, 1966, NSF, LBJL. Furthering the process of American acquiescence to British plans was Wilson's skill in dredging up past and present sins against Britain that had to be atoned for. Soon after the conclusion of the 1966 defense review, the prime minister wrote Johnson on February 27, 1966 to announce he had dissolved Parliament and called for a general election on March 31. "I am not proposing to ask you to come and help us during the election. There are, of course, abundant precedents. Eisenhower in 1955 agreed to Eden's request for an early Summit meeting to which in fact Eisenhower was strongly opposed. In 1959 he conferred the same electoral benefit on Macmillan and indeed allowed himself to be toted through 14 London marginal constituencies in an open car with Macmillan beside him. I have no such requests except that if you were thinking of doing anything which might be positively unhelpful, I hope that you would at any rate give me a little notice." [Wilson to Johnson, February 27, 1966, FRUS 1964–8, XII: 530–2].

75 "Administrative History", United Kingdom, pp. 8–11.

76 Francis M. Bator, July 14, 1966, MPWWR, Volume 8 [1 of 2], July 1–15, 1966, NSF, LBJL.

77 Wilson to Johnson, July 20, 1966, MPWWR, 9 [3 of 3], July 16–31, 1966, NSF, LBJL.

78 WWR to Johnson, July 20, 1966, MPWWR, 9 [3 of 3], July 16–31, 1966, NSF, LBJL.

79 Bator to Johnson, July 28, 1966 CFNSF, United Kingdom, PM Wilson Visit 7/29/66 [1 of 2], LBJL.

80 See, for instance, Bator to Johnson, June 21, 1967, MPWWR, 32 [2 of 2], June 21–30, 1967, NSF, LBJL.

81 J. B. Kelly, *Arabia, the Gulf and the West* (London: Weidenfeld & Nicolson, 1980), 33.

82 Fitzpatrick to ministry of defense, January 31, 1968, FCO 8/781/BS 10/1 149.

83 *Daily Telegraph*, February 13, 1968, FCO 8/781/BS 10/1 w 144; see also Brenchley, "Armoured Cars for Saudi Arabia–Daily Telegraph Article", FCO 8/780 BS 10/1 136: "The loss of this contract is a serious setback, as is the possibility that naval sales may also be affected. There seems little doubt that the decision was a political one . . . and stemmed from king Faisal's resentment at what he regards as our successive betrayal of the South Arabian Government and the Gulf rulers."

84 Balfour-Paul, *The End of Empire in the Middle East*, 123.

85 Kelly, *Arabia*, 48.

86 Cmnd. 3357, 5.

87 Elisabeth Monroe, "British Bases in the Middle East: Assets or Liabilities?", *International Affairs* 42, 1 (February, 1966): 24–34.

88 Michael Howard, "Britain's Strategic Problem East of Suez", *International Affairs* 42, 2 (April, 1966): 179–83.

89 Christopher Mayhew, *Britain's Role Tomorrow* (London: Hutchinson, 1967), 54, 113.

90 Denis Healey, *The Time of My Life* (London: Michael Joseph, 1989), 277.

91 Michael Stewart, *Life and Labour: An Autobiography* (London: Sidgwick & Jackson, 1980).

92 Brown, *In My Way*, 141.

93 Roy Jenkins, *A Life at the Centre* (London: Macmillan, 1991), 225.

94 Ziegler, *Wilson*, 211.

95 Jeffrey Pickering, *Britain's Withdrawal from East of Suez: The Politics of Retrenchment* (London: Macmillan Press, 1998), 168–9; Pieragostini, *Britain, Aden and South Arabia*, 183.

96 Balfour-Paul, *The End of Empire in the Middle East*, 124.

97 F. Gregory Gause, "British and American Policies in the Persian Gulf, 1968–1973", *Review of International Studies* 11 (1985): 247–73.

98 Administrative history, Great Britain, 15.

99 Yergin, *The Prize*, 566.

100 Healey quoted from Kelly, *Arabia*, 50–1.

101 Rusk to Johnson, May 31, 1967, NSFCF, UK: Visit of PM Harold Wilson [1 of 2], 6/2/67, LBJL; Roger Morris observed in a briefing paper for the president that "South Arabia is of little economic importance (the port of Aden is its only real resource) to us". The United States was but little concerned apart from the impact on pro-American regimes by a violent, radical take over of

South Arabia. ["South Arabia", May 29, 1967, NSFCF, UK: Visit of PM Harold Wilson [1 of 2], 6/2/67].
102 Roger Morris, "Visit of United Kingdom Prime Minister Harold Wilson, June 1967: East of Suez", May 29, 1967, NSFCF, in *ibid.*
103 "Administrative History", United Kingdom, 12–15.
104 Rusk to Brown, April 21, 1967, FRUS 1964–8, XII: 566–8.
105 Wilson to Johnson, July 13, 1967, FRUS 1964–8, XII: 576– 8.
106 Ziegler, *Wilson*, 385.
107 Johnson to Wilson, n.d., NSF, Special Head of State Correspondence (hereafter cited as SHSC), United Kingdom [2 of 4], LBJL.
108 Johnson to Wilson, January 11, 1968, NSH, SHSC, UK [2 of 4], LBJL.
109 Summary Notes 587th NSC Meeting, June 5, 1968, NSC Meetings, vol. 5 Tab. 69, 6/5/68, NSF, LBJL.
110 Brief by D. J. Swan, September 12, 1968, FCO 7/772/AU 2/13
111 Secretary of state for defence, *Supplementary Statement on Defence Policy 1968* (HMSO, July, 1968), 6.

5 Leaving Aden, October 1964 to November 1967

1 J. D. Stoddart, "British Defense Interests: Persian Gulf, Trucial States and Aden", January 25, 1966, Conference Files, box 399, NARG 59.
2 Brian Lapping, *The End of Empire* (London: Granada Publishing Limited, 1985) 278–89.
3 Curtis Jones to State Department, August 30, 1965, POL 2 Aden; Lapping, *End of Empire*, 298.
4 Jones to State Department, February 26, 1967, POL 15 Aden.
5 CIA intelligence memorandum, "South Arabia", FRUS 1964–8, XXI: 218.
6 Julian Paget, *Last Post Aden 1964–1967* (London: Faber & Faber, 1969), 114.
7 David Holden, *Farewell to Arabia* (London: Faber & Faber, 1966), 64.
8 John B. Kelly, *Arabia, the Gulf and the West* (New York: Basic Books, 1980), 21.
9 Karl Pieragostini, *Britain, Aden and South Arabia: Abandoning Empire* (London: Macmillan, 1991), 103.
10 R. S. Crawford, "Aden and the Persian Gulf", November 4, 1964, FO 371/179751/B 1052/26 G.
11 Healey to colonial secretary, March 31, 1965, PREM 13/112; see also Denis Healey, *The Time of My Life* (London: Michael Joseph, 1989), 284.
12 Burke Trend to Wilson, March 23,1965, PREM 13/112.
13 United States State Department, briefing paper, "Visit of British Foreign Secretary Washington, March 21–24, 1965", March 19, 1965, POL 2-3 Yemen.
14 Wheelock to State Department, reporting mc with general Charles Harrington, commander-in-chief, United Kingdom Middle Eastern force, March 29, 1965, POL 19 Aden.
15 Wheelock to State Department, April 12, 1965, POL 2-3 Aden.
16 Wheelock to State Department, May 10, 1965, POL 23-1 Saud.
17 Greenwood to Healey, August 2, 1965, PREM 13/113.
18 Curtis Jones, principal officer American consulate Aden, to State Department; August 30, 1965, POL 2 Aden.

19 Jones to State Department, September 6, 1965, POL 2 Aden.

20 Jones to State Department, September 20, 1965, POL 2 Aden.

21 Pieragostini, *Britain, Aden and South Arabia*, 136.

22 *Ibid.*, 140; Thompson to Brown, September 14, 1966, FO 371/190212/ VG 1053/17/ G.

23 Mc Harrison M. Symmes and Mahmoud Riad, Foreign Minister Egypt, October 8, 1965, POL 19 Aden.

24 On this see George Brown, *In My Way: The Political Memoirs of Lord George-Brown* (London: Victor Gollancz, 1971), 137, 230.

25 Thompson to Brown, September 14, 1966.

26 Rusk circular telegram, September 28, 1965, POL 19 Aden; Komer to Johnson, September 30, 1965, MPMGB, vol. 15 [2 of 2], 9/23-10/14/65. Komer wrote Johnson, "Our interests are involved because we've relied on the Brits to police the oil-rich Gulf".

27 Defence and Oversea Policy Committee, Defence Review Working Party, October 12, 1965, CAB 148. O.P.D.(O) (D. R) (W. P) (65) 15th mtg.

28 Wriggins-Sanders to Rostow, December 1, 1966, United Arab Republic, vol. V. Memos, 9/66-5/67, CFNSF, LBJL. Rusk put it more directly to the Egyptian Ambassador Kamel on July 13, 1966: "The US, continued the Secretary, had exhausted its capability to go on its knees bearing gifts. We did not necessarily want gratitude. We could live with silence but not with abuse," FRUS 1964–8, XVII: 615–17.

29 Mc Greenwood and George Moore (United States) *et al.*, October 19, 1965, POL 19 Aden.

30 Jones to State Department, October 25, 1965, POL 2 Aden.

31 Mc Wilson and advisors, November 24, 1965, PREM 13/681.

32 Mc Wilson and Johnson, December 16, 1965, PREM 13/686.

33 George Moore, "UK Position in Aden and the Persian Gulf", January 27, 1966, U.K. Defense Review, 1/27/66, United Kingdom, CFNSF, LBJL; Healey and Stewart to Wilson, January 28, 1966, PREM 13/801. Healey and Stewart noted that Rusk and McNamara "did not question our decision to leave Aden by 1968 or sooner".

34 Rusk to American embassy, Cairo, February 19, 1966, POL 19 Aden.

35 Lapping, *The End of Empire*, 300; Kelly, *Arabia*, 26.

36 Mc Christopher Everett (United Kingdom) and Rodger Davies (United States), October 19, 1966, FRUS 1964–8, XXI: doc. 80.

37 Healey, *The Time of My Life*, 280.

38 American embassy to State Department, March 2, 1966, POL 19 Aden.

39 Glen Balfour-Paul, *The End of Empire in the Middle East: Britain's Relinquishment of Power in Her Last Three Arab Dependencies* (Cambridge: Cambridge University Press, 1991), 85–6.

40 Lapping, *The End of Empire*, 298–9.

41 D. J. McCarthy to Sir Richard Beaumont, November 20, 1967, FCO 8/253 BA 1/103.

42 Kelly, *Arabia*, 26.

43 G. G. Arthur to Allen (with Allen's handwritten comments), November 21, 1966, FO 371/185250/BA 103145/12.

44 Brown to cabinet, August 2, 1966, CAB 128/41 CC (66) 41ˢᵗ Conclusions.
45 Jones to State Department, September 18, 1966, POL 13-3 Aden.
46 Paul Gore-Booth to Patrick Dean, October 4, 1966, FO 371/185172/B 103145/ 7G.
47 Bruce to State Department, October 21, 1966, POL 19 Aden.
48 Jones to State Department, November 21, 1966, POL 19 Aden.
49 Jones to State Department, November 22, 1966, POL 19 Aden.
50 Katzenbach to American embassy Jidda, December 7, 1966, POL Aden.
51 Stewart to Brown, 16 March 1967, FCO 8/220/BA 1/71.
52 US embassy London to State Department, January 27, 1967, FRUS 1964–8, XXI: doc. 84.
53 Brown to cabinet, March 16, 1967, CAB 128/42 CC (67) 13th Conclusions.
54 Brenchley to Allen, "Factors Involved in a Crash Withdrawal from South Arabia", February 17, 1967, FCO 8/301/BA 2/14.
55 Thompson to Brown, March 17, 1967, FCO 8/220/BA 1/71/9.
56 Thompson to Brown, March 17, 1967, FCO 8/220/BA 1/71/8.
57 Kelly, *Arabia*, 33.
58 Balfour-Paul, *End of Empire*, 87.
59 Crossman's diaries from Balfour-Paul, *End of Empire*, 88.
60 Mc Faisal and Wilson *et al.*, May 15, 1967, FCO 8/819/ BS 22/6.
61 Department of state to American consul, Aden, March 15, 1967, FRUS 1964–8, XXI: 197.
62 Mc Wilson and Brown, March 20, 1967, FCO 8/196/BA 1/49.
63 D. J. McCarthy to Brenchley, March 13, 1967, FCO 8/196/ BA 1/49.
64 Mc Wilson and Brown.
65 Lapping, *End of Empire*, 303.
66 M. S. Weir to Brenchley, April 12, 1967, FCO 8/571/BC 1/ 4.
67 J. A. Thompson to McCarthy, May 2, 1967, FCO 8/253/ BA 1/103.
68 Mc Wilson and Faisal et al., May 15, 1967, FCO 8/819/BS 22/6/128.
69 *Ibid.*
70 Mc Wilson and Faisal *et al.*, May 23, 1967, FCO 8/819/BS 22/6/147. Balfour-Paul, *The End of Empire* observes that the aid package was only a fig leaf to expedite British withdrawal from Aden, p. 88.
71 *Ibid.*
72 Mc Healey and Sheik Kamal Adham, May 23, 1967, FCO 8/760/BS 2/4.
73 State Department, "Future of South Arabia", n.d., Briefing Papers for National Security Council Meeting, May 24, 1967, Meeting Notes file, LBJL; see also Rostow to Johnson, May 23, 1967 in *ibid.*
74 Rostow to Johnson, June 15, 1967, MPWWR, 32 [2 of 2], June 13–20, 1967, LBJL.
75 State Department to United States embassy London, October 2, 1967, FRUS 1964–8: XXI: doc. 103.
76 David Holden and Richard Jones, *The House of Saud* (London: Pan Books, 1983), 272.
77 Brown to British embassy, Jidda, September 29, 1967, FCO 8/356/BA 3/9.
78 D. J. McCarthy, Foreign Office to Jidda, September 20, 1967, FCO 8/356/BA/3/9.

79 Brown to cabinet, September 7, 1967, CAB 128/42 CC (67) 54th Conclusions.
80 Brown to cabinet, October 30, 1967, CAB 128/42 CC (67) 62nd Conclusions.
81 Brown to cabinet, October 31, 1967, CAB 129/134 C(67) 172.
82 Humphrey Trevelyan, *The Middle East in Revolution* (London: Macmillan, 1971), 252–3, 265–6.
83 Brown to Trevelyan, September 25, 1967, FCO 8/356/BA 3/9.
84 Mc Rusk and Dean, November 1, 1967, FRUS 1964–8, XXI: 232–3.
85 Brown to Jidda.
86 Weir to Brown, October 23, 1967, FCO 8/756/BS 211.
87 McCarthy to Richard Beaumont, November 20, 1967, FCO 8/253/BA 1/103.
88 Cmnd., 14, 15–16.
89 Kelly, *Arabia.*
90 Alistair Horne, *Macmillan*, vol. II, *1957–1986* (London: Macmillan, 1989), 421.
91 Michael Carver, *War since 1945* (London: Weidenfeld & Nicolson, 1980), 81.

6 *Doctrinaire Socialists as Feudal Overlords: Saudi Arabia, 1964–1967*

1 Administrative history of the State Department, Chapter 4 (The Near East and South Asia), section G. Yemen, Box 2, LBJL.
2 American embassy Jidda to State Department, October 5, 1965, POL 7 Saud-UK.
3 American embassy, Jidda to State Department, November 12, 1964, DEF 12-5 Saud.
4 Brenchley, "Assurances to Saudi Arabia", November 23, 1964, FO 371/174676/BS 1051/ 11.
5 Memorandum by R. S. Crawford, November 25, 1964 in *ibid.*
6 *Ibid.*
7 Rusk to American embassy Jidda, January 4, 1965, DEF 12-5 Saud-UK.
8 Mc John Jernegan and John Lindley, vice president Litton Industries, February 24, 1965, POL 7 Saud.
9 Brenchley, "Arms for Saudi Arabia", March 17, 1965, FO 371/179888/BS 1192/44.
10 *Ibid.*
11 Moore to Symmes, May 7, 1965, DEF 12-5 Saud-UK.
12 Frank Brenchley, *Britain and the Middle East: An Economic History, 1945–87* (London: Lester Crook Academic Publishing, 1989), 140.
13 Man to Foreign Office, July 19, 1965, FO 371/179890/BS 1192/92.
14 Komer to Johnson, June 16, 1965, FRUS 1964–8, XXI: doc. 248.
15 Stewart to Foreign Office, September 25, 1965, FO 371/179890/BS 1192/111.
16 Ball to American embassy Jidda, December 16, 1965, DEF 12-5 Saud.
17 S. W. Treadgold, "Saudi Arabia Air Defence Scheme", May 8, 1967, FCO 8/818/BS 22/6.
18 Rusk to American embassy Jidda, December 17, 1965, DEF 12-5 Saud.
19 Rusk circular telegram, December 11, 1965, DEF 12-5, Saud.
20 Mc Owen and Symmes, December 13, 1965, DEF 12 Saud. ARAMCO's role in Anglo-American relations on the Arabian Peninsula in the 1950s is explored in Tore T. Petersen, *The Middle East between the Great Powers:*

Anglo-American Conflict and Cooperation, 1952–7 (London: Macmillan Press, 2000).

21 William Eagleton to Symmes, January 10, 1966, DEF 12 Saud.

22 Rusk to American Embassy, March 5, 1966, DEF 12-5 Saud.

23 Stewart to Rusk, March 11, 1966, FO 371/185485/ BS 1051/23/G.

24 Rusk to Stewart, March 23, 1966, DEF 12-5 Saud.

25 Rostow to Johnson, May 3, 1966, MPWWR, vol. 2 [2 of 2], May 1–15, 1966, NSF, LBJL.

26 US embassy Saudi Arabia to State Department, December 18, 1964, FRUS, 1964–8, XXI: doc. 235.

27 Rostow to Johnson, May 30, 1966, MPWWR, vol. 5 [3 of 5], 5/27-6/10/66, NSF, LBJL.

28 Briefing paper for Johnson, "Major Elements of Saudi Foreign Policy", June 7, 1966, CFNSC, LBJL.

29 Rostow to Johnson, July 14, 1966, MPWWR, vol. 8 [1 of 2], July 1–15, 1966, NSF, LBJL.

30 Administrative history, Yemen, p. 12.

31 Mc Johnson, Faisal *et al.*, June 21, 1966, FRUS, 1964–8, XXI: doc. 276.

32 Rostow to Johnson, June 18, 1966, FRUS, 1964–8, XXI: doc. 272.

33 Rusk to Jidda and London, August 5, 1966, DEF 12-5 Saud.

34 State Department, research paper, "Internal Cohesion in Saudi Arabia", September 7, 1966, POL Saud 1/1/64.

35 Man, "Saudi Arabia: Annual Review for 1966", January 17, 1967, FCO 8/ BS 1/1.

36 Malcolm Kerr, *The Arab Cold War: Gamal 'Abd al-Nasir and His Rivals, 1958–1970* (London: Oxford University Press, 1977), 113.

37 Jidda to State Department, November 16, 1966, POL 27 Yemen.

38 Jidda to State Department, November 30, 1966, POL 7 Saud.

39 London to State Department, December 29, 1966, POL 32-1 Saud Trucial States.

40 Kerr, *The Arab Cold War*, 126; David Holden and Richard Johns, *The House of Saud* (London: Sidgwick & Jackson, 1981), 247; Burton I. Kaufman, *The Arab Middle East and the United States: Inter-Arab Rivalry and Superpower Diplomacy* (New York: Twayne, 1996), 47.

41 Nadav Safran, *Saudi Arabia: The Ceaseless Quest for Security* (London: Cornell University Press, 1991), 201–2.

42 Rodger Davies to Rusk, January 4, 1967, POL 31-1 Saud-UAR.

43 Eilts to State Department, January 17, 1967, POL 27 Saud-UAR.

44 Man, "Saudi Arabia 1966".

45 Rusk to Jidda, January 20, 1967, POL 27 Saud-UAR

46 Rusk to Jidda, January 28, 1967, POL 27 Saud-UAR.

47 Administrative history, Yemen, 16.

48 British embassy, Washington to Foreign Office, February 17, 1967, FCO 8/765/ BS 3/5.

49 Jidda to State Department, February 1, 1967, DEF 1-4 Saud.

50 Rusk to Jidda, February 25, 1967, POL 27 Saud-UAR.

51 Weir to Thompson, February 23, 1967, FCO 8/756/BS 2/1.

52 Gore-Booth to Faisal via Harry Kern, May 17, 1967, FCO 8/356/BA 3/9.

53 Daily Express, January 31, FCO 8/765/BS/3/5; clippings from FCO.

54 Gore-Booth to Faisal.

55 Weir, briefing memorandum on Buraimi, March 30, 1967, FCO 8/59/B 42/2.

56 Ibid., Brenchley's handwritten comments.

57 Treadgold, "Saudi Arabia Air Defence Scheme".

58 Man to private secretary, prime minister, May 5, 1967, PREM 13/1775.

59 Harold Wilson, The Labour Government 1964–1970 (London: Weidenfeld & Nicolson, 1971), 396.

60 Mc Wilson and Faisal, May 23, 1967.

61 Jidda to Foreign Office, May 17, 1967, Foreign and Commonwealth Office [hereafter cited as FCO with appropriate filing designations] 8/765/BS 3/5.

62 Rusk to Jidda, May 14, 1967, POL 27 Saud-UAR.

63 Rusk to Jidda, May 14, 1967, POL 27 Yemen.

64 Administrative history, Yemen, p. 23; rumors had reached the State Department on May 15, 1967 that Egypt used poison on Yemeni villages on May 15, 1967, see Rusk circular telegram, May 15, 1967, POL 27 Saud-UAR.

65 Memorandum for the record, IRG meeting, April 12, 1967, FRUS, 1964–8, XXI: doc. 288.

66 Gore-Booth to Brenchley, May 17, 1967, FCO 8/356/BA 3/G.

67 State Department paper, "Near East Oil: How Important Is It?", February 8, 1967, FRUS, 1964–8, XXI: document 19 (this volume is taken from the Internet, where they use document identification not pagination, hereafter cited as doc. and number).

68 Saunders to Rostow, May 16, 1967, FRUS 1964–8: XXI, doc. 20.

69 CIA, Memorandum for the record, August 16, 1967, in ibid., doc. 24.

70 Mc Faisal and Wilson et al., May 22, 1967, FCO 8/819/BS 22/6.

71 Mc Faisal and Wilson et al., May 23, 1967, FCO 8/819/BS 22/(P) 147, PRO.

72 Gore-Booth to Brenchley, May 17, 1967, FCO 8/356/BA 3/9.

73 Brown to Man, June 22, 1967, FCO 8/820/BS 22/6.

74 Man to Brown, June 26, 1967, FCO 8/760/BS 2/4.

75 Man to Foreign Office, September 4, 1967, FCO 8/356/BA 3/9.

76 Foreign Office to Man, September 18, 1967, FCO 8/356/BA 3/9/25.

77 Jidda to Foreign Office, September 28, 1967, FCO 8/356/BA 3/9.

78 Roberts to Foreign Office, September 29, 1967, FCO 8/356/BA 3/9.

79 Jidda to State Department, October 28, 1967, POL 19 Aden.

80 Rusk to London, October 30, 1967, POL 19 Aden.

7 The Withdrawal from the Persian Gulf

1 Morris to Michael Stewart, November 2, 1964, FO 371/174489/B 1052/27.

2 Weir to McCarthy, August 13, 1968, FCO 8/572/BC 1/4.

3 Report by Major R. J. F. Brown on Dhofar, March 31, 1968, FCO 8/572/BC 1/4.

4 On Dhofar, see for instance: John Akehurst, We Won a War: The Campaign in Oman, 1965–1975 (Southampton: Michael Russel, 1984); Ranulph Fiennes, Where Soldiers Fear to Tread (London: Hodder & Stoughton, 1977); David Lee, Flight from the Middle East (London: HMSO, 1980); Michael Dewar,

Brush Fire Wars: Minor Campaigns of the British Army since 1945 (New York: St. Martin's Press, 1984).

5 Safran, *Saudi Arabia*, 125, 129.

6 Bruce Hoffman, "British Air Power in Peripheral Conflict, 1919–1976" (Rand/Air Force Report, October, 1989), 97.

7 Meeting Stewart and Foreign Office, December 3, 1964, FO 371/174489/B 1052/136-46.

8 CIA intelligence memorandum, "Britain's Government Expenditures East of Suez", June 7, 1965, United Kingdom vol. IV, Memos 5/65-6/65, CFNSF, LBJL.

9 Patrick Gordon Walker, *The Cabinet* (London: Fontana, 1972), 140.

10 Cmnd. 2901, 1.

11 Crawford to Brown, December 30, 1966, PREM 13/2209.

12 Jeffrey Pickering, *Britain's Withdrawal from East of Suez: The Politics of Retrenchment* (London: Macmillan Press, 1998), ch. 7; David Reynolds, *Britannia Overruled: British Policy and World Power in the 20th Century* (London: Longman, 1991), 230–1.

13 Ben Pimlott, *Harold Wilson* (London: HarperCollins Publishers, 1992), 388.

14 Alan P. Dobson, *Anglo-American Relations in the Twentieth Century: Of Friendship, Conflict and the Rise and Decline of Superpowers* (London: Routledge, 1995), 136.

15 Cmnd. 3357, 4–5.

16 Denis Healey, *The Time of My Life* (London: Michael Joseph, 1989), 293.

17 Cmnd, 3540, 2, 3.

18 Frank Brenchley, *Britain and the Middle East: An Economic History, 1945–87* (London: Lester Crook Academic Publishing, 1989), 357 n. 2.

19 Daniel Yergin, *The Prize: The Epic Quest for Oil, Money and Power* (New York: Simon & Schuster, 1992), 566.

20 Faisal to Wilson, May 23, 1967, FCO 8/819/BS 22/6.

21 Cmnd. 2592, 9.

22 "Administrative History of the Department of State", Chapter 4, The Near East and South Asia, Section F. The Persian Gulf: "The Issue of British Withdrawal", p. 1, Box 2 [1 of 2], LBJL.

23 *Ibid.*, 2–3.

24 Weir to Brenchley (with Brenchley's handwritten comments), October 31, 1967, FCO 8/94/B 13/6.

25 Wilson to Johnson, November 16, 1967, PREM 13/1447.

26 Mc Wilson, Healey and Brown, December 20, 1967, PREM 13/1466.

27 Jenkins to cabinet, January 3, 1968, CAB 129/135 C(68) 5.

28 Brown and commonwealth secretary to cabinet, January 3, 1968, CAB 129/35, C (68) 7 (revise).

29 Roy Jenkins, *A Life at the Centre* (London: Macmillan, 1991), 225.

30 Administrative history, Persian Gulf, pp. 2–3, LBJL.

31 Rusk to Brown, January 6, 1968, PREM 13/2209; administrative history, Persian Gulf, p. 3, LBJL.

32 Rusk quote in Brown to British embassy, Washington, January 6, 1968, PREM 13/2209.

33 Administrative history, Persian Gulf, p. 3.
34 *Ibid.*, p. 4.
35 Administrative history, United Kingdom, p. 16.
36 Brown to Foreign Office, January 11, 1968, CAB 129/135 C(68), 22.
37 Mc Rusk and Brown, n.d., United Kingdom, vol. XIII, memos 1/68-7/68, CFNSF, LBJL.
38 Brown to Foreign Office, January 11, 1968, CAB 129/135 C(68), 22.
39 Administrative history; Persian Gulf, pp. 4–5; United Kingdom (for LBJ to Wilson), p. 17.
40 United Kingdom embassy Tehran to Foreign Office, January 7, 1968, FCO 8/145/B22/15.
41 Background paper, "Persian Gulf", February 2, 1968, United Kingdom, 2/7-9/68, Visit of PM Wilson, Briefing Book, CFNSF, LBJL.
42 Mc Wilson and Johnson, February 2, 1968, PREM 13/2455.
43 Johnson gave an exclusive interview to place his objections on the record [Tomkins to Foreign Office, February 22, 1968, FCO 7/857/AU 13/1], and at an Anglo-American conference for parliamentarians, some American Congressmen complained bitterly about the British lack of consultation, and wondered "whether this was part of socialist policy to make England a tight little island" [Diggins, "Ditchley Park Conference", February 15, 1968, FCO 7/792/AU 2/38].
44 Crawford to Brown, November 22, 1967, FCO 8/144/B 22/14.
45 Mc Faisal and Roberts, January 10, 1968, FCO 8/47/B 3/19.
46 Crawford to Foreign Office, January 11, 1968, FCO 8/47/B 3/19.
47 Healey to Parliament, February 13, 1968, FCO 8/85 B10/17.
48 *Daily Telegraph*, January 25, 1968 in FCO 8/48/BS 3/19.
49 Michael A. Palmer, *Guardians of the Gulf: A History of America's Expanding Role In the Persian Gulf* (New York: Free Press, 1992), 86–7.
50 Administrative history, Persian Gulf, pp. 9–10, 11–12, 17 (for quote), 18 (fragile).
51 Katzenbach to NSC, February 21, 1968, NSC Meetings, vol. 5, Tab 64, 2/21/68, Near East Region, NSC Meetings File, NSF, LBJL.
52 D. J. D. Maitland to Arbuthnott, March 4, 1968, FCO 8/102/B 14/11.
53 Nadav Safran, *Saudi Arabia: The Ceaseless Quest for Security* (London: Cornell University Press, 1991), 134.
54 Foreign Office, Anglo-American discussions on Persian Gulf, March 27, 1968, FCO 8/37/B 3/7.
55 John B. Kelly, *Arabia, the Gulf and the West* (New York: Basic Books, 1980), 78–86; Glen Balfour-Paul, *The End of Empire in the Middle East: Britain's Relinquishment of Power in Her Last Three Arab Dependencies* (Cambridge: Cambridge University Press, 1991), 128–33.
56 Denis Wright, United Kingdom ambassador Iran 1963–71 observed: "Many, especially those of us serving at the time, deplored this sudden *volte face*. We believed the decision to be premature, given the lack of political cohesion among the sheikhdoms, their Lilliputian size and the many unresolved disputes both between themselves and with their larger neighbors, notably Iran and Saudi Arabia." [Denis Wright and Elizabeth Monroe, *The Changing Balance*

of Power in the Persian Gulf (New York: American Universities Field Staff, 1972), 14.]

57 Brenchley, *Britain and the Middle East*, 172.

58 McCarthy to Bernard Burroughs, August 19, 1968, FCO 8/89/B 10/24.

59 Man to Brown, January 15, 1968, FCO 8/750/BS 1/1.

60 Brenchley to D. Allen, February 15, 1968, FCO 8/780/BS 10/1.

61 Richard Beeston, "Why Faisal Turns Away Again", *Daily Telegraph*, February 13, 1968, in FCO 8/781/ BS 10/1.

62 Mc MoD officials (Brown and Craig) and Sultan, March 21, 1968, FCO 8/798/ BS 10/9.

63 Shackleton to Wilson, May 2, 1968, PREM 13/2401.

64 *Ibid.*; see also Trevelyan to Shackleton, n.d., PREM 13/2401.

65 Jidda to Foreign Office, August 31, 1968, FCO 8/357/BA 3/9.

66 Foster to Rostow, March 21, 1968, NSFCF, Middle East Yemen, Cables vol. II, 7/64-12/68, LBJL.

67 John W. Foster, NSC to Rostow, May 21, 1968, FRUS 1964–8: XXI: doc. 145.

68 State Department briefing paper, June 22, 1968, POL 7 Saud.

69 Mc Nixon, Prince Fafd and Omar Saqqaf, Saudi Arabia, October 16, 1969, POL Saud-US 42.

70 Douglas Little, "Gideon's Band: America and the Middle East since 1945", *Diplomatic History* 18, 4 (Fall, 1994): 513–40.

71 Butler to Home, April 20, 1964, PREM 11/4718.

72 Kitchen to Rusk, "Discussions with the British on Indian Ocean Island Facilities", March 3, 1964, FRUS 1964–8, XXI: doc. 34; see also Karl Pieragostini, *Britain, Aden and South Arabia: Abandoning Empire* (London: Macmillan Academic and Professional Ltd, 1991), 161.

73 Rusk to Johnson, July 15, 1964, FRUS 1964–8, XXI: doc. 37.

74 McNamara to secretary of the Air Force, June 14, 1965, FRUS 1964–8, XXI: doc. 39.

75 McNaughton to McNamara, August 2, 1966, in *ibid.*, doc. 43 (including McNamara's approval on August 4).

76 *Ibid.*, Nietze to McNamara, February 24, 1967, doc. 44.

77 *Ibid.*, Joint Chiefs of Staff to McNamara, July 25, 1967, doc. 45.

78 Healey, *The Time of My Life*, 284; see also Healey to McNamara, November 18, 1967, FRUS 1964–8, XII: 585–6.

79 Pieragostini, *Britain, Aden and South Arabia*, 175–6.

80 Rusk to American embassy, London, July 3, 1968, FRUS 1964–8, XXI: doc. 49.

81 US embassy, London to State Department, Sept. 4, 1968, in *ibid.*, doc. 50.

8 The End of the Anglo-American Middle East?

1 FCO memorandum, "Political and Security Factors Affecting the Process of British Military Withdrawal from the Persian Gulf", October 7, 1969, FCO 8/985/NB 10/27.

2 Comment by A. D. Parson, FCO, June 26, 1972, FCO 8/1806/NB 3/30401.

3 David Holden, "The Persian Gulf: After the British Raj", *Foreign Affairs* (July, 1971): 721–35.

4 Heath to cabinet, July 23, 1970, CAB 128/47 pt. I, CM (70) 8th Conclusions; F. Gregory Gause, "British and American Policies in the Persian Gulf, 1968–1973", *Review of International Studies* 11 (1985): 247–73.

5 G. G. Arthur, "Persian Gulf: Annual Review for 1970", FCO 8/1570/NB1/2; foreign minister Douglas Home to prime minister Edward Heath, November 12, 1970, PREM 15/538; Nadav Safran, *Saudi Arabia: The Ceaseless Quest for Security* (London: Cornell University Press, 1991), 137.

6 Noyes, testimony, February 2, 1972, "U.S. Interests in and Policy toward the Persian Gulf", Hearings before the Subcommittee on the Near East of the Committee on Foreign Affairs, House of Representatives, 92 Cong: 2nd Sess. (Washington: GPO, 1972), p. 6.

7 R. M. Burrell and Alvin J. Cotrell, "Iran, the Arabian Peninsula and the Indian Ocean", *National Strategy Information Center* (New York, 1972), 21.

8 John Duke Anthony, *Arab States of the Lower Gulf: People, Politics, Petroleum* (Washington: Middle East Institute, 1975), 228.

9 Mc William Rogers and Home, July 11, 1970, FCO 7/1828/ALUSJ/548/12.

10 Henry Kissinger, *Years of Upheaval* (London: Weidenfeld & Nicolson and Michael Joseph, 1983), 141.

11 British embassy Jidda to FCO, April 3, 1969, FCO 8/1122/NB S2/2.

12 Memorandum by Morris, May 5, 1969, FCO 8/1181/1/NBS 3/548/1.

13 Morris, Jidda to D. J. McCarthy, December 9, 1969, FCO 8/1110/NBN3/372/2.

14 British embassy Jidda to FCO, April 3, 1969, FCO 8/1172/NB S2/2.

15 Douglas Little, "Gideon's Band: America and the Middle East since 1945", *Diplomatic History* 18, 4 (Fall, 1994): 513–40.

16 American embassy Jidda to State Department, December 3, 1969, POL 17 Saud-UAR.

17 Kissinger to Nixon, April 22, 1970, UAR Vol. III, 1 Feb.–30 April, 1970, Richard Nixon Presidential Materials Staff, National Security File (hereafter cited as RNNSC), National Archives, College Park, Maryland.

18 Henry Kissinger, *White House Years* (Boston: Little Brown & Company, 1979), 347 (for quote), 378.

19 Nixon to Nasser in Kissinger to Nixon, March 29, 1969, UAR vol. I, Jan. 1969–31 Aug. 1969, RNNSC.

20 John Lewis Gaddis, *Strategies of Containment: A Critical Appraisal of Postwar American National Security Policy* (New York: Oxford University Press, 1982), 298–9; Raymond L. Garthoff, *Détente and Confrontation: American–Soviet Relations from Nixon to Reagan* (Washington: Brookings Institution, 1985), 1078; Walter LaFeber, *America, Russia and the Cold War, 1945–1990* (New York: McGraw-Hill, 1991), 262.

21 James A. Bill, *The Eagle and the Lion: The Tragedy of American–Iranian Relations* (London: Yale University Press, 1988), 192; Garthoff, *Détente*, 74; LaFeber, *America*, 263.

22 Bill, *The Eagle and the Lion*, 202–3, 381–2; Kelly, *Arabia*, 300–9.

23 Bill, *ibid.*, 280–1; Garthoff, *Détente*, 316.

24 Safran, *Saudi Arabia*, 138.

25 Bill, *The Eagle and The Lion*, 204–7; Garthoff, *Détente*, 316.

26 Henry Kissinger, *Years of Upheaval* (London: Weidenfeld & Nicolson and Michael Joseph, 1982), 975.

27 Bill, *The Eagle and the Lion*, 204–7; Garthoff, *Détente*, 1108.

28 Statement by senator Frank Church, March 18, 1975, *Multinational Corporations and United States Foreign Policy*, Hearings before the Subcommittee on Multinational Corporations of the Committee on Foreign Relations, United States Senate, pt. 9 (Washington: GPO, 1975), 259–60.

29 Anthony Sampson, *The Arms Bazaar: The Companies, the Dealers, the Bribes: From Vickers to Lockheed* (London: Hodder & Stoughton, 1977), 294.

30 James H. Noyes, *The Clouded Lens: Persian Gulf Security and U.S. Policy* (Stanford: Hoover University Press, 1979), 21.

31 Henry Kissinger, *Years of Renewal* (New York, 1999), 603.

Bibliography

Public Record Office, Kew
CAB – Records of the Cabinet Office.
The Defence and Oversea Policy Committee (CAB 148).
FO 371 – Records of the Foreign Office.
FCO – Records of the Foreign and Commonwealth Office.
PREM – Prime Minister's Office.

US National Archives, College Park, Maryland
United States Department of State, decimal file, record group 59.
United States Department of State, central file (subject-numeric file).
POLitical affairs and relations.
DEFense.
PETroleum.
Nixon Presidential Materials Staff, National Security Council File.

Dwight D. Eisenhower Presidential Library, Abilene, Kansas
Eisenhower, Dwight D., papers as president (Ann Whitman File).
White House Central Files.
White House Office, Office of the Special Assistant for National Security Affairs.
White House Office, Office of the Staff Secretary.
International Trips and Meetings Series.

John Fitzgerald Kennedy Presidential Library, Boston, Massachusetts
National Security Files.
National Security Action Memorandum.
Meetings and Memoranda, Staff Memoranda.
Presidential Office Files.

Lyndon Baines Johnson Presidential Library, Austin, Texas
National Security File, Country File.
National Security File, Head of State Correspondence.
National Security File, Special Head of State Correspondence.
National Intelligence Estimates.
National Security Council Meetings.
White House Central Files.

White House Confidential File.
Administrative Histories.

Published Records and Official Sources

Beschloss, Michael R. (ed.), *Taking Charge: The Johnson White House Tapes, 1963–1964* (New York: Simon & Schuster, 1997).
——, *Reaching for Glory: Lyndon Johnson's Secret White House Tapes* (New York: Simon & Schuster, 2001).
Farid, Abdel Magid, *Nasser: The Final Years* (Reading: Ithaca Press, 1996).
Hyam, Ronald and Louis, Wm. Roger, *The Conservative Government and the End of Empire 1957–1964*, vol. 4, part I, *High Policy, Political and Constitutional Change*; part II, *Economics, International Relations, and the Commonwealth* (London: Stationery Office, 2000).
May, Ernest R. and Zelikow, Philip D. (eds), *The Kennedy Tapes: Inside the White House during the Cuban Missile Crisis* (London: Belknap Press of Harvard University Press, 1997).
Multinational Corporations and United States Foreign Policy, Hearings before the Subcommittee on Multinational Corporations of the Committee on Foreign Relations, United States Senate, pt. 9 (Washington: GPO, 1975).
Neustadt, Richard E., *Report to JFK: The Skybolt Crisis in Perspective* (London: Cornell University Press, 1999).
Secretary of State for Defence, *Statement on the Defence Estimates, 1965* (Her Majesty's Stationery Office, 1965) [hereafter cited as HMSO], Cmnd. 2592; *idem*, *Statement on the Defence Estimates, 1966: The Defence Review*, part I, Cmnd. 2901 and part II, Cmnd. 2902 (HMSO, 1966); *idem*, *Supplementary Statement on Defence Policy, 1967* (HMSO, 1967), Cmnd. 3357; *idem*, *Statement on the Defence Estimates, 1968* (HMSO, 1968), Cmnd. 3540; *idem*, *Supplementary Statement on Defence Policy 1968* (HMSO, July, 1968).
Shuckburgh, Evelyn, *Descent to Suez: Diaries, 1951–56* (London: Weidenfeld & Nicolson, 1986).
United States Department of State, *Papers Relating to the Foreign Relations of the United States, 1955–1957*, vol. XVI, *Suez Crisis, July 26–December 31, 1956* (Washington: Government Printing Office [hereafter cited as GPO], 1990).
"U.S. Interests in and Policy toward the Persian Gulf", Hearings before the Subcommittee on the Near East of the Committee on Foreign Affairs, House of Representatives, 92 Cong: 2nd Sess. (Washington: GPO, 1972).
United States Department of State, *Papers Relating to the Foreign Relations of the United States, 1961–1963*, vol. XIII, *Western Europe and Canada* (Washington: GPO, 1994); vol. XVII, *Near East, 1961–1962* (Washington: GPO, 1995); vol. XVIII, *Near East, 1962–1963* (Washington: GPO, 1995).
United States Department of State, *Papers Relating to the Foreign Relations of the United States, 1964–1968*, vol. VIII *International Monetary and Trade Policy* (Washington: GPO, 1998); vol. IX, *International Development and Economic Defense Policy: Commodities* (Washington: GPO, 1997); vol. XII, *Western Europe* (Washington: GPO, 2001); vol. XIII, *Western Europe Region* (Washington: GPO, 1995); vol. XVIII, *Arab–Israeli Dispute, 1964–1967* (Washington: GPO, 2000); vol. XX, *Arab–Israeli Dispute, 1967–1968* (GPO,

Washington, 2001); vol. XXI, *Near East Region; Arabian Peninsula* (Washington: GPO, 2000); vol. XXIII, *Iran* (Washington: GPO, 1999); vol. XXXIV, *Energy Diplomacy and Global Issues* (Washington: GPO, 1999).

Memoirs

Ball, George W., *The Past Has Another Pattern* (New York: Norton & Company, 1972).

Brown, George, *In My Way: The Political Memoirs of Lord George-Brown* (London: Victor Gollancz, 1971).

Butler, Richard Austin, *The Art of the Possible: The Memoirs of Lord Butler* (London: Hamish Hamilton, 1971).

Cairncross, Alec, *Managing the British Economy in the 1960s: A Treasury Perspective* (London: Macmillan Press, 1996).

Dobrynin, Anatoly, *In Confidence: Moscow's Ambassador to America's Six Cold War Presidents* (New York: Random House, 1995).

Douglas-Home, Alexander Frederick, *The Way the Wind Blows: An Autobiography* (London: Collins, 1975).

Hart, Parker T., *Saudi Arabia and the United States: Birth of a Security Partnership* (Bloomington: Indiana University Press, 1998).

Healey, Denis, *The Time of My Life* (London: Michael Joseph, 1989).

Jenkins, Roy, *A Life at the Centre* (London: Macmillan, 1991).

Johnson, Lyndon Baines, *The Vantage Point: Perspectives of the Presidency, 1963–1969* (New York: Holt, Rinehart & Winston, 1971).

Johnston, Charles Hepburn, *The View from the Steamer Point: Being an Account of Three Years in Aden* (New York: Frederick A. Praeger, 1964).

Kissinger, Henry, *White House Years* (Boston: Little Brown Company, 1979).

——, *Years of Upheaval* (London: Weidenfeld & Nicolson and Michael Joseph, 1982).

——, *Years of Renewal* (New York: Simon & Schuster, 1999).

Macmillan, Harold, *Pointing the Way, 1959–1961* (London: Macmillan, 1972).

——, *At the End of the Day* (London: Macmillan, 1973).

Murphy, Robert, *Diplomat among Warriors* (New York: Pyramid Books, 1964).

Rusk, Dean, *As I Saw It: A Secretary of State's Memoirs* (London: I.B. Tauris & Co Ltd, 1991).

Schlesinger, Arthur M., *A Thousand Days: John F. Kennedy in the White House* (New York: Fawcett Premier, 1992).

Smiley, David, *Arabian Assignment* (London: Leo Cooper, 1975).

Sorensen, Theodore C., *Kennedy* (New York: Smithmark, 1995).

Stewart, Michael, *Life and Labour: An Autobiography* (London: Sidgwick & Jackson, 1980).

Stonehouse, John, *Death of an Idealist* (London: W. H. Allen, 1975).

Trevaskis, Kennedy, *Shades of Amber: A South Arabian Episode* (London: Hutchinson, 1968).

Trevelyan, Humphrey, *The Middle East in Revolution* (London: Macmillan, 1971).

Wilson, Harold, *The Labour Government 1964–1970* (London: Weidenfeld & Nicolson, 1971).

Books

Akehurst, John, *We Won a War: The Campaign in Oman, 1965–1975* (Southampton: Michael Russel, 1984).

Aldous, Richard and Lee, Sabine (eds), *Harold Macmillan and Britain's World Role* (London: Macmillan, 1996).

Al-Jahny Shiry, Ali Faiz, "South Yemen and the Soviet Union, 1967–1986: A Study of a Small Power in an Alliance", PhD dissertation, George Washington University, 1991.

Almadhagi, Ahmed Noman Kassim, *Yemen and the United States: A Study of a Small Power and Super-State Relationship 1962–1994* (London: I. B. Tauris, 1996).

Ambrose, Stephen E., *Eisenhower: The President* (New York: Simon & Schuster, 1984).

Anthony, John Duke, *Arab States of the Lower Gulf: People, Politics, Petroleum* (Washington: Middle East Institute, 1975).

Ashton, Nigel John, *Eisenhower, Macmillan and the Problem of Nasser: Anglo-American Relations and Arab Nationalism, 1955–59* (London: Macmillan Press, 1996), 225.

——, *Kennedy, Macmillan and the Cold War: The Irony of Independence* (London: Palgrave, Macmillan, 2002).

Balfour-Paul, Glen, *The End of Empire in the Middle East: Britain's Relinquishment of Power in Her Last Three Arab Dependencies* (Cambridge: Cambridge University Press, 1991).

Ball, George W. and Douglas, B., *The Passionate Attachment: America's Involvement with Israel 1947 to the Present* (New York: W. W. Norton & Company, 1992).

Bass, Warren, *Support Any Friend: Kennedy's Middle East and the Making of the U.S.–Israeli Alliance* (New York: Oxford University Press, 2003).

Baylis, John (ed.), *Documents in Contemporary History: Anglo-American Relations since 1939: The Enduring Alliance* (Manchester: Manchester University Press, 1997).

Beling, Willard A. (ed.), *King Faisal and the Modernization of Saudi Arabia* (London: Croom Helm, 1980).

Ben-Zvi, Abraham, *John F. Kennedy and the Politics of Arms Sales to Israel* (London: Frank Cass, 2002).

Bernstein, Irving, *Guns or Butter: The Presidency of Lyndon Johnson* (New York: Oxford University Press, 1996).

Bill, James A., *The Eagle and the Lion: The Tragedy of American Iranian Relations* (London: Yale University Press, 1988).

Brands, H. W., *The Wages of Globalism: Lyndon Johnson and the Limits of American Power* (New York: Oxford University Press, 1995).

—— (ed.), *Beyond Vietnam: The Foreign Policies of Lyndon Johnson* (Texas A&M University Press, 1999).

Brenchley, Frank, *Britain and the Middle East: An Economic History, 1945–87* (London: Lester Crook Academic Publishing, 1989).

Breslauer, Georg W., *Soviet Strategy in the Middle East* (Boston: Unwin Hyman, 1990).

Brown, Judith and Louis, Wm. Roger (eds), *The Oxford History of the British Empire, vol. IV, The Twentieth Century* (New York: Oxford University Press, 1999).

Burns, William J., *Economic Aid and American Policy toward Egypt, 1985–1981* (New York: State University Press of New York, 1985).

Caro, Robert A., *The Years of Lyndon Johnson: Means of Ascent* (London: Bodley Head, 1990).

——, *The Years of Lyndon Johnson: Master of the Senate* (New York: Vintage Books, 2003).

Carver, Michael, *War since 1945* (London: Weidenfeld & Nicolson, 1980).

Churba, Joseph, *The Politics of Defeat: America's Decline in the Middle East* (New York: Cyrco Press, 1977).

Citino, Nathan J., *From Arab Nationalism to Opec: Eisenhower, King Saud, and the Making of U.S.–Saudi Relations* (Bloomington: Indiana University Press, 2002).

Cohen, Michael J., *Strategy and Politics in the Middle East, 1954–1960: Defending the Northern Tier* (London: Frank Cass, 2005).

Cohen, Michael J. and Kolinsky, Martin (eds), *The Demise of the British Empire in the Middle East: Britain's Response to the Nationalist Movements, 1943–1955* (London: Frank Cass, 1998).

Cohen, Warren I. and Tucker, Nancy Bernkopf (eds), *Lyndon Johnson Confronts the World: American Foreign Policy 1963–1968* (New York: Cambridge University Press, 1994).

Coopey, R., Fielding, S. and Tiratsoo, N. (eds), *The Wilson Governments 1964–1970* (London: Pinter, 1993).

Copeland, Miles, *The Game of Nations* (New York: Simon & Schuster, 1969).

Dalleck, Robert, *Flawed Giant: Lyndon Johnson and His Times* (New York: Oxford University Press, 1998.

Darby, Phillip, *British Defence Policy East of Suez* (London: Oxford University Press, 1973).

Darwin, John, *The End of the British Empire: The Historical Debate* (Oxford: Blackwell, 1991).

De Gaury, Gerald, *Faisal: King of Saudi Arabia* (London: Arthur Baker, 1966).

Dewar, Michael, *Brush Fire Wars: Minor Campaigns of the British Army since 1945* (London: Robert Hale, 1990).

Dickie, John, *The Uncommon Commoner: A Study of Sir Alec Douglas-Home* (London: Pall Mall Press, 1964).

Divine, Robert A., *The Johnson Years, vol. 3, LBJ at Home and Abroad* (University Press of Kansas, 1994).

Dobson, Alan P., *Anglo-American Relations in the Twentieth Century: Of Friendship, Conflict and the Rise and Decline of Superpowers* (London: Routledge, 1995).

Dockrill, Saki, *Britain's Retreat from East of Suez: The Choice between Europe and the World* (London: Palgrave, 2002).

Dresch, Paul, *A History of Modern Yemen* (Cambridge: Cambridge University Press, 2000).

English, Richard and Kenny, Michael (eds), *Rethinking British Decline* (London: Macmillan Press, 2000).

Ennes, James M. Jr., *Assault on the Liberty: The True Story of the Israeli Attack on an American Intelligence Ship* (New York: Random House, 1979).

Farouk-Sluglett, Marion and Sluglett, Peter, *Iraq since 1958: From Revolution to Dictatorship* (London: I. B. Tauris, 1990).

Fiennes, Ranulph, *Where Soldiers Fear to Thread* (London: Hodder & Stoughton, 1977).

Freedman, Lawrence, *Kennedy's Wars: Berlin, Laos, and Vietnam* (Oxford: Oxford University Press, 2000).

Freedman, Robert O., *Soviet Policy toward the Middle East since 1970* (New York: Praeger, 1982).

Gaddis, John Lewis, *Strategies of Containment: A Critical Appraisal of Postwar American National Security Policy* (New York: Oxford University Press, 1982).

——, *We Now Know: Rethinking Cold War History* (Oxford: Clarendon Press, 1998).

Garthoff, Raymond L., *Détente and Confrontation: American–Soviet Relations from Nixon to Reagan* (Washington: Brookings Institution, 1985).

Gat, Moshe, *Britain and the Conflict in the Middle East, 1964–1967: The Coming of the Six-Day War* (London: Praeger, 2003).

Gause, F., Gregory III, *Saudi–Yemeni Relations: Domestic Structures and Foreign Influence* (New York: Columbia University Press, 1990).

Gavin, R. J. *Aden under British Rule, 1839–1967* (London: C. Hurst & Co., 1975).

Gerges, Fawaz A., *The Superpowers and the Middle East: Regional and International Politics, 1955–1967* (Boulder, CO: Westview Press, 1994).

Golan, Galia, *Soviet Policies in the Middle East from World War II to Gorbachev* (New York: Cambridge University Press, 1990).

Green, Stephen, *Taking Sides: America's Secret Relations with a Militant Israel* (Vermont: Amana Books, 1988).

Hahn, Peter L., *The United States, Great Britain and Egypt, 1945–1956: Strategy and Diplomacy in the Early Cold War* (London: University of North Carolina Press, 1991).

——, *Caught in the Middle East: U.S. Policy toward the Arab–Israeli Conflict, 1945–1961* (London: University of North Carolina Press, 2004).

Halliday, Fred, *Arabia without Sultans* (Middlesex: Penguin Books, 1979).

Hamilton, Nigel, *JFK: Reckless Youth* (New York: Random House, 1992).

Hammond, Paul Y., *LBJ and the Presidential Management of Foreign Relations* (Austin: University of Texas Press, 1992).

Hennessy, Peter, *Muddling Through: Power, Politics and the Quality of Government in Postwar Britain* (London: Victor Gollancz, 1996).

Heren, Louis, *No Hail, No Farewell* (London: Weidenfeld & Nicolson, 1970).

Herring, George C., *LBJ and Vietnam: A Different Kind of War* (Austin: University of Texas Press, 1994).

Hersh, Seymour, *The Dark Side of Camelot* (New York: Little, Brown & Co. 1997).

Hogan, Michael J. (ed.), *America in the World: The Historiography of American*

Foreign Relations since 1941 (Cambridge: Cambridge University Press, 1995).

Holden, David, *Farewell to Arabia* (London: Faber & Faber, 1966).

Holden, David and Jones, Richard, *The House of Saud* (London: Sidgwick & Jackson, 1981).

Horne, Alistair, *Macmillan, 1957–1986* (London: Macmillan, 1989).

Howard, Anthony, *RAB: The Life of R. A. Butler* (London: Jonathan Cape, 1987).

Ingram, Edward, *The British Empire as a World Power* (London: Frank Cass, 2001).

Jones, Clive, *Britain and the Yemen Civil War, 1962–1965. Ministers, Mercenaries and Mandarins: Foreign Policy and the Limits of Covert Action* (Brighton and Portland: Sussex Academic Press, 2004).

Joyce, Miriam, *Kuwait 1945–1996: An Anglo-American Perspective* (London: Frank Cass, 1998).

——, *Ruling Shaiks and Her Majesty's Government, 1960–1969* (London: Frank Cass, 2003).

Kaiser, David, *American Tragedy: Kennedy, Johnson, and the Origins of the Vietnam War* (London: Belknap Press of Harvard University Press, 2000).

Kaiser, Wolfram and Staerck, Gillian (eds), *British Foreign Policy, 1955–64: Contracting Options* (London: Macmillan Press, 2000).

Kaufman, Burton I., *The Arab Middle East and the United States: Inter-Arab Rivalry and Superpower Diplomacy* (New York: Twayne, 1996).

Kelly, John B., *Arabia, the Gulf and the West* (New York: Basic Books, 1980).

Kennedy, Paul, *The Rise and Fall of the Great Powers: Economic Change and Military Conflict from 1500 to 2000* (New York: Random House, 1987).

Kerr, Malcolm H., *The Arab Cold War: Gamal 'Abd al-Nasir and His Rivals, 1958–1970* (London: Oxford University Press, 1977).

Kissinger, Henry, *Diplomacy* (New York: Simon & Schuster, 1994).

Kunz, Diane B. (ed.), *The Diplomacy of the Crucial Decade: American Foreign Relations during the 1960s* (New York: Columbia University Press, 1994).

LaFeber, Walter, *America, Russia and the Cold War, 1945–1900* (New York: McGraw-Hill, Inc., 1991).

Lankford, Nelson D., *The Last American Aristocrat: The Biography of David K. E. Bruce, 1898–1977* (Boston: Little Brown & Co., 1996).

Lapping, Brian, *End of Empire* (London: Granada Publishing, 1985).

Ledger, David, *Shifting Sands: The British in South Arabia* (London: Peninsula Publishing, 1983).

Lee, Air Chief Marshall Sir David, *Flight from the Middle East* (London: HMSO, 1980).

Levin, Bernard, *The Pendulum Years: Britain and the Sixties* (London: Sceptre, 1970).

Louis, Wm. Roger and Owen, Roger (eds), *Suez 1956: The Crisis and Its Consequences* (New York: Clarendon Press, 1989).

Lucas, W. Scott, *Divided We Stand: Britain, the US and the Suez Crisis* (London: Hodder & Stoughton, 1991).

Lunt, James, *The Barren Rocks of Aden* (London: Herbert Jenkins, 1966).

Mayhew, Christopher, *Britain's Role Tomorrow* (London: Hutchinson Herbert, 1967).

McIntyre, W. David, *British Decolonization, 1946–1997: When, Why and How Did the British Empire Fall?* (London: Macmillan, 1998).

McMullen, Christopher J., *Resolution of the Yemen Crisis, 1963: A Case Study in Mediation* (Washington: Institute for the Study of Diplomacy, School of Foreign Service, Georgetown University, 1980).

McNamara, Robert, *Britain, Nasser and the Balance of Power in the Middle East, 1952–1967* (London: Frank Cass, 2003).

Morgan, Austen, *Harold Wilson* (London: Pluto Press, 1992).

Neff, Donald, *Warriors at Suez: Eisenhower Takes America into the Middle East* (New York: Simon & Schuster, 1981).

Noyes, James H., *The Clouded Lens: Persian Gulf Security and U.S. Policy* (Stanford: Hoover University Press, 1979).

Nunnerly, David, *President Kennedy and Britain* (London: Bodley Head, 1972).

Nutting, Anthony, *Nasser* (New York: Dutton, 1972).

O'Ballance, Edgar, *The War in Yemen* (Hamden, CT: Archon Books, 1971).

Oren, Michael B., *Six Days of War: June 1967 and the Making of the Modern Middle East* (Oxford: Oxford University Press, 2002).

Paget, Julian, *Last Post: Aden 1964–1967* (London: Faber & Faber, 1969).

Palmer, Michael A., *Guardians of the Gulf: A History of America's Expanding Role In the Persian Gulf* (New York: Free Press, 1992).

Paterson, Peter, *Tired and Emotional: The Life of Lord George-Brown* (London: Chatto & Windus, 1993).

Paterson, Thomas G. (ed.), *Kennedy's Quest for Victory: American Foreign Policy, 1961–1963* (New York: Oxford University Press, 1989).

Pearce, Edward, *Denis Healey: A Life in Our Times* (London: Little, Brown, 2002).

Petersen, Tore T., *The Middle East between the Great Powers: Anglo-American Conflict and Cooperation, 1952–7* (London: Macmillan, 2000).

Pickering, Jeffrey, *Britain's Withdrawal from East of Suez: The Politics of Retrenchment* (London: Macmillan, 1998).

Pieragostini, Karl, *Britain, Aden and South Arabia: Abandoning Empire* (London: Macmillan, 1991).

Pimlott, Ben, *Harold Wilson* (London: HarperCollins, 1992).

Ponting, Clive, *Breach of Promise: Labour in Power* (London: Hamish Hamilton, 1989).

Pridham, B. R., *Contemporary Yemen: Politics and Historical Background* (New York: St. Martin's Press, 1984).

Quandt, William B., *Peace Process: American Diplomacy and the Arab–Israeli Conflict since 1967* (Los Angeles: University of California Press, 1993).

Reeves, Richard, *President Kennedy: Profile of Power* (New York: Simon & Schuster, 1993).

Reeves, Thomas C., *A Question of Character: A Life of John F. Kennedy* (New York: Free Press, 1991).

Reynolds, David, *Britannia Overruled: British Policy and World Power in the 20th Century* (London: Longman, 1991).

Richter, James G., *Khrushchev's Double Bind: International Pressures and Domestic Coalition Politics* (Baltimore: Johns Hopkins University Press, 1994).

Rostow, W. W., *The Diffusion of Power: An Essay in Recent History* (New York: Macmillan, 1972).

Safran, Nadav, *Saudi Arabia: The Ceaseless Quest for Security* (London: Cornell University Press, 1991).

Sampson, Anthony, *The Seven Sisters: The Great Oil Companies and The World They Shaped* (New York: Bantam Books, 1976).

——, *The Arms Bazaar: The Companies, the Dealers, the Bribes: from Vickers to Lockheed* (London: Hodder & Stoughton, 1977).

Sanders, David, *Losing an Empire, Finding a Role: British Foreign Policy since 1945* (London: Macmillan,1990).

Schmidt, Dana Adams, *Yemen: The Unknown War* (New York: Holt, Rinehart & Winston, 1968).

Schoenbaum, Thomas J., *Waging Peace and War: Dean Rusk in the Truman, Kennedy and Johnson Years* (New York: Simon & Schuster, 1988).

Schwartz, Thomas Alan, *Lyndon Johnson and Europe: In the Shadow of Vietnam* (London: Harvard University Press, 2003).

Smith, Simon C., *Britain's Revival and Fall in the Gulf: Kuwait, Bahrain, Qatar, and the Trucial States, 1950–1971* (London: Routledge Curzon, 2004).

Stivers, William, *America's Confrontation with Revolutionary Change in the Middle East, 1948–83* (London: Macmillan Press, 1986).

Stookey, Robert W., *America and the Arab States: An Uneasy Encounter* (New York: John Wiley & Sons, Inc., 1975).

Strange, Susan, *Sterling and British Policy: A Political Study of an International Currency in Decline* (London: Oxford University Press, 1971).

Taylor, Alan R., *The Superpowers and the Middle East* (New York: Syracuse University Press, 1991).

Thorpe, D. R., *Alec Douglas-Home* (London: Sinclair-Stevenson, 1996).

Thucydides, *History of the Peloponnesian War* (London: Penguin Books, 1972).

Walker, Patrick Gordon, *The Cabinet* (London: Fontana, 1972).

Wilkinson, John C., *Arabia's Frontiers: The Story of Britain's Boundary Drawing in the Desert* (London: I. B. Tauris, 1991).

Winks, Robin W. (ed.), *The Oxford History of the British Empire, vol. V, Historiography* (New York: Oxford University Press, 1999).

Wright, Denis and Monroe, Elizabeth, *The Changing Balance of Power in the Persian Gulf* (New York: American Universities Field Staff, 1972).

Yaqub, Salim, *Containing Arab Nationalism: The Eisenhower Doctrine and the Middle East* (Chapel Hill: University of North Carolina Press, 2004).

Yergin, Daniel, *The Prize: The Epic Quest for Oil, Money and Power* (New York: Simon & Schuster, 1992).

Zeiler, Thomas W., *Dean Rusk: Defending the American Mission Abroad* (Wilmington, DE: A Scholarly Resources, Inc. imprint, 2000).

Ziegler, Philip, *Wilson: The Authorized Life of Lord Wilson of Rievaulx* (London: Weidenfeld & Nicolson, 1993).

Zubok, Vladislav and Pleshakov, Constantine, *Inside Kremlin's Cold War: From Stalin to Khrushchev* (Cambridge, MA: Harvard University Press, 1996).

Articles

Ashton, Nigel John, "'A Great New Venture?' – Anglo-American Cooperation in the Middle East and the Response to the Iraqi Revolution July 1958", *Diplomacy and Statecraft* 4, 1 (March, 1993).

——,"A Microcosm of Decline: British Loss of Nerve and Military Intervention in Jordan and Kuwait, 1958 and 1961", *Historical Journal* 40, 4 (December, 1997): 1069–83.

——,"Britain and the Kuwaiti Crisis, 1961", *Diplomacy and Statecraft* 9, 1 (March, 1998): 163–81.

Bar-Siman-Tov, Yaacov, "The United States and Israel since 1948: A 'Special Relationship'?", *Diplomatic History* 22, 2 (Spring, 1998): 231–72.

Brands, Henry William, "What Eisenhower and Dulles Saw in Nasser: Personalities and Interest in U.S.–Egyptian Relations", *American–Arab Affairs* 17 (Summer, 1986): 44–54.

Bishku, Michael B., "The Kennedy Adminstration, the U.N. and the Yemeni Civil War", *Middle East Policy* I (1992): 116–28.

Boyle, Kevin, "The Price of Peace: Vietnam, the Pound, and the Crisis of the American Empire", *Diplomatic History* 27, 1 (January, 2003): 37–72.

Burell, R. M. and Alvin J. Cottrell, "Iran, the Arabian Peninsula, and the Indian Ocean", *National Strategy Information Center* (New York, 1972).

Cohen, Warren I., "Balancing American Interests in the Middle East: Lyndon Baines Johnson vs. Gamal Abdul Nasser", in Warren I. Cohen and Nancy Bernkopf Tucker (eds), *Lyndon Johnson Confronts the World: American Foreign Policy 1963–1968* (New York: Cambridge University Press, 1994): 279–309.

Dobson, Alan P., "The Years of Transition: Anglo-American Relations, 1961–1967", *Review of International Studies* 16 (1990): 239–58.

Dumbrell, John, "The Johnson Administration and the British Labour Government: Vietnam, the Pound and East of Suez", *Journal of American Studies* 30 (1996): 211–31.

Fain, W. Taylor, "'Unfortunate Arabia': The United States, Great Britain and Yemen, 1955–63", *Diplomacy and Statecraft* 12, 2 (June, 2000): 125–52.

Fielding, Jeremy, "Coping with Decline: US Policy toward the British Defense Reviews of 1966", *Diplomatic History* XXIII, 4 (Fall, 1999): 633–56.

Gause, F. Gregory, "British and American Policies in the Persian Gulf, 1968–1973", *Review of International Studies* 11 (1985): 247–73.

Gerges, Fawaz A., "The Kennedy Administration and the Egyptian–Saudi Conflict in Yemen: Co-opting Arab nationalism", *Middle East Journal* 49, 2 (Spring, 1995): 292–311.

Heiss, Mary Ann, "The United States, Great Britain, and the Creation of the Iranian Oil Consortium, 1953–1954", *International History Review* XVI, 3 (August, 1994): 511–35.

Hoffman, Bruce, "British Air Power in Periphal Conflict, 1919–1976", United States Air Force/R and Publication Series (Santa Monica, 1989), 87–96.

Holden, David, "The Persian Gulf: after the British Raj", *Foreign Affairs* (July, 1971): 721–35.

Howard, Michael, "Britain's Strategic Problem East of Suez", *International Affairs* 42, 2 (April, 1966): 179–83.

Kaufman, Burton I., "John F. Kennedy as World Leader: a Perspective on the Literature", in Michael J. Hogan (ed.), *America in the World: The Historiography of American Foreign Relations since 1941* (Cambridge: Cambridge University Press, 1995): 326–57.

Kunz, Diane B., "'Somewhat Mixed Up Together': Anglo-American Defence and Financial Policy during the 1960s", *Journal of Imperial and Commonwealth History* 27, 2 (1999): 213–32.

Lefebvre, Jeffrey A., "The United States and Egypt: Confrontation and Accommodation in Northeast Africa, 1956–60", *Middle Eastern Studies* 29, 2 (April, 1993): 321–38.

Little, Douglas, "The New Frontier on the Nile: JFK, Nasser, and Arab Nationalism", *The Journal of American History* 75: 2 (September, 1988): 501–527.

——, "From Even-Handed to Empty-Handed: Seeking Order in the Middle East", in Thomas G. Paterson (ed.), *Kennedy's Quest for Victory: American Foreign Policy, 1961–1963* (New York, 1989).

——, "Choosing Sides: Lyndon Johnson and the Middle East", in Robert A. Divine, *The Johnson Years, Volume Three: LBJ at Home and Abroad* (Lawrence: University Press of Kansas, 1994): 150–97.

——, "A Fool's Errand: America and the Middle East, 1961–1969", in Diane B. Kunz (ed.), *The Diplomacy of the Crucial Decade: American Foreign Relations during the 1960s* (New York: Columbia University Press, 1994): 283–319.

——, "Gideon's Band: America and the Middle East since 1945", *Diplomatic History* 18: 4 (Fall, 1994): 513–540.

——, "Ike, Lebanon, and the 1958 Middle East Crisis", *Diplomatic History* 20:1 (Winter, 1996): 27–54.

——, "Nasser Delenda Est: Lyndon Johnson, the Arabs, and the Six-Day War", in Brands, H. W., (ed.), *Beyond Vietnam: The Foreign Policies of Lyndon Johnson* (Texas A&M University Press, 1999).

Louis, Wm. Roger, "The Tragedy of the Anglo-Egyptian Agreement of 1954", in Louis, Wm Roger and Owen, Roger (eds), *Suez 1956: The Crisis and Its Consequences* (New York: Clarendon Press, 1989), 43–71.

——, "The Dissolution of the British Empire in the Era of Vietnam", *American Historical Review* 107, 1 (February, 2002): 1–25.

Louis, Wm. Roger and Robinson, Ronald, "The Imperialism of Decolonization", *Journal of Imperial and Commonwealth History* 22, 3 (1994): 462–511.

——, "The British Withdrawal from the Gulf, 1967–1971", *Journal of Imperial and Commonwealth History* 31, 1 (January, 2003): 83–108.

Martel, Gordon, "The Meaning of Power: Rethinking the Decline and Fall of Great Britain", *International History Review* XIII, 4 (November, 1991): 662–94.

McNamara, Robert, "Britain, Nasser and the Outbreak of the Six Day War", *Journal of Contemporary History* 35, 4 (October, 2000): 619–39.

Middeke, Michael, "Britain's Global Military Role, Conventional Defence and Anglo-American Interdependence after Nassau", *Journal of Strategic Studies* 24, 1 (March, 2001): 143–64.

Monroe, Elisabeth, "British Bases in the Middle East: Assets or Liabilities?", *International Affairs* 42, 1 (February, 1966): 24–34.

Nadelmann, Ethan, "Setting the Stage: American Policy toward the Middle East, 1961–1966", *International Journal of Middle East Studies* 14 (1982): 435–57.

O'Hara, Glen, "The Limits of US Power: Transatlantic Financial Diplomacy under the Johnson and Wilson Administrations, October 1964–November 1968", *Contemporary European History* 12, 3 (August, 2003): 257–78.

Oren, Michael B., "A Winter of Discontent: Britain's Crisis in Jordan, December 1955–March 1956", *International Journal of Middle East Studies* 22 (May, 1990): 174–84.

Ovendale, Ritchie, "Great Britain and the Anglo-American Invasion of Jordan and Lebanon in 1958", *International History Review* XVI, 2 (May, 1994): 284–303.

Petersen, Tore T., "Anglo-American Rivalry in the Middle East: the Struggle for the Buraimi Oasis, 1952–1957", *International History Review* XIV: 1 (February, 1992): 71–91.

——, "Transfer of Power in the Middle East", *International History Review* XIX, 4 (November, 1997): 852–65.

——, "Crossing the Rubicon? Britain's Withdrawal from the Middle East, 1961 1968: A Bibliographical Review", *International History Review* XXX, 2 (June, 2000): 318–40.

——, "How Not to Stand up to Arabs and Israelis", *International History Review* XXV, 3 (September, 2003): 616–35.

Snell-Mendoza, Morice, "In Defence of Oil: Britain's Response to the Iraqi Threat towards Kuwait, 1961", *Contemporary Record* 10, 3 (Autumn, 1996): 39–62.

Tal, David, "Symbol Not Substance?: Israel's Campaign to Acquire Hawk Missiles, 1960–1962", *International History Review* XXII, 2 (June, 2000): 304 17.

Thornhill, Michael, "Britain and the Politics of the Arab League, 1943–50", in Cohen, Michael J. and Kolinsky, Martin (eds), *The Demise of the British Empire in the Middle East: Britain's Response to the Nationalist Movements, 1943–1955* (London: Frank Cass, 1998): 41–63.

Warner, Geoffrey. "The United States and the Suez Crisis", *International Affairs* 67 (April, 1991): 303–17.

Wrigley, Chris "Now You See It, Now You Don't: Harold Wilson and Labour's Foreign Policy Foreign Policy 1964–70", in Coopey, R., Fielding, S. and Tiratsoo, N. (eds), *The Wilson Governments 1964–1970* (London: Pinter, 1993): 123–35.

Index